PROTOCOLS FOR HIGH-SPEED NETWORKS VI

IFIP - The International Federation for Information Processing

IFIP was founded in 1960 under the auspices of UNESCO, following the First World Computer Congress held in Paris the previous year. An umbrella organization for societies working in information processing, IFIP's aim is two-fold: to support information processing within its member countries and to encourage technology transfer to developing nations. As its mission statement clearly states,

IFIP's mission is to be the leading, truly international, apolitical organization which encourages and assists in the development, exploitation and application of information technology for the benefit of all people.

IFIP is a non-profitmaking organization, run almost solely by 2500 volunteers. It operates through a number of technical committees, which organize events and publications. IFIP's events range from an international congress to local seminars, but the most important are:

- The IFIP World Computer Congress, held every second year;
- open conferences;
- working conferences.

The flagship event is the IFIP World Computer Congress, at which both invited and contributed papers are presented. Contributed papers are rigorously refereed and the rejection rate is high.

As with the Congress, participation in the open conferences is open to all and papers may be invited or submitted. Again, submitted papers are stringently refereed.

The working conferences are structured differently. They are usually run by a working group and attendance is small and by invitation only. Their purpose is to create an atmosphere conducive to innovation and development. Refereeing is less rigorous and papers are subjected to extensive group discussion.

Publications arising from IFIP events vary. The papers presented at the IFIP World Computer Congress and at open conferences are published as conference proceedings, while the results of the working conferences are often published as collections of selected and edited papers.

Any national society whose primary activity is in information may apply to become a full member of IFIP, although full membership is restricted to one society per country. Full members are entitled to vote at the annual General Assembly, National societies preferring a less committed involvement may apply for associate or corresponding membership. Associate members enjoy the same benefits as full members, but without voting rights. Corresponding members are not represented in IFIP bodies. Affiliated membership is open to non-national societies, and individual and honorary membership schemes are also offered.

PROTOCOLS FOR HIGH-SPEED NETWORKS VI

IFIP TC6 WG6.1 & WG6.4 /
IEEE ComSoc TC on Gigabit Networking
Sixth International Workshop on
Protocols for High-Speed Networks (PfHSN '99)
August 25-27, 1999, Salem, Massachusetts, USA

Edited by

Joseph D. Touch
University of Southern California,
Information Sciences Institute
USA

James P.G. Sterbenz
BBN Technologies, GTE
USA

SPRINGER-SCIENCE+BUSINESS MEDIA, B.V.

ISBN 978-1-4757-6318-8 ISBN 978-0-387-35580-1 (eBook)
DOI 10.1007/978-0-387-35580-1

Library of Congress Cataloging-in-Publication Data

Printed on acid-free paper.

CONTENTS

COMMITTEE MEMBERS

WORKSHOP CO-CHAIRS:

James P. G. Sterbenz	*BBN Technologies, GTE, U.S.A.*
Joseph D. Touch	*USC / ISI, U.S.A.*

PROGRAM COMMITTEE:

Sujata Banerjee	*Univ. of Pittsburgh, U.S.A.*
Ernst Biersack	*Eurecom, France*
Gregor von Bochmann	*University of Ottawa, Canada*
Jon Crowcroft	*UCL, United Kingdom*
Christophe Diot	*Sprint Advanced Technology Lab, U.S.A.*
Julio Escobar	*SENACYT, Panama*
Per Gunningberg	*Uppsala University, Sweden*
Marjory Johnson	*RIACS/NASA Ames Research Center, U.S.A.*
Guy Leduc	*University of Liege, Belgium*
Bryan Lyles	*Sprint Advanced Technology Lab, U.S.A.*
Gerald Neufeld	*Siara Systems, U.S.A.*
Craig Partridge	*BBN Technologies, GTE, U.S.A.*
Harry Rudin	*IBM Zurich Research Lab, Switzerland*
Douglas C. Schmidt	*Washington University, U.S.A.*
Ahmed Tantawy	*IBM, U.S.A.*
Martina Zitterbart	*Tech. University Braunschweig, Germany*

PREFACE

This year marks the 10th anniversary of the IFIP International Workshop on Protocols for High-Speed Networks (PfHSN). It began in May 1989, on a hillside overlooking Lake Zurich in Switzerland, and arrives now in Salem Massachusetts 6,000 kilometers away and 10 years later, in its sixth incarnation, but still with a waterfront view (the Atlantic Ocean). In between, it has visited some picturesque views of other lakes and bays of the world: Palo Alto (1990 – San Francisco Bay), Stockholm (1993 – Baltic Sea), Vancouver (1994 – the Strait of Georgia and the Pacific Ocean), and Sophia-Antipolis / Nice (1996 – the Mediterranean Sea).

PfHSN is a workshop providing an international forum for the exchange of information on high-speed networks. It is a relatively small workshop, limited to 80 participants or less, to encourage lively discussion and the active participation of all attendees. A significant component of the workshop is interactive in nature, with a long history of significant time reserved for discussions. This was enhanced in 1996 by Christophe Diot and Wallid Dabbous with the institution of Working Sessions chaired by an "animator," who is a distinguished researcher focusing on topical issues of the day. These sessions are an audience participation event, and are one of the things that makes PfHSN a true "working conference."

This year, we received twice as many papers as we could accommodate, and have a record number of Working Sessions, the latter including charging and accounting, multicast, wireless, as well as a retrospective of this workshop. We have half as many countries represented as we have papers, making this a truly international year for PfHSN.

During the past ten years we have seen high-speed networking grow from a niche research area to commodity commercial products, such as Gigabit Ethernet, OC-192 SONET, and ATM. PfHSN has tracked the evolution of high-speed network research, from protocol concepts to their implementation, from applications to switching, from OSI to TCP and ATM. On the way, we have visited a diverse set of research areas, including parallelization, copy reduction, hardware protocols, congestion control, host–network interface design, video, quality of service, and layer integration.

Harry Rudin and Robin Williamson brought us that first workshop, and in their preface hoped that we would be able to discuss issues in designing and implementing high-level protocols, to bring the promise of high-speed networking to fruition. As we sit at our desktops, using 100 Mbps and Gbps commercial LANs connected by Gbps service provider connections, it is clear that their vision has become real. It is also clear that the challenges of high-performance networking are ever more present, as the World-Wide Web continues to be nick-named the "World-Wide Wait."

The issue, raised ten years ago, was whether we need new protocols to support high-speed networks, or whether clever tuning would suffice. Ten years of research has not completely answered that question. We do know that networks will continue to get faster, that protocols will continue to provide richer capabilities, and that the trade-offs will shift, as technology evolves. So it goes with all computing.

Five years later, when we were in the midst of the ATM hype, James Sterbenz presented the keynote address which questioned *Protocols for High Speed Networks: Life after ATM?* ATM had taken experimental fast packet switching research in the mid 1980's, to a set of standards prematurely cast with serious technical flaws, to a bandwagon on which both researchers and vendors were jumping and thinking that ATM *was* high speed networking. Even before the ATM bubble burst, PfHSN remained focused on high-speed networking in general, rather than any particular technology in particular (such as ATM). In fact, of the PfHSN papers from the mid 90's which did concentrate on ATM, a substantial number were focused on the problems with ATM, both in isolation and as a second network layer under IP.

This workshop owes its existence and its longevity to Harry Rudin, who continued to shepherd it through IFIP as chair of WG 6.1, until passing the torch to Guy Leduc earlier this year. We thank them, as well as the past Workshop Co-Chairs Harry Rudin, Robin Williamson, Marjory Johnson, Per Gunningberg, Björn Pehrson, Stephen Pink, Mabo Ito, Gerald Neufeld, Wallid Dabbous, and Christophe Diot for the initiative and work to keep PfHSN going for ten years. We would also like to thank the authors, and all the participants, for making this workshop productive and worthwhile. We thank the Program Committee for taking the time to personally review papers and for their collaboration in creating this year's Working Sessions. We thank the authors for their interest, active participation, and assistance with the process of publishing their work herein. We thank Jeanine Yamazaki and Sungita Patel for their help in pulling PfHSN '99 all together.

Finally, some notes about the future: High-speed networking has become a pervasive aspect of network research, partly due to the success of this workshop. IFIP's Conference on High-Performance Networks (HPN), and IEEE's Gigabit Networking Workshop (GBN), to name only a few. With such success comes an opportunity: IFIP is considering a merger of PfHSN IFIP Conference on High-Performance Networking (HPN). Part of this merger will involve a name shift, some unification of the titles of both. But we hope it will retain part of the unique character of PfHSN, particularly the animated Working Session, and the open forum for discussion it provides. These sessions, like orchestral performances, are conducted by a distinguished person, but are created only as the result of the participation and collaboration of the entire group. We hope these sessions, which we feel embody the best aspects of PfHSN, will continue, whatever the name of the forum.

In this light, the current volume contains a full contents and author index of the last ten years of PfHSN workshop. We hope that this will serve not only as a useful index to past PfHSNs, but also encourage people to look back at the evolution of high speed networking research over the last ten years and think about the future.

While the end-to-end and higher layer issues remain as elusive as ever for high speed networking, a new set of challenges at the lower layers are emerging. These not only motivate new research at the lover layers, but continue to drive research at the end-system, end-to-end protocols, middleware, and the application interface. Some of these new challenges include:

1. Wireless networks are of increasing importance in the arena of smart spaces and wearable networks. The scale and density of networks in which each individual may have 10 to 100 nodes is daunting (consider a stadium with 100 000 people and 10 000 000 networked devices in range). There is no reason to believe that the demand for bandwidth will not vastly exceed what is readily available in the radio spectrum.

2. Optical technology is finally maturing to the degree that the prospect of all-optical portions of the Internet are conceivable, and are worthy of research. There are significant issues remaining, not only in how to do all-optical networking, but how to do this in the context of the Internet as we know it.

3. We are now considering how to extend the Internet to Mars for the upcoming Mars space missions; it is only sensible to do this in the context of how to build an Interplanetary Internet. Not only do latencies on the order of 10 to 100 minutes cause us to rethink how we can do interactive applications because the usual tricks to effectively beat the speed of light break down, but current protocols simply break (for example timers and end-to-end state synchronization). While space bandwidths are currently low relative to fiber standards, the hint of free space laser communications causes us to consider the prospect of bandwidth-×-delay products of petabits or exabits in flight.

So, just as we said at the first PfHSN in 1989, and mid-decade in 1994, there is much interesting research to be done. We will continue to struggle with the issue Harry Rudin and Robin Williamson raised in 1989: whether new protocols are needed or clever re-engineering of current protocols will suffice, and it will likely continue to be a combination of the two.

Finally, two things have happened in the high-speed networking community: First, an increasing amount of networking research involves performance as a fundamental aspect, and thus researchers who would have not originally identified themselves as part of the high-speed community are concerned with these issues on a daily basis. Second, many of us who were focused on high-speed networking *per se* have moved on to orthogonal disciplines, of which high-speed networking is a significant component. And while we suffer from the problem that "nothing is *just* high speed networking, and everything is high speed networking", there remains a community of people who are deeply interested in high-speed networking as a discipline. Hopefully, we will continue to be able to meet and work at forums such as PfHSN.

James P. G. Sterbenz

Joseph D. Touch

PART 1

KEYNOTE AND WORKING SESSIONS

THE OPTICAL FUTURE OF HIGH-SPEED NETWORKS

C. Qiao
State University of New York, Buffallo

Abstract:

With the ever increasing optical transmission rate, now exceeding 1 Tb/s on a single fiber thanks to Wavelength Division Multiplexing (WDM) technologies, electronic routing/switching is quickly becoming a performance bottleneck in high-speed backbone networks. WDM optical networking, though rooting in the physical and link layers, is by no means yet another ordinary low layer technology as it may affect the designs of the upper electronic layer. Specifically, WDM optical networks can be configured to bypass intermediate electronic components by switching/routing data in the optical domain. This will not only reduce electronic processing and I/O loads, but also provide bit-rate and coding format transparency. However, this may also lead to unexpected "shortest" and "alternate" paths in the electronic layer. In addition, primitive optical logic, and especially the lack of optical memory (buffer) are major challenges in order to realize the vision of building a bandwidth-abundant infrastructure, which is ubiquitous and yet efficient, based on WDM optical networks. In this talk, I will describe these issues and along relevant optical switching paradigms, namely wavelength-routing (as a form of optical circuit switching), optical packet switching, and optical burst switching (OBS), and discuss how the next generation Optical Internet may support QoS and provide multicast services in the WDM optical layer.

Chunming Qiao earned his BS degree in Computer Science and Engineering from University of Science and Technology of China (USTC) in Hefei, P.R. China. He received the Andrew-Mellon Distinguished doctoral fellowship award from University of Pittsburgh and later earned his Ph.D. degree in Computer Science there in 1993. He was an Assistant Professor in the ECE Department, and now an Associate Professor in the newly created CSE Department at SUNY at Buffalo. His research interests cover the two converging areas of computers and communications and currently, he is conducting research on Wavelength Division Multiplexed (WDM) networks and internetworks (e.g. IP over WDM) which has been funded by NSF and Telcordia Technologies (formerly Bellcore). Dr. Qiao has published more than 50 papers in IEEE Trans. on Computers, Trans on Parallel and Distributed Systems, Trans. on Communications and Trans. on Networking as well as other journals and conference proceedings. He has served as a Co-Chair for the annual All-optical Networking conference since 1997, a Program Vice Co-Chair for the 1998 International Conf. on Computer Communications and Networks (IC3N), panel/session organizer at the IEEE Globecom'99 and IEEE MILCOM'96, and program committee members and session chairs in over a dozen of other conferences and workshops. He has been featured in a couple of interviews shown in the Alcatel's Communications Week and SPIE's OE Reports. He is also an editor of the Journal on High-Speed Networks (JHSN) and the new Optical Networks Magazine, and a member of IEEE Computer Society and IEEE Communications Society.

PfHSN '99 WORKING SESSIONS

The working session is a key feature of Protocols for High-Speed Networks. The sessions for 1999 are described below.

PROTOCOL ISSUES FOR CHARGING, PRICING, AND ACCOUNTING

Animator: Bryan Lyles, Sprint Advanced Technology Lab, U.S.A.

MULTICAST ISSUES

Animator: Marjory Johnson, RIACS/NASA Ames Research Center, U.S.A.
Panelists: Radia Perlman, Sun Microsystems, U.S.A.
Kevin Almeroth, U.C. Santa Barbara, U.S.A.

10 YEARS OF PFHSN: WHERE HAVE WE BEEN, WHERE ARE WE GOING?

Animators: James P. G. Sterbenz, BBN Technologies, GTE, U.S.A.
Joe Touch, USC/ISI, U.S.A.

WIRELESS ISSUES

Animator: Julio Escobar, SENACYT, Panama

PART 2

SWITCHING AND ROUTING

A SURVEY OF RECENT IP LOOKUP SCHEMES [1]

V. Srinivasan, G. Varghese
Microsoft Research, UCSD
cheenu@ccrc.wustl.edu, varghese@ccrc.wustl.edu

Abstract

Internet (IP) address lookup is a major bottleneck in high performance routers. IP address lookup is challenging because it requires a *longest matching prefix* lookup. It is compounded by increasing routing table sizes, increased traffic, higher speed links, and the migration to 128 bit IPv6 addresses.

We survey recent approaches to do fast IP lookups. We compare algorithms based on their lookup speed, scalability, memory requirement and update speed. While our main interest lies in the worst case lookup time, competitive update speeds and theoretical worst case bounds are also important. In particular we consider binary search on prefixes, binary search on prefix lengths, LC-tries, controlled prefix expansion and Lulea tries. We consider both software and hardware environments. We conclude that with these recent developments, IP lookups at gigabit speeds is a solved problem and that terabit lookup chips can be designed should the need arise.

1. INTRODUCTION

From the present intoxication with the Web to the future promise of electronic commerce, the Internet has captured the imagination of the world. It is hardly a surprise to find that the number of Internet hosts triple approximately every two years [7]. Also, Internet traffic is doubling every 3 months [28], partly because of increased users, but also because of new multimedia applications. The higher bandwidth need requires faster communication links and faster network routers. Gigabit fiber links are commonplace[2], and yet the fundamental limits of optical transmission have hardly been approached. Thus the key to improved Internet performance is faster routers. This market opportunity has led to a flurry of startups (e.g., Avici, Juniper,Torrent) that are targeting the gigabit and terabit router market.

What are the fundamental impediments to improved router performance? An Internet message (called a packet) arrives at an input link. A processor[3] examines the destination address of the packet in a Forwarding Database to determine the output link. In some cases, the processor may also perform "firewall" transit checks that require a lookup in a database of firewall rules. If the checks succeed, the processor instructs a switching system to switch the packet the corresponding output link. Many routers also do a form of scheduling at the output link to ensure fairness among competing packet streams, and to provide delay bounds for time critical traffic such as video.

Thus the three central bottlenecks in router forwarding are lookups, switching, and output scheduling. Switching is well studied, and good solutions like fast busses and crossbar switches (e.g., [14, 30]) have been developed. Similarly, most vendors feel that full scale fair queuing[4] is not required for a few years until video usage increases. In the interim, cheaper approximations such as weighted and deficit round robin [23] ensure fairness and can easily be implemented. So IP lookups remain a major bottleneck. In this survey, we look at recent algorithms for IP address lookups.

2. THE INTERNET LOOKUP PROBLEM

Internet address lookup would be simple if we could lookup a 32 bit IP destination address in a table that lists the output link for each assigned Internet address. In this case, lookup could be done by hashing, but a router would have to keep millions of entries. To reduce database size and routing update traffic, a router database consists of a smaller set of prefixes. This reduces database size, but at the cost of requiring a more complex lookup called *longest matching prefix*. It also requires a more complex update procedure when prefixes are added and deleted.

A metaphor can explain the compression achieved by prefixes. Consider a flight database in London. We could list the flights to a thousand U.S. cities in our database. However, suppose most flights to the U.S. hub though Boston, except flights to California that hub through LA. We can reduce the flight database from thousand entries to two prefix entries (USA* $\rightarrow$ Boston; USA.CA.* $\rightarrow$ LA). We use "*" to denote a wildcard that can match any number of characters. The flip side of this reduction is that a destination city like USA.CA.Fresno will now match both the USA* and USA.CA.* prefixes; we must return the longest match (USA.CA.*).

The Internet address lookup problem is similar except that that we use bit strings instead of character strings. The currently deployed version of the Internet (v4) uses 32 bit destination addresses; each Internet router can have a potentially different set of prefixes, each of which we will denote by a bit string (e.g., 01*) of up to 32 bits followed by a "*". Thus if the destination address began with 01000 and we had only two prefix entries (01* $\rightarrow$ L1; 0100* $\rightarrow$ L2), the packet should be switched to link L2.

The Internet began with a simpler form of hierarchy in which 32 bit addresses were divided into a network address and a host number, so that routers could only store entries for networks. For flexible address allocation, the network addresses came in variable sizes: Class A (8 bits), Class B (16 bits), and Class C (24 bits). Organizations that required more than 256 hosts were given class B addresses; these organizations further structured their Class B addresses ("subnetting") for internal routing. Finally, Class B addresses began to run out. Thus larger organizations needed multiple Class C addresses. To reduce backbone router table size, the CIDR scheme [21] now allocates larger organizations multiple *contiguous* Class C addresses that can be aggregated by a common prefix. In summary, the forces of subnetting and CIDR "supernetting" have led to the use of prefixes for the Internet. While the currently deployed IPv4 protocol uses 32 bit addresses, the next generation IPv6 protocol uses 128 bit addresses and continues to use longest matching prefix.

Best matching prefix is also used in the OSI Routing scheme [18]. Best matching prefix appears to be a fundamental problem for routers, and not just an artifact of the way the Internet has evolved.

3. PERFORMANCE MODEL

The choice of a lookup algorithm depends crucially on assumptions about the routing environment and the implementation environment. We also need a performance model with precise metrics to compare algorithms.

Routing Databases

The Internet consists of local domains which are interconnected by a backbone consisting of multiple Internet Service Providers (ISPs). Accordingly, there are two interesting kinds of routers [1]: enterprise routers (used in a campus or organization) and backbone routers (used by ISPs). The performance needs of these two types of routers are different.

Backbone routers today [1] can have databases of up to 45,000 prefixes (growing every day, several of them with multiple paths). The prefixes contain almost all lengths from 8 to 32; however, because of the evolution from Class B and Class C addresses, there is considerable concentration at 24 and 16 bit prefix lengths. Because backbone routers typically run the Border Gateway Protocol [22], and some implementations exhibit considerable instability, route changes can occur up to 100 times a second [1, 11], requiring algorithms for handling route updates that take 10 msec or less. Backbone routers may require frequent reprogramming as ISPs attempt to deal with customer requirements such as virus attacks. The distribution of packet sizes is bimodal, with peaks corresponding to either 64 byte control packets or 576 byte data packets.

Enterprise routers have smaller databases (up to 1000 prefixes) because of the heavy use of default routes for outside destinations. Routes are also typically much more stable, requiring route updates at most once every few seconds. The packet sizes are bimodal and are either 64 bytes or 1519 bytes[5]. However, large multi-campus enterprise routers may look more like backbone routers.

Address space depletion has lead to the next generation of IP (IPv6) with 128 bit addresses. While there are plans for aggressive aggregation to reduce table entries, the requirement for both provider based and geographical addresses, the need for connections to multiple ISPs, plans to connect control devices on the Net, and the use of features like Anycast [3], all make it unlikely that backbone prefix tables will be smaller than in IPv4.

We use four publically available prefix databases for our comparisons. These are made available by the IPMA project [15] and are daily snapshots of the routing tables used at some major Network Access Points (NAPs). The largest of these, MaeEast (about 38,000 prefixes), is a reasonable model for a large backbone router; the smallest database, PAIX (around 713 prefixes), can be considered a model for an Enterprise router. We will compare lookup schemes using these four databases with respect to three metrics: search time (most crucial), storage, and update times.

Implementation Model

In this paper, we will compare lookup algorithms using a software platform. Software platforms are more flexible and have smaller initial design costs. For example, BBN [6] uses DEC Alpha CPUs in each line card. However, hardware platforms are higher performance and cheaper after volume manufacturing. For example, Torrent [6] uses a hardware forwarding engine. We will briefly discuss hardware platforms in Section 6.

Thus for the majority of this paper, we will consider software platforms using modern processors such as the Pentium [9] and the Alpha [24]. These CPUs execute simple instructions very fast (few clock cycles) but take much longer (thirty to fifty clock cycles) to make a random access to main memory. The only exception is if the data is in either the Primary (L1) or Secondary Cache (L2), which allow access times of a few clock cycles. The distinction arises because main memory uses slow cheap Dynamic Memory (DRAM, 60-100 nsec access time) while cache memory is expensive but fast Static Memory (SRAM, 10-20 nsec). When a READ is done to memory of a single word, the entire *cache line* is fetched into the cache. This is important because the remaining words in the cache line can be accessed cheaply for the price of a single memory READ.

Thus an approximate measure of the speed of any lookup algorithm, is the number of main memory (DRAM) accesses required, because these accesses often dominate search times. To do so, we must have an estimate of the total storage required by the algorithm to understand how much of the data structures can be placed in cache. Finally, both cache accesses and clock cycles for instructions are important for a more refined comparison. To measure these, we must fix an implementation platform and have a performance tool capable of doing dynamic instruction counts that incorporate pipeline and superscalar effects.

We chose a commodity 300 Mhz Pentium II running Windows NT that has a 8 Kbyte L1 data cache, a 512 KByte L2 cache, and a cache line size of 32 bytes. Since prefix databases are fairly large and the L1 cache is quite small, we (pessimistically) chose to ignore the effects of L1 caching. Thus our model assumes that *every* access leads to a L1 cache miss. When there is a L1 miss, the time to read in the first word in the cacheline from the L2 cache is 15 nsec. When there is a L2 miss, the total time to read in the word from memory (including the effects of the L2 miss) is 75 nsec. While many of our experiments use a 512 Kbyte L2 cache size, we also present a few projected results assuming an L2 cache size of 1024 Kbytes.

We chose the Pentium platform because of the popularity of Wintel platforms, and the availability of useful tools. We believe the results would be similar if run on other comparable platforms such as the Alpha. We have implemented several previously known schemes on this platform. Further, we use a tool called Vtune [8] that gives us access to dynamic instruction counts, cache performance, and clock cycles for short program segments. Thus for careful analytical worst-case comparisons, we use speed measurements given to us by Vtune. In addition, we also do a test of average speed using accesses to a million randomly chosen IP addresses.

The analytic worst case measurements we use are much more conservative than what would be obtained by actually running the program on the Pentium II PC. This is because we assume that the L1 cache always misses, that branch prediction always fails, and that the worst possible branching sequence in the code is taken. A second reason for using Vtune is the difficulty of otherwise measuring the time taken for short code segments. A standard technique is to run C lookups to the same address D, measure (using the coarse-grained system clock) the time taken for these lookups, and then to divide by C to estimate the time taken for a single lookup. Unfortunately, such measurements are optimistic because repeated lookups to the same address are likely to result in the few relevant parts of the data structure (i.e., the parts used to lookup D) entering the L1 cache.

4. EARLIER SCHEMES

We describe previous schemes for IP lookup and compare them using our software performance model. We divide these schemes into four categories: conventional algorithms, hardware and caching solutions and protocol based solutions. For the rest of this paper, we use BMP as a shorthand for Best Matching Prefix and W for the length of an address (32 for v4, and 128 for v6).

The most commonly available IP lookup implementation is found in the BSD kernel, and is a radix trie implementation [25]. If W is the length of an address, the worst-case time in the basic implementation can be shown to be $O(W)$. Thus the implementation can require up to 32 or 128 worst-case costly memory accesses for IPv4 and IPv6 respectively.

Even in the best case, with binary branching and 40,000 prefixes, this trie implementation can take $\log_2(40,000) = 16$ memory accesses. A modified binary search technique is described in [12]. However, this method requires $O(\log_2 2n)$ steps, with n being the number of routing table entries. With 40,000 prefixes, the worst case would be 17 memory accesses. Using our crudest model, and 75 nsec DRAM, a trie or binary search scheme will take at least 1.2 usec.

Content-addressable memories(CAMs) that do exact matching can be used to implement best matching prefix. A scheme in [13] uses a separate CAM for each possible prefix length. This can require 32 CAMs for IPv4 and 128 CAMs for IPv6, which is expensive. It is possible to obtain CAMs that allow "don't care" bits in CAM entries to be masked out. Such designs only require a single CAM. However, the largest such CAMs today only allow around 8000 prefixes. While such a CAM may be perfectly adequate for an enterprise router, it is inadequate for a backbone router. Finally, CAM designs have not historically kept pace with improvements in RAM memory. Thus any CAM solution runs the risk of being made obsolete in a few years by software running on faster processors and memory.

Caching has not worked well in the past in backbone routers because of the need to cache full addresses (it is not clear how to cache prefixes). This potentially dilutes the cache with hundreds of addresses that map to the same prefix. Also, typical backbone routers may expect to have hundreds of thousands of flows to different addresses. Some studies have shown cache hit ratios of around 50-70 percent [16]. Caching can help but does not avoid the need for fast lookups.

The main idea in Protocol Based solutions (IP and Tag Switching) is to replace best matching prefix by an exact match by having a previous hop router pass an index into the next router's forwarding table. This leads to a much faster lookup scheme (1 memory access), but the cost is additional protocol and potential set up delays. IP switching [16] relies on switching long lived flows. This solution may be ineffective with short-lived flows such as web sessions. Tag switching [2, 20] does not work at the boundaries of administrative domains. Both schemes require large parts of the network to make the required protocol changes before performance will improve. Both schemes also increase the vulnerability of an already fragile set of Internet routing protocols (see [11]) by adding a new protocol that interacts with every other routing protocol. Also, neither completely avoids the BMP problem.

5. NEW ALGORITHMS

Several new techniques [4, 17, 31, 26] for best matching prefix were invented in the past two years. The expanded trie scheme [26] implements multibit tries based on what is called *controlled prefix expansion.* The Lulea Scheme [4] is based on implementing multibit tries but compresses trie nodes to reduce storage to fit in cache. While the worst case is still $O(W)$ memory accesses where W is the address length, these accesses are to fast cache memory. The LC-trie scheme [17] is also based on implementing multibit tries but compresses them using what the authors call level compression.

The binary search on prefix lengths scheme [31] is based on binary search of the possible prefix lengths and thus takes a worst case of $\log_2 W$ hashes, where each hash is assumed to be a single access to memory. It is much harder to determine the new schemes currently being designed or used by router vendors because they regard their schemes as trade secrets. However, Rapid City [6] and Torrent [29] use schemes based on hashing that claim good average performance but have poor worst case times (16 memory accesses for the Torrent ASIK scheme). A technique based on controlled prefix expansion for improving the worst case lookup performance of the binary search of prefix lengths was introduced in [26] and we refer to this scheme as 'Binary search on levels with expansion'.

Table 1 Prefix databases as on 12 Sep 97

Database	Number of Prefixes	Number of 24 bit prefixes
MaeEast	38816	22872
MaeWest	14065	7850
Pac	3811	2455
Paix	713	377

If we rule out pure caching and protocol based solutions, it is important to compare the other schemes using a common implementation platform and a common set of databases. We extracted the BSD lookup code using Patricia tries into our Pentium platform; we also implemented 6-way search [12] and binary search on hash tables [31] using the largest (MaeEast) database. We project the worst case evaluation presented in [4] and the average case numbers in [17] to the 300 Mhz Pentium II platform with 15 nsec L2 cache (recall that 15 nsec is the time taken for the first word in the cacheline to be read when there is a L1 cache miss). Projections were done using the numbers reported in the papers describing the schemes, and by scaling the earlier results to account for the (faster) clock cycle times in our platform. The results are shown in *Table 2*. We also plot the worst case lookup times of various schemes in *Figure 1*.

Table 2 Lookup times for various schemes on a 300 MHz pentium II for the MaeEast database. The times for binary search on hash tables are projected assuming good hash functions can be found. The average performance is determined by the time taken when the best matching prefix is a 24 bit prefix as there are very few prefixes with length 25 and above. Note that for the Lulea scheme, the numbers have been recalculated with 300 MHz clock and 15 nsec latency L2 cache. For binary search on levels, memory is estimated assuming minimal perfect hash functions and $log_2 W = 5$ hashes. To be fair to the other schemes, we would like to point out that the numbers for our schemes are from highly optimized code and it might be possible to speedup other schemes simply by optimizing the implementation

	Average (24 bit prefix (nsec)	Worst case (nsec)	Memory required for MaeEast database (KBytes)
Patricia trie	1500	2500	3262
LC trie scheme	800	1000	700
Binary Search on prefix lengths	250	650	1600
6-way search on prefixes	490	490	950
Lulea scheme	349	409	160
Binary search on prefix lengths with expansion	250	250	3200
Expanded tries	130	196	500

Comparing Multibit Trie Schemes

The Lulea scheme [4] uses a clever scheme to compress multibit trie nodes using a bitmap. It uses a trie with fixed strides of 16,8,8; they are able to compress large trie nodes without slow linear search using a fast method of counting the number of bits set in a large bitmap. However, updating this bitmap is a slow operation. Also the Lulea approach pushes the prefix information to the leaves in the trie, which causes insertion to be O(N). The Lulea scheme also optimizes the information associated with prefixes by noting that there are (typically) only a small number of next hops. All these cause the Lulea scheme to have a slow insertion time.

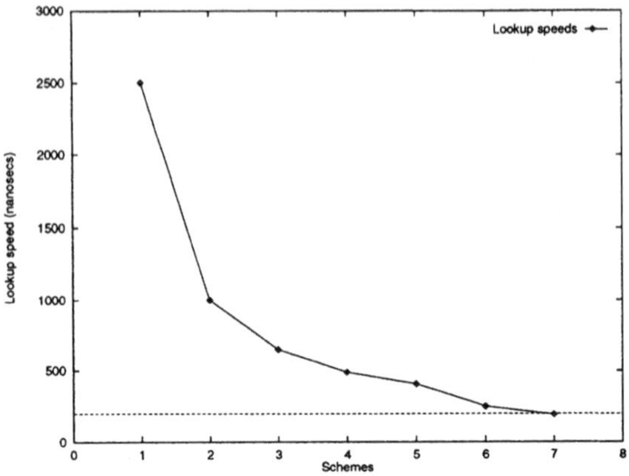

Figure 1 The lookup speeds of various schemes in nanoseconds. The scheme numbers used are 1. Patricia tries 2. LC-tries 3. Binary search on prefix lengths 4. Multiway search on prefixes 5. Lulea tries 6. Binary search prefix lengths with expansion and 7. Expanded tries. The dotted line corresponds to a lookup speed of 200 nanoseconds.

When compared to these other schemes, expanded multibit trie schemes have greater tunability and faster insertion/deletion times. Both the Lulea [4] and binary search on prefix lengths [31] schemes are competitive in lookup speeds, but have an insertion cost of O(N). So we conclude that in a software environment, expanded tries give the best performance while allowing fast incremental updates.

6. IP LOOKUPS IN HARDWARE

While this paper has focused on software comparisons, it is also important to consider how IP lookup schemes could be implemented in hardware. Many vendors today are using hardware IP lookup engines because of the cheaper cost and the higher speeds offered by such engines. Thus in this section, we first present a hardware model and the relevant metrics for hardware. We then briefly consider the schemes described in this paper from a hardware implementation perspective.

We assume a cheap forwarding engine (say 50 dollars assuming high volumes) operating at a clock rate of 2-10 nsec. We assume the chip can place its data structure in SRAM (with say 10 nsec access times) and/or DRAM (60-100 nsec access times). In memory comparisons, it is important to observe that SRAM is several times more expensive than DRAM. For example, following current prices, SRAM costs six times as much as DRAM per byte. Finally, some forwarding engines may have a few megabits of on-chip memory that is extremely fast (say 5 nsec access times).

Also, modern memory technologies like SDRAM and RAMBUS [19] provide a way to hide the long access times of DRAMs. They do so by providing a single chip with multiple DRAM banks to which accesses can be interleaved. Thus an access for bank $B1$ can be started while the results of a previous access to bank $B0$ are still forthcoming. Such technology lends itself naturally to pipelining, with the memory for each pipeline stage in a separate bank. At the same time, the forwarding engine only needs a single set of address pins to drive the multiple memory banks of a single RAMBUS or SDRAM.

Besides the search time measured in memory accesses, two other crucial measures for a hardware implementation are *worst case* memory usage and update times. While we have described the memory usage of different algorithms on "typical databases", it would be better to have a hardware implementation that can specify the worst case number of prefixes it can support, given a bounded amount of fast memory. For single chip forwarding engines, fast update times are also crucial. Besides the problem of backbone instability alluded to earlier, a chip that can do database updates entirely in hardware is much more attractive to customers. For example, consider an IP lookup chip that can do wire speed forwarding at OC-48 rates (one lookup every 166 nsec), can handle 50,000 arbitrary prefixes, and can do an update every msec. Such a chip would be extremely valuable today compared to CAM solutions that can only handle around 8000 prefixes. In *Table 3* we present a comparison of the theoretical worst case bounds for lookup time, memory required and the update complexity of the schemes considered.

None of the schemes described in this paper have good worst case memory usage. However, it is easy to add worst case memory bounds for multibit tries using a technique called path compression, first described in [32]. In this technique, trie nodes with only one pointer are removed and substituted with an equivalent bit string. Path compression differs slightly from the more standard technique for compressing one-way branches using a skip count, is described in [10] and used in [25]. An important advantage of path compression over skip count compression is that path compression does not require backtracking [25, 27] during search.

Using path compression, the number of trie nodes used to store n prefixes can be shown to be no more than $2n$. Path compression [32] can be applied to all the multibit trie schemes considered in this survey to

Table 3 W is the number of bits in the address and N is the number of prefixes in the database. For trie based schemes, k is the number of bits looked at in a single trie level. In the multiway search on prefixes, k is the degree of the search tree used.

	Worst case lookup	Memory required	Update Complexity
Multiway search on prefixes	$O(log_k N)$	$O(N)$	$O(N)$
Patricia trie	$O(W)$	$O(NW)$	$O(1)$
LC-trie	$O(W/k)$	$O(2^k NW/k)$	$O(2^k)$
Lulea trie	$O(W/k)$	$O(2^k NW/k)$	$O(N)$
Expanded trie	$O(W/k)$	$O(2^k NW/k)$	$O(2^k)$
Binary search on prefix lengths	$O(log_2 W)$	$O(N log_2 W)$	$O(N)$
Binary search on prefix lengths with expansion	$O(log_2(W/k))$	$O(N(log_2(W/k) + 2^k))$	$O(N2^k)$

provide worst case memory bounds.

A simple observation is that any search tree, whether a trie or a binary search tree, can be pipelined by splitting its levels into pipeline stages. The idea is that each level of the tree corresponds to a pipeline stage. The address is fed to the first stage which contains the root. The comparison at the first stage stage tells which pointer to follow (e.g., to node $N1$ or $N2$). The address is then passed to the second stage *along* with the pointer to say node $N2$. The second stage contains both nodes $N1$ and $N2$. Since the passed pointer says $N2$, the address is compared with $N2$ and the resulting pointer is passed to the third stage, and so on. Pipelining allows a speed of one lookup per memory access at the cost of possibly increased complexity. As we have seen, memory technologies such as SDRAM and RAMBUS lend themselves naturally to pipelining, by providing a single set of pins that drive multiple memory banks. In summary, *all* the schemes described in this paper can be pipelined to provide one lookup per memory access.

Given this modification, the expanded trie schemes are best applicable to hardware implementations that use external DRAM. This is because DRAM is cheap and inexpensive, and the increased memory needs of expanded tries are not a significant issue. However, since even the fastest trie schemes take 3-4 memory accesses, implementations (e.g., routers that support OC-48 links) that require lookup times faster will require pipelining. As link speeds continue to increase (e.g., terabit forwarding), DRAM memory access times will become a bottleneck. At such speeds, the entire IP lookup database will need to be stored in SRAM or on-chip memory. In such environments, where memory is again limited, schemes that compress trie nodes such as [4] will do better than multibit expanded tries (with relevant modifications to support high update speeds).

7. CONCLUSIONS

We believe with [31] and [4] that IP lookup technology can be implemented in software, at least up to gigabit speeds. We also believe that fast lookup algorithms make the arguments for tag and IP switching less compelling. We also believe that terabit lookup chips can be designed if such a need should arise. Finally, we believe that routers of the future may be less vertically integrated than at present; instead they will be assembled from special chips for functions (e.g., lookups, switching, and scheduling) and commodity routing software, just as computers evolved from mainframes to PCs. We hope the lookup technology described by us and others will contribute to this vision of the future.

We would like to thank Sanjay Cherian (Ascend), Zubin Dittia (Washington University), Will Eatherton (Washington University), Chaitanya Kodeboyina (Microsoft), Geoff Ladwig (Bay Labs), Craig Partridge (BBN), and Marcel Waldvogel (ETH) for invaluable feedback.

Notes

[1] George Varghese is supported by NSF Grant NCR-9405444 and an ONR Young Investigator Award. This work was done while both authors were at Washington University, St. Louis. George Varghese is now a professor at the University of California, San Diego.

[2] MCI and UUNET have upgraded their Internet backbone links to 622 Mbits/sec

[3] Some designs have a processor per input link; others use a processor per router. Some designs use a general purpose processor; others use dedicated hardware.

[4] Fair queuing [5] is a form of output scheduling that guarantees bandwidth fairness and tight delay bounds.

[5] 576 byte data packets arise in ISPs because of the use of a default size of 576 bytes for wide area traffic; 1519 byte size packets in the enterprise network probably arises from Ethernet maximum size packets

REFERENCES

[1] Scott Bradner. *Next Generation routers Overview.* Presented at Networld Interop'97, Atlanta, Georgia, 1997.

[2] G. Chandranmenon and G. Varghese. Trading packet headers for packet processing. *IEEE/ACM Transactions on Networking*, (April):141–152, 1996.

[3] S. Deering and R. Hinden. *Internet Protocol, Version 6 (IPv6) Specification RFC 1883*. IETF http://www.ietf.org/rfc/, 1995.

[4] M. Degermark, A. Brodnik, S. Carlsson, and S. Pink. Small Forwarding Tables for Fast Routing Lookups. *Proceedings SIGCOMM 97*, (October):3–14, 1997.

[5] A. Demers, S. Keshav, and S. Shenker. Analysis and Simulation of a fair queuing algorithm. *Proceedings of Sigcomm 89*, (September):1–12, 1989.

[6] Craig Partridge et. al. A 50-Gb/s IP Router. *IEEE/ACM Transactions on Networking*, (June):237–248, 1998.

[7] M. Gray. *Internet Growth Summary*. http://www.mit.edu/people/ mkgray/net/ internet-growth-summary.html, 1996.

[8] Intel. *VTune Performance Enhancement Environment*. Intel Corporation, Santa Clara, CA, USA, 1997.

[9] Intel. *Pentium Pro and Pentium II processors and related products*. Intel Corporatation, Santa Clara, CA, USA, 1998.

[10] D. Knuth. *Fundamental Algorithms vol 3: Sorting and Searching*. Addison-Wesley, 1973.

[11] C. Labovitz, G. Malan, and F. Jahanian. Internet Routing Instability. *Proceedings of SIGCOMM 97*, (October):115–126, 1997.

[12] B. Lampson, V. Srinivasan, and G. Varghese. IP Lookups using Multi-way and Multicolumn Search. *Proceedings of IEEE Infocom 98*, (April):1248–1256, 1998.

[13] A. McAuley, P. Tsuchiya, and D. Wilson. Fast multilevel heirarchical routing table using content-addressable memory. U.S. Patent serial number 034444, 1995.

[14] Nick McKeown, Martin Izzard, Adisak Mekkittikul, Bill Ellersick, and Mark Horowitz. The Tiny Tera: A Packet Switch Core. *IEEE Micro*, (January):26–33, 1997.

[15] Merit. Ipma statistics. *http://nic.merit.edu/ipma*, (Snapshot on 12 September 97), 1997.

[16] P. Newman, G. Minshall, and L. Huston. IP Switching and Gigabit Routers. *IEEE Communications Magazine*, (January):64–69, 1997.

[17] S. Nilsson and G. Karlsson. Fast Address Look-Up for Internet Routers. *Presented at the IEEE Broadband Communications'98, Stuttgart, Germany*, (April), 1998.

[18] R. Perlman. *Interconnections, Bridges and Routers*. Addison-Wesley, 1992.

[19] Rambus. http://www.rambus.com/, 1998.

[20] Y. Rechter, B. Davie, D. Katz, E. Rosen, and G. Swallow. Cisco Systems' Tag Switching Architecture Overview. Technical Report RFC 2105, 1997.

[21] Y Rechter and T Li. *An Architecture for IP Address Allocation with CIDR RFC 1518.* IETF http://www.ietf.org/rfc/, 1993.

[22] Y. Rechter and T. Li. *A Border Gateway Protocol 4 (BGP-4) RFC 1771.* IETF http://www.ietf.org/rfc/, 1995.

[23] M. Shreedhar and G. Varghese. Efficient fair queuing using deficit round robin. *IEEE/ACM Transactions on Networking*, (June):375–385, 1996.

[24] Richard Sites and Richard Witek. *Alpha AXP Architecture Reference Guide.* Butterworth Heinemann, 1995.

[25] K. Sklower. A Tree-Based Routing Table for Berkeley Unix. *Presented at the 1991 Winter Usenix Conference, Dallas TX*, 1991.

[26] V. Srinivasan and G. Varghese. Faster Address Lookups using Controlled Prefix Expansion. *ACM Transactions on Computer Systems*, (February):1–40, 1999.

[27] W. Stevens. *TCP/IP Illustrated, Volume 1 The Protocols.* Addison-Wesley, 1994.

[28] A. Tammel. *How to survive as an ISP.* Presented at Networld Interop'97, Atlanta, Georgia, 1997.

[29] Torrent. *Torrent Systems, Inc.* Torrent Systems Cambridge MA, http://www.torrent.com/, 1998.

[30] J. Turner. Design of a Gigabit ATM Switch. *Proceedings of IEEE Infocom 97*, (March):2–11, 1997.

[31] M. Waldvogel, G. Varghese, J. Turner, and B. Plattner. Scalable High Speed IP Routing Lookups. *Proceedings of SIGCOMM 97*, (October):25–36, 1997.

[32] H. Wilkinson, G. Varghese, and N. Poole. Compressed prefix matching database searching. U.S. Patent 5781772, 1998.

SPACE DECOMPOSITION TECHNIQUES FOR FAST LAYER-4 SWITCHING

Milind M. Buddhikot,
Lucent Bell Labs
Subhash Suri,
Washington University in St. Louis
Marcel Waldvogel,
ETH, Zürich
milind@dnrc.bell-labs.com, suri@cs.wustl.edu, mwa@tik.ee.ethz.ch

ABSTRACT

Packet classification is the problem of matching each incoming packet at a router against a database of filters, which specify forwarding rules for the packets. The filters are a powerful and uniform way to implement new network services such as firewalls, Network Address Translation (NAT), Virtual Private Networks (VPN), and per-flow or class-based Quality of Service (QOS) guarantees [4]. While several schemes have been proposed recently that can perform packet classification at high speeds, none of them achieves fast worst-case time for adding or deleting filters from the database [3, 8, 9]. In this paper, we present a new scheme, based on space decomposition, whose search time is comparable to the best existing schemes, but which also offers fast worst-case filter update time. The three key ideas in this algorithm are as follows: (1) innovative data-structure based on quadtrees for a hierarchical representation of the recursively decomposed search space, (2) fractional cascading and pre-computation to improve packet classification time, and (3) prefix partitioning to improve update time. Depending on the actual requirements of the system this algorithm is deployed in, a single parameter α can be used to tradeoff search time for update time. Also, this algorithm is amenable to fast software and hardware implementation.

1. INTRODUCTION

In recent years the Internet has transformed from a early day low speed network connecting predominantly educational institutions to a gargantuan fast growing commercial infrastructure. The diverse users of the Internet now range from ordinary home users downloading recipes to large corporations conducting sensitive transactions over the net. The expectations in terms of security, privacy, performance, and reliability of these diverse users are dramatically different. Realizing this, Internet Service Providers (ISP) are envisioning new differentiated network services that can meet demands of the full spectrum of clients. For example, a corporation that has multiple sites may want to connect its internal networks using the Internet but request strict bandwidth and delay guarantees and require that all its packets be encrypted as they flow through the Internet. To provide this new network service, commonly termed as *Virtual Private Networks* (VPN), the routers must be able to recognize packets originating from or destined to corporation sites and process them differently than other packets. However, IP routers that provide the best-effort Internet service of today differentiate packets based only on the IP destination address, the minimum requirement to get the packet closer and closer to its destination. To realize a service such as VPN requires the router to look at additional network layer information such as the source address, protocol type, and transport protocol fields such as source, destination ports [8, 9]. This new paradigm for packet forwarding based on network (ISO/OSI Layer 3) and transport (Layer 4) level information is termed as *Layer 4 Forwarding* or *Layer 4 Switching* and is central to realization of new differentiated network services such as firewalls, Network Address Translation, Virtual Private Networks, and per-flow or class-based Quality of Service (QOS) guarantees. A router supporting Layer 4 Switching maintains a table of rules for classifying packets, commonly called *filters*. Each rule also has an *action* item associated with it. Two important aspects of Layer 4 packet classification are: (1) *filter search* — classify/match every incoming packet to a lowest cost/highest priority filter and performs the associated action on the packet. (2) *filter update* — update filter table in the event of a filter addition or deletion. To be ready for the growing demands of users and ISPs, a Layer 4 router must be perform the filter matching operation at Gigabit per second rate. However, it is becoming increasingly evident that in addition to this, services such as firewalls and NAT require the router to support insertion and deletion of filters with sub-second latency. Unfortunately, recent packet classification algorithms reported in the literature only support fast filter search and require prohibitively large update time that grows at least linearly with the number of filters in the database or even require a complete rebuild of the lookup structure [8, 9, 3]. In addition, for a filter database with N entries, some of these algorithms [3, 9] require $O(N^2)$ space which is prohibitively high.

Contributions

In this paper, we describe a class of algorithms called (PACARS) — **PA**cket **C**lassification **A**lgorithms using **R**ecursive **S**pace-decompositions and present in detail a specific instance called Area-based Quad Tree (AQT). We focus primarily on 2-dimensional prefix based filters. However, our scheme can be extended to multi-dimensional filters using well known techniques in [8].

For N two-dimensional filters, our scheme requires $O(N)$ space, $O(\alpha W)$ worst-case search time, and $O(\alpha \sqrt[\alpha]{N})$ worst-case update (insert/delete) time. Using α as a tunable parameter, we can tradeoff lookup time for faster update time and thus, tune our algorithm to the requirements of dominant services. For example, with $\alpha = 2$, we get a search time of $O(2W)$ and update time of $O(2\sqrt{N})$, which are suitable for applications that require fast searches and reasonably fast updates. With $\alpha = 3$, the search time is increased to $3W$ but the update time is reduced to $O(3\sqrt[3]{N})$.

2. RELATED WORK

The problem of Layer 4 packet classification has received significant attention in the recent past. Existing commercial implementations of firewalls that use layer-3/4 filters often use linear search and hence do not scale to large databases. Caching based approaches are not scalable, since each cache miss requires a linear search of the database, which can be a big bottleneck.

Among other recently proposed schemes, Stiliadis et al. [9] present two algorithms: their first scheme is hardware oriented and requires wide data buses. It can handle general K-dimensional filters, but requires $O(N^2)$ space and expensive hardware. Their second algorithm is a 2D scheme that is more appropriate for software implementation but it does not handle general filters. Also, the worst case update time of both the schemes is $O(N)$.

In [8], Srinivasan et al. present a fast 2D scheme, called *Grid-of-Tries*, with $O(N)$ space requirement and attractive worst case search time of $O(W)$. By maintaining four such grid-of-tries, they can handle 5-dimensional filters. The worst-case update time of this scheme is also $O(N)$ and requires complicated *lazy update* schemes to improve average case performance.

Decasper et al. [3] present a packet classification scheme based on finite state machines. This scheme, though fast for lookups, requires $O(N^2)$ memory and is thus completely impractical for the number of filters that are expected in the future.

A more recent scheme called Tuple Space Search [6] proposed by Srinivasan-Suri-Varghese can handle arbitrary general filters, and has fast update time, but its worst-case bounds on both the search and update time are very poor.

In recent years, a new form of Content-Addressable Memories (CAM) called ternary CAMs have been proposed for use in packet classification and routing. However, they suffer from high cost, large power dissipation, and $O(N)$ worst case update time.

3. PACKET CLASSIFICATION, SPATIAL DECOMPOSITION, AND QUADTREES

This section presents the basics of the packet classification problem, and how to approach it using recursive search space decomposition, and the quadtree data structure.

Overview of Packet Classification Problem

Before we discuss our algorithms, we briefly review the multidimensional packet classification problem [8]. We assume that the router maintains a filter database or table that consists of N filters $F_1, F_2, \ldots, F_N$, each with K fields corresponding to the packet headers which it should match. In case of IPv4 packets, fields such as IP source address (SA, 32 bits), IP destination address (DA, 32 bits), protocol identification number (PID, 8 bits), Type-of-Service (TOS, 8 bits), and transport protocol level source/destination port (SP, DP, 16 bits each) have been considered as relevant fields. Each of the header fields is assigned one of the four match types: *exact match*, *wildcard match*, *prefix match*, and *range match*. For an exact match, the field in the header must completely match the specified filter field. Wildcard matches allow the database to contain either a fully specified field or a match-all (wildcard) symbol. In a prefix match, the packet's field must match the first *prefix length* bits of the filter's field, where the prefix length is also specified in the filter. In a range match, the value of field in the packet header must fall in the range specified in the filter. Each filter has associated *action* that is taken when the packet matches it. Consider an example of a 5-tuple firewall filter (SA, DA, PID, SP, DP) = $(1110*, 101*, \text{TCP}, [1110\ldots6000], [2000\cdots4000])$ with associated action *Allow the packet*. A packet $(1110\ldots, 10111\cdots, \text{TCP}, 2000, 3000)$ matches this filter and will be allowed to pass through the router but $(1110\ldots, 10111\ldots,$ $\text{TCP}, 1009, 3000)$ does not match the filter and hence will be dropped, unless it matches another filter.

Our algorithm allows for matching against a database of prefix pairs and range pairs, respectively. It can be augmented in a straightforward way to also match against a small number of fields with wildcard matches and a limited number of ranges. Due to space limitations, in the remaining discussion, we exclusively focus on 2D prefix based filters. We will first describe the basic ideas in our algorithm, namely the geometric interpretation of filters and hierarchical quadtree based representation of decomposed space.

Space Decomposition and Quadtrees

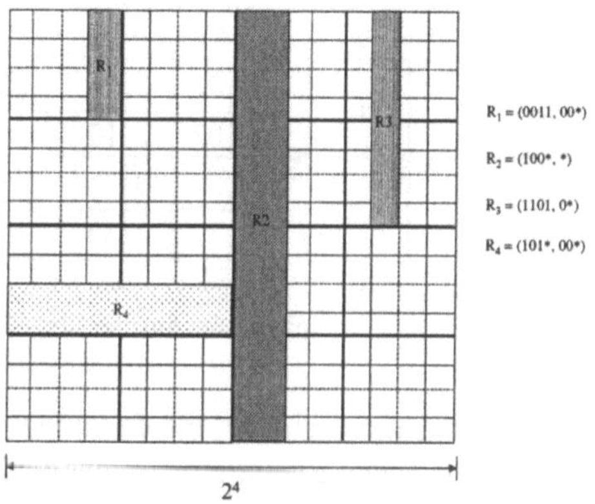

Figure 1 Geometric interpretation of filters: An example

The geometric interpretation of 2D filters forms the foundation of our scheme. If W is maximum prefix length, a prefix filter can be viewed as a rectangle in the $2^W \times 2^W$ search space. For example, a filter $F = (S*, D*)$, where S is a i bit prefix and D is a j bit prefix, can be represented by a $2^{W-i} \times 2^{W-j}$ rectangle. Figure 1 illustrates this using an example of four filters R_1, R_2, R_3, R_4 with a maximum prefix length $W = 4$. Here the filter $R_2 = (100*, *)$, represents a rectangle of size $2^1 \times 2^4$ in the search space of size $2^4 \times 2^4$. An incoming packet with a fully specified source and destination address, defines a point in the space. In the rest of the paper, we will use the terms filter and rectangle as well as point and packet interchangeably. Note that in a geometric representation of a general filter database, rectangles (filters) can potentially overlap and the point (packet) can thus belong to multiple rectangles (filters).

In the fields of image processing, computer graphics, and remote sensing such 2-dimensional point and region data is commonly represented using quadtrees. A quadtree is a representation of a recursive partitioning of an address space where regions are split until there is a constant amount of information to be stored in them. Several variants of the basic quadtree that differ in the type of data they store and the semantics of tree construction and search have been reported in literature [5]. A basic quadtree is a *4-way branching tree* that represents a recursive binary decomposition of space wherein at each level we divide a square subspace into four equal size squares – the north-east (NE), north-west (NW), south-east (SE), and south-west (SW) quadrants. Each node v in the tree corresponds to a square in the decomposition and its four children correspond to the four sub-squares obtained by dividing the square of v. Figure 2 illustrates this decomposition scheme.

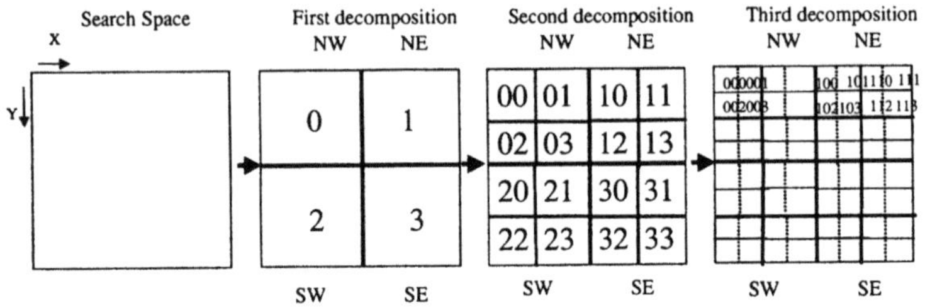

Figure 2 Recursive spatial decomposition

In our basic packet classification scheme, the decomposition is induced by a set of filters. We continue to divide a square recursively using binary decomposition until all packets mapped to that square are classified by the same filter and no more decomposition is required. Since the corresponding quadtree represents search space, every fixed point in the space has fixed location in this tree. Therefore, given a point's coordinate, this data structure will help us answer questions such as does it belong to a specific area in the space. Specifically, starting at the root of the tree, we can use successive bits of the X and Y co-ordinates of the point to make branching decisions at the nodes along the search path terminating at a leaf node and use the information therein to answer the query. The runtime and number of memory accesses for this search are proportional to the height h of the quadtree.

However, this naive scheme has the memory explosion problem — N filters in the worst case can lead to N^2 space. In the next section we present a scheme that requires $O(N)$ space.

4. AREA-BASED QUAD TREES (AQT)

In this section, we will first describe the key insight that leads to the concept of a *crossing filter set* (CFS) and then describe the quadtree data structure called Area-based Quad Tree (AQT) based on this insight.

Crossing Filter Set (CFS)

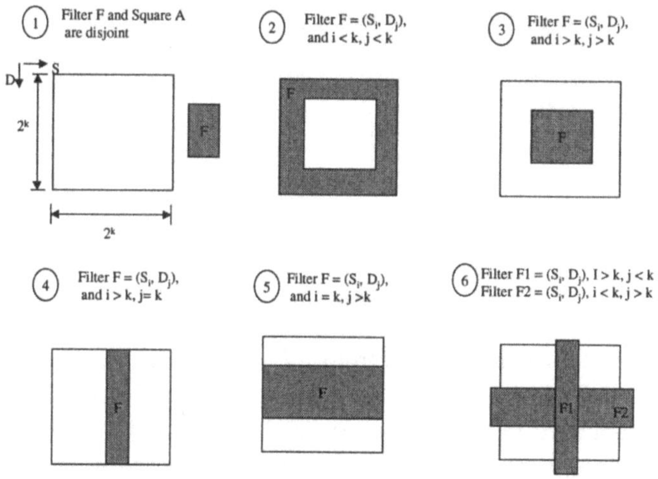

Figure 3 Filter overlaps

Our key insight is as follows (Refer Figure 3): consider a square A of size $2^k \times 2^k$ in the quadtree subdivision, and a filter $F = (S, D)$, where S is i bits long, and D is j bits long. There are several ways in which A and F can be inter-related: (a) If F and A are disjoint, then F is irrelevant to square A (case 1). (b) If the rectangle F completely contains A, then we don't need to pass F down to nodes that correspond to smaller squares. Of all the filters whose rectangles completely contain A, it suffices to just keep track of the lowest cost filter. This happens if both i and j are smaller than k (case 2). (c) If F lies entirely inside A, then of course, we continue to subdivide A and pass F down. This happens if both i and j are greater than k (case 3). (d) Last, the most interesting case is when F falls in none of the cases considered so far. In this case, F intersects square A, but neither contains the other completely. Because our filters are prefix filters, and since each square in the quadtree decomposition has size $2^l \times 2^l$ for some l, it follows easily that the rectangle F can intersect A in only one way — crossing A completely in one dimension. Figure 3 (4, 5, 6) shows various cases of overlaps to illustrate this point. Clearly, if $i \geq k$ and $j \leq k$, then F crosses A in the D dimension (case 4, 6 (F1)). Cases 5 and 6(F2) are complimentary cases in S dimension. In all these cases, we say that F_i *crosses* A. We call the set of all filters that cross a given region A as its *Crossing Filter Set* (CFS). We use this basic idea to construct a quadtree representation of the search space, called Packet Classification using Recursive Space-decomposition, (PACARS), as follows (Figure 4): Given a filter set FD, start with the root of the tree that corresponds to the entire search space.

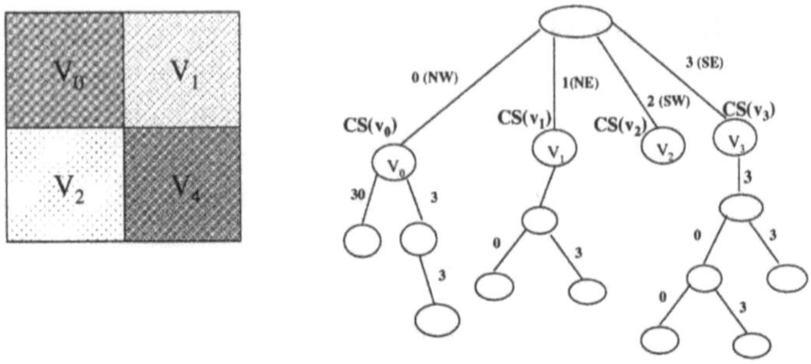

Figure 4 Basic PACARS Data Structure

Compute the CFS of the root and store it in a Crossing Filter Set Data Structure (CFSDS). Remove these filters from FD and recursively divide the search space into four children v_1, v_2, v_3, v_4. Compute the set $F(v_i)$ of filters that are completely contained in the space associated with v_i and then repeat the process of computing CFS at v_i. Do this recursively at each v_i and its children until the node (region) under consideration has only one or zero filters left. The method of space decomposition decides the height h of the quadtree and type of the PACARS algorithm. Now, our basic algorithm in the form of pseudo-code is as follows:

Algorithm 4.1 *Constructing the* PACARS *quadtree*

1 r = InitQuadTreeRoot()
2 A(r) = Square area ($2^W \times 2^W$) associated with r
3 F(r) = FD; //The set of input filters
4 C(r) = Set of filters in F(r) that cross A(r)
5 BuildCFSDS($C(r), r$)); //Build a crossing filter data structure on C(r)
6 $F(r) = F(r) - C(r)$; //Remove C(r) filters from current set
7 $v = r$;
8 Divide A(v) into four children sub-squares: $A(v_1), A(v_2), A(v_3), A(v_4)$;
9 $F(v_i)$ = Filters in F(v) that lie entirely in $A(v_i)$
10 **for** $i = 1$ **to** 4 **do**
11 BuildCFSDS($C(v_i), v_i$));
12 $F(v_i) = F(v_i) - C(v_i)$;
13 **if** $(F(v_i) == \phi)$
14 **then continue** ; // F(v_i) is empty, do nothing
15 **else** //F(v_i) has > 1 filter, recursively compute decomposition for v_i
16 Recurse from 8
17 **fi**
18 **od**

The main novel idea here is the use of crossing filter sets. This idea ensures that the memory requirement is $O(N)$, because each filter F is stored exactly once, at the highest node for which F is a crossing filter. Now, we will describe the crossing filter data structure (CFSDS), and how the query algorithm works.

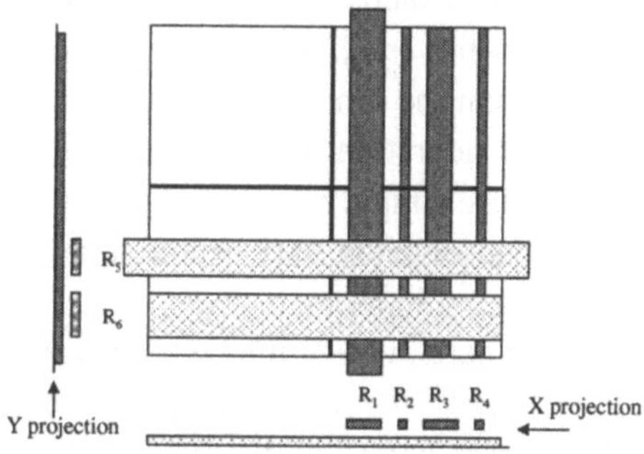

Figure 5 Crossing filter lookup

Consider what a CFS set C(v) must look like (Figure 5). The filters of C(v) can be divided into two groups, CX(v) and CY(v). The former is the set of filters that cross the square A(v) perpendicular to the X axis; and the set Y(v) is the set of filters that cross A(v) perpendicular to the Y axis. In our example, R_5, R_6 belong to CY(v), whereas R_1, R_2, R_3, R_4 belong to CX(v). We can exploit this special structure of the CFS to efficiently find the filter match at each node. Observe that for each CFS, we can project the component filters along X and Y axis, and since, the filters are specified using prefixes, these projections are also prefixes. This therefore reduces the problem of filter match to problem of finding the best matching prefix (BMP) along X and Y axis and selecting the one corresponding to the high priority (lowest cost) filter. The problem of finding best-matching-prefix has been widely researched. We look at three possible ways to solve this problem at each CFS.

Store the prefixes in a binary trie: This approach reported in [7] can find a BMP in $O(W)$ time with very small constant, where W is the maximum prefix length.

Binary search based on prefix length: In this approach reported in [10], a modified binary search is performed among prefixes sorted using the length of the prefixes. This scheme finds a BMP in $O(\log W)$ time.

Binary search on prefix endpoints: Note that each prefix $X*$ covers a range of numbers $[(X0\cdots0)\ldots(X1\cdots1)]$. Therefore, we can store m prefixes as $2m$ numbers or keys. With each key we store, two prefix ids

— *equal* and *less-than*, which are used to decide the matching prefix if the point/packet under search is equal to or less-than than the key under consideration. This formulation reduces the BMP problem to finding the successor element which is the smallest entry greater than the search value. If the key found exactly matches the key under consideration, the prefix ID stored in the *equal* field defines the most-specific or the best matching prefix. On the other hand, if the successor key is greater than the key under consideration, the *less-than* field defines the matching prefix ID. We can use simple binary search to obtain the matching or successor key and thus, solve the BMP problem in $O(\log N)$.

Now that we have all the parts, we summarize the search procedure: Given an incoming packet $P = (S, D)$, we form a location code L_p by interleaving S and D bit strings. The search begins at the root of the quadtree. We initialize a variable – $match$ to remember the least-cost filter along the search path. Starting at the most significant bit (MSB), we use the successive 2-bit values of L_p to make the branching decisions at the nodes that the search visits. At each node, the we search the CFS structure for the best matching (least-cost or highest priority) filter $bestf$ at that node. If the filter matches 'better' than the filter recorded in $match$, we replace value of $match$ with $bestf$ and continue. If we exhaust the bits or reach a quadtree leaf node, indicating end of the search path, the search is complete and $match$ represents the filter match. This suggests that in this naïve formulation we can solve filter matching problem in $O(h \log W)$ or $O(h \log N)$.

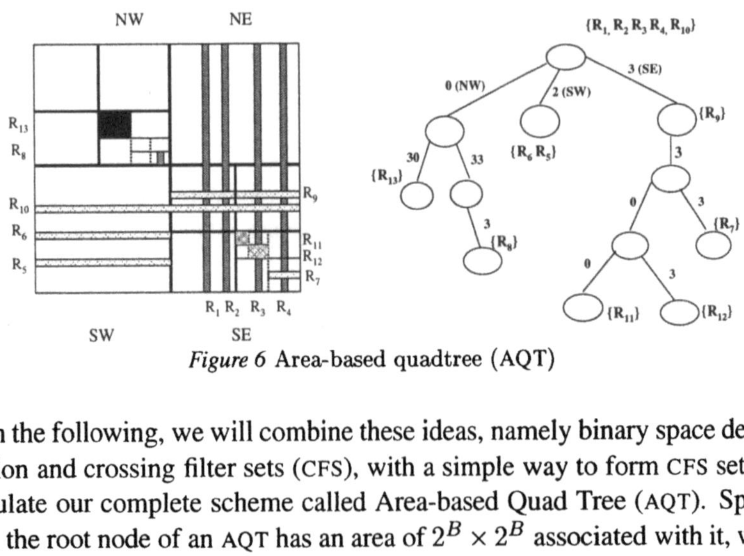

Figure 6 Area-based quadtree (AQT)

In the following, we will combine these ideas, namely binary space decomposition and crossing filter sets (CFS), with a simple way to form CFS sets and formulate our complete scheme called Area-based Quad Tree (AQT). Specifically, the root node of an AQT has an area of $2^B \times 2^B$ associated with it, where as each of its 4 children has squares of area $2^{B-1} \times 2^{B-1}$ associated with them. In general, a node at level i has a square with an area of $2^{B-i} \times 2^{B-i}$ associated with it (the root node is at level 0). We store a rectangle R at a quadtree node, if the square associated with the node is the *smallest* square that fully contains R. We can see that every filter passed down to the node at level i has at least one prefix of length i bits. This observation leads to the following rule for placing filters in quadtree nodes: A rectangle R represented as $(X_{w_1}*, Y_{w_2}*)$, where w_1 is the length of the X prefix and w_2 is the length of the Y prefix, should be placed at a node at level $i = min(w_1, w_2)$. The square $SQ = (X_i*, Y_i*)$ associated with this node, where X_i (Y_i) is a prefix of X_{w_1} (Y_{w_2}), represents the *smallest* square that fully contains the rectangle R. If W is the maximum prefix length, we can see that the worst-case height of the area-based quadtree is W. Since, every filter is stored at only one node, the space complexity of this quadtree is $O(N)$.

Figure 6 illustrates an example of an AQT with 13 rectangles constructed using this rule. In this figure, rectangles in the form of vertical strips R_1, R_2, R_3, R_4, and horizontal strips R_{10} are fully contained in the square of size $2^B \times 2^B$ and are therefore listed at the root of the quadtree. Similarly, south-west quadrant of size $2^{B-1} \times 2^{B-1}$ contains rectangles R_5, R_6 and hence, the two are listed at the node reached by bit string $10(2)$.

Optimizing the Average Case Search Time

Several optimizations are possible to improve the average case performance of the naïve search procedure. First optimization that relies on pre-computation is based on following two simple observations: (1) Note that if a filter with small area is *fully contained* in another larger filter, the node at which the smaller filter is stored will always be at a lower level than the the node at which the larger filter is stored. (2) Also, if two filters have partial *intersection* overlap, they are stored either at the same node or different nodes. We use these observations to *pre-compute* a variable *MaxPriID* at each node, which records the ID of the highest priority filter among all filters found in a subtree rooted at the node. When the search visits a node, before searching its filter list, we first check if the priority of the filter currently matched by the partial search is greater than *MaxPriID*. If it is, then we conclude that no higher priority filters exist in the subtree rooted at the node that can match the packet under consideration. So we abort the search and report $match$ as the best filter match, else we continue the search along the path to a leaf node. Clearly, if this comparison fails at each node, the search ends up visiting every node along the path to the leaf node. Therefore, this optimization does not improve the worst case performance of our basic search.

However, it is possible that quadtree nodes will be unevenly populated with filter prefixes i.e. some of the nodes in the quadtree will be empty and constitute only branching points in the tree, whereas others will contain a large number of prefixes. In fact study of real routing tables has revealed that prefix lengths are not uniformly distributed but have peaks at lengths 8, 16, and 24 which correspond to prefix lengths of the original Class A, B, and C networks [10]. This suggests that we can use $k = 8$ or more bits instead of just two bits to make branching decision at each node. This can reduce the worst case complexity dramatically to $O((2W/k)\log N)$ at the cost of increasing space requirement by 2^k. However, it is still not comparable to the search time of the state-of-the-art search algorithms such as [8, 9].

However, the AQT can take advantage of a well known technique called *Fractional Cascading* [2] to reduce the $O(W \log N)$ worst case search complexity to $O(W + \log N)$, comparable to other algorithms. Also, since $\log N \leq W$, the worst case complexity is bounded by $O(2W)$. By combining k-bit trie and fractional cascading, we can reduce the worst case complexity further to $O(W/k + W)$. The details of application of fractional cascading to AQT are not presented here due to space limitations and can be found in [1].

5. EFFICIENT FILTER INSERTION AND DELETIONS

In this section, we discuss insertion, deletions or changes to a filter database represented using AQT quadtree. We will first present an overview of changes to AQT datastructure that are necessary to effect a filter insertion or deletion and then present our schemes to reduce the overheads in implementing these changes.

Overview of Implications of Insert/Delete

The insertion of a new filter $(X*, Y*)$ to a filter database represented by a AQT requires following set of operations:

1. **Find a quadtree node to which the filter belongs:** We first use the filter placement rule to find in $O(W)$ time the smallest square that will fully contain this rectangle. This in turn defines the node in the quadtree to which this the new filter belongs to. If the node does not exist, a new quadtree node is initialized and inserted.

2. **Insert the prefixes in the projection lists:** The endpoints of the X and Y prefixes of this filter are inserted to the list of prefix keys at the node using ordinary binary search procedure.

3. **Update *equal* and *less-than* fields of keys:** The insertion of a new prefix into the X and Y prefix lists at the node can alter the *equal* and *less-than* fields of each key in the prefix endpoint list at the node. So these fields must be modified consistent to the new prefix overlaps. This problem is same as inserting a new prefix to a prefix database [10].

4. **Update the fractional cascading structure:** The addition of new keys to the prefix endpoint lists alters the augmented lists at the node and possibly changes the keys that need to be passed to the parents.

Clearly, Step 1 in the procedure above can be accomplished in $O(W)$ time whereas Step 2 takes at the most $\log n$ time if the number of keys in the augmented list is n (n is bounded by N and $\log N$ is bounded by W). In the third step, in the worst case we may have to modify every existing key record and thus, may require $O(N)$ time. Note that in the last step, passing new keys to parent lists can alter the *Successor-in -original-list* information for potentially all keys in the list and thus, in the worst case can take $O(N)$ time. Therefore, the worst case complexity of inserts in the naïve implementation is $O(N)$.

When a filter is deleted, we follow the complement of the 4-step process described above. In the following we will discuss how we can reduce complexity of steps 3 and 4 above using the *prefix partitioning* framework.

Prefix Partitions

The scheme introduced below, *Recursive Prefix Partitioning*, reduces the cost of prefix updates significantly at a modest cost being paid in search time. Additionally, it offers a tunable tradeoff between the penalty incurred for updates and searches, which makes it very convenient for a wide range of applications.

Basic Partitioning

The idea of prefix partitioning is to group N prefixes in a shallow tree of height α instead of a general binary tree of height $log(N)$. To understand the concept and implications of partitioning, we start with $\alpha = 1$ ie a single layer of partitions. We will use a simple example illustrated in Figure 7 (a): Assume an address space of 4 bits with addresses ranging from 0 to 15. This space also contains nine prefixes, labeled $a1$ to $c3$. For the fractional cascading to work, each left endpoint of a range contains the information what is covered by prefixes in higher layers. This is referred to as the less-than pointer and is the data that requires update whenever the closest covering prefix is changed.

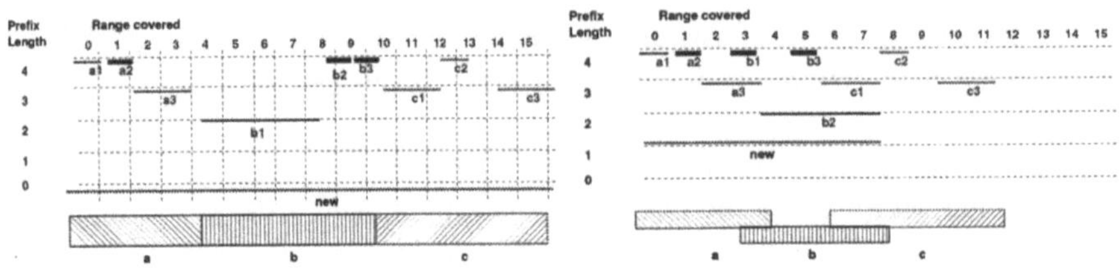

(a) Simple partitioning example *(b)* Partitions with overlaps

Figure 7 Prefix partitioning explained

Assume the prefix designated *new* is inserted. Traditional approaches would require the insert procedure to walk through all the prefixes and correct their less-than pointer, taking up to N steps. The *Prefix Partitioning* scheme groups these prefixes together. Assume we had grouped prefixes $a1$ to $a3$ in group a, prefixes $b1$ to $b3$ in b, and $c1$ to $c3$ in c. Note that the prefixes in the group are disjoint and hence, we can store a single overlapping prefix or less-than pointer information for all of them instead of each of them. Thus, in this example, we would remember only three such entries — one per group or partition. This improves the update time from updating each entry to just updating the information common to the group. In our example above (Figure 7 (a)), when adding the *new* prefix, we see that it entirely covers the partitions a, b and c. Thus, our basic scheme works well as long as the partition boundaries can be chosen so that no prefix overlaps them and the new prefix covers entire groups.

Consider one more example in Figure 7 (b), where partition A contains prefixes a_1, a_2, a_3, partition B contains prefixes b_1, b_2, b_3 and partition C contains prefixes c_1, c_2, c_3. Clearly, the partition boundaries now overlap. Although in this example it is possible to find partitioning without overlaps, in a general case prefixes that cover a large part of the address space would severely limit the ability to find enough partitions. In other words, in a general case, the boundaries between the splits are no longer well-defined; there are overlaps. The key insight that solves this problem is as follow: Instead of introducing a special case for these overlaps, we observe that only the less-than field of the key inserted for the left prefix endpoint contains information about the enclosing region. This starting address of the range covered by the prefix is thus the only relevant part. Therefore, it is not necessary to keep information about the covered range and the information about the starting point is sufficient. Since we only deal with individual addresses now, there is no need to treat overlaps and partitions can split the database at any arbitrary point. For ease of explanation, we nevertheless define a range for the partition, defined by the minimum and maximum starting address of the covered prefixes.

Continuing our example above (Figure 7 (b)), when adding the *new* prefix, we see that it entirely covers the partitions a, b and partially covers c. For all the fully covered partitions, we update the partitions' Best Match. Only for the partially covered partitions, we need to process their individual elements. The changes for the less-than pointers are outlined in bold in the Table 1. The real value of the less-than pointer is the entry's value, if it is set, or the partition's value otherwise. If neither the entry nor the entry's containing partition contain any information, as is the case for $c3$, the packet does not match a prefix (filter) at this level.

Table 1 Updating Less-Than Pointers

Entry /Group	Old<	New<
a1	—	—
a2	a1	a1
a3	a2	a2
a	—	**new**

Entry /Group	Old<	New<
b1	a3	a3
b2	b1	b1
b3	b2	b2
b	—	**new**

Entry /Group	Old<	New<
c1	b2	b2
c2	c1	c1
c3	—	—
c	—	—

Generalizing to p partitions of e entries each, we can see that any prefix will cover at most p partitions, requiring at most p updates.Thanks to the starting-address rule, all partitions are now disjoint. Therefore at most two partitions can be partially covered, one at the start of the new prefix, one at the end. In a simple-minded implementation, at most e entries need to be updated in each of the split partitions. If more than $e/2$ entries require updating, instead of updating the majority of entries in this partition, it is also possible to relabel the container and update the minority to store the container's original value. This reduces the update to at most $e/2$ per partially covered prefix, resulting in a worst-case total of $p + 2e/2 = p + e$ updates.

As $p * e$ was chosen to be N, minimizing $p + e$ results in $p = e = \sqrt{N}$. Thus, the optimal splitting solution is to split the database into $\sqrt{N}$ sets of $\sqrt{N}$ entries each. This reduces update time from $O(N)$ to $O(\sqrt{N})$ at the expense of at most a single additional memory access during search. This memory access is needed only if the entry does not store its own less-than value and we need to revert to checking the container's value.

Extensions of this basic to multiple layers of partitioning and the update behavior are described in more detail in [10, 1].

6. PERFORMANCE ESTIMATION

Table 2 shows the worst-case update and search times we expect to see for our algorithm when running on a typical processor used in workstations or PCs. Our calculations assume that the processor accesses are from 10ns SRAMs which are cheap and widely used in PCs. Besides that, we assume worst case conditions: No data cache hits in the processor improve the performance, and the data structure is laid out in the worst possible case with almost all the entries in a single quadtree node at the bottom of the tree. All these worst-case assumptions are very unlikely to hold. We therefore expect real-world average performance to be about an order of magnitude better. Still, our numbers compare well with even the search time results of the other known schemes. Please note that the worst-case search time is independent of the actual database size.

Table 2 Worst-case search and update times for PACARS

Update ($\alpha \sqrt[\alpha]{N}$)	$\alpha = 2$	$\alpha = 3$x	$\alpha = 4$
$N = 10,000$	$3 \ldots 4\mu s$	$1.2 \ldots 1.8\mu s$	$.4 \ldots .6\mu s$
$N = 100,000$	$7 \ldots 9\mu s$	$1.6 \ldots 2.6\mu s$	$.8 \ldots 1.3\mu s$
$N = 1,000,000$	$20 \ldots 30\mu s$	$4 \ldots 6\mu s$	$1.5 \ldots 2.4\mu s$
Search (αW)	$.64\mu s$	$1.28\mu s$	$1.92\mu s$

7. CONCLUSIONS

A number of results on multi-dimensional packet classification have appeared in recent years. Some of them have been geared for hardware implementation, some for software, all of them delivering fast classification, but none of them has been designed with efficient updates in mind.

In this paper we presented space and time efficient algorithm for fast-packet filtering that use *space decomposition* to efficiently represent the search space. For N two-dimensional filters specified using prefixes of up to W bits in length, our *Area-based Quadtrees* (AQT) data structure requires $O(N)$ space, $O(\alpha W)$

search time, and $O(\alpha \sqrt[\alpha]{N})$ update complexity. Both the average and worst-case search times and memory consumption are comparable or better than other schemes known in the literature. Our algorithm clearly outperforms them when it comes to updating the database by inserting or deleting entries. Note that using well-known approaches such as *lazy deletes*, and *multibit tries*, performance of our basic schemes can be improved even further.

We have also devised an alternate scheme, called Median-based Quad Tree (MQT), that supports arbitrary filters and efficient search and update operations. One of the applications of these algorithms we are focusing on is a dynamically adapting firewall, which is currently being developed and requires sub-second update latency.

REFERENCES

[1] Buddhikot, M., Suri, S., and Waldvogel, S., "Space Decomposition Techniques for Fast Layer-4 Switching," *Bell Labs Technical Memorandum*, BL011345-990726-06TM, Lucent Bell Labs, Holmdel, NJ, 1999.

[2] Chazelle, B., and Guibas, J., L., "Fractional Cascading," *Digital Systems Research Center* Technical Report, Palo Alto, June 1986.

[3] Decasper, D., Dittia, Z., Parulkar, G., and Plattner, B., "Router Plugins: A Software Architecture for Next Generation Routers," *Proceedings of ACM SIGCOMM 98*, Vancouver, Canada, pp. 229-240, Sept. 1998.

[4] Kumar, V., P., Lakshman, T., V., and Stiliadis, D., "Beyond Best-Effort: Gigabit Routers for Tomorrow's Internet," *IEEE Communications Magazine*, pp. 152-164, May 1998.

[5] Samet, H., "Design and Analysis of Spatial Data Structures," Addison Wesley, ISBN 0-201-50255-0, 1990.

[6] Srinivasan, V., Suri, S., and Varghese, G., "Tuple Search for Fast Layer-4 Packet Classification," To appear *ACM Sigcomm'99*, Boston, Sept. 99.

[7] Srinivasan, V., and Varghese, G., "Fast Address Lookups Using Controlled Prefix Expansion," *ACM Transactions on Computer Systems (TOCS)*, pp. 1-40, Feb. 1999.

[8] Srinivasan, V., Varghese, G., Suri, S., and Waldvogel, M., "Fast and Scalable Layer Four Switching," *Proceedings of SIGCOMM '98*, Vancouver, Canada, pp. 191-202, Sept. 1998.

[9] Stiliadis, D., and Lakshman, T., V., "Multidimensional Range Matching for Fast Packet Classification," *Proceedings of SIGCOMM '98*, Vancouver, Canada, pp. 203-214, Sept. 1998.

[10] Waldvogel, M., "Fast Prefix Matching: Algorithms, Analysis, and Applications," *Ph.D. Dissertation*, Dept. of Electrical Engg., ETH, Zürich, July 1999.

HOW MANY WAVELENGTHS DO WE REALLY NEED IN AN INTERNET OPTICAL BACKBONE?

Joe Bannister, Joe Touch, Alan Willner
University of Southern California/ISI and Dept. of EE-Systems
joseph@isi.edu, touch@isi.edu, willner@solar.usc.edu

Stephen Suryaputra
Nortel Networks
ssuryapu@nortelnetworks.com

ABSTRACT

Coupling Internet protocol (IP) routers with wavelength-selective optical crossconnects makes it possible to support existing Internet infrastructure in a wavelength-division multiplexing optical network. Because optical wavelength routing is transparent to IP, very high throughput and low delay can be achieved when packets are made to bypass the IP forwarding process by being switched directly through the optical cross-connect. One version of this approach is called packets over wavelengths (POW). This paper presents the POW architecture in detail and discusses its salient features. Realistic simulations of the POW that use actual packet traces in a well-known Internet backbone network reveal the level of performance that can be expected from POW under various options. Specifically, the fraction of packets that are switched through the crossconnect is evaluated as a function of the number wavelengths and the degree of flow aggregation that can be achieved. The resulting analysis, conducted in the context of the very-high bandwidth network service (vBNS) Internet backbone, suggests that as few as four wavelengths combined with a high degree of traffic aggregation can carry more than 98% of IP packets in the streamlined switched mode. In cases where it is not possible to aggregate traffic, the deployment of wavelength-merging technology would increase the fraction of IP packets carried in streamlined switched mode by up to 52%.

1. INTRODUCTION

The deployment of wavelength-division multiplexing (WDM) links has begun [7], and it is highly desirable to use these links to interconnect the routers that comprise the global Internet. Consider a network architecture — called packets over wavelengths (POW) and described in full below — in which packets can be forwarded by both Internet protocol (IP) routers and optical crossconnect switches. The goal of such an architecture is to switch as much traffic as possible directly by means of optical crossconnect switches, because IP forwarding is relatively expensive by comparison. Wavelength routing through an optical crossconnect switch is limited by the fact that only a few (four to 64) WDM channels per link are supported by today's commodity technology. This paper characterizes the expected performance of POW in such a sparse-WDM environment. Different options are examined for recognizing which packets should be switched through an optical crossconnect switch and which packets should be forwarded by an IP router. Simulations determine the level of WDM needed to carry a substantial fraction of packets in a switched (rather than a routed) mode.

POW shares features with IP switching [14], tag switching [16], and multiprotocol label switching [6], all of which are henceforth referred to by the vendor-neutral term "label switching." Label switching is used when an IP router includes a switching fabric that can be used to bypass IP forwarding. Because switching speeds are much greater than forwarding speeds (estimated by some [14, 12] to be 20 times greater for comparably priced hardware), the goal is to place as large a fraction of packets as possible on the streamlined switched path and to leave as small a fraction of packets as possible on the slower forwarded path. This feat requires some above-average intelligence in the switch–router. The router must have software that recognizes that a flow of packets can be passed through the switching fabric. A signaling protocol then notifies switches that the recognized flow should be carried over a switched path rather than a routed path. Eventually a hop-by-hop sequence of switches carries the flow of packets from one router to another. WDM equipment is on the verge of deployment in the Internet, and there are a number of projects to evaluate and implement label switching or burst switching in WDM networks [3, 15, 19], so it is crucial to fully understand fully their engineering tradeoffs.

This paper examines whether optical label switching is feasible and beneficial in the near-to-medium term. This necessitates investigating the behavior of real Internet traffic in an optical label-switching backbone with a limited number of wavelengths. It also requires the evaluation of the performance improvement achieved by schemes that aggregate traffic to increase the utilization of WDM channels.

The remainder of this paper is organized into four sections. Section 2 describes the POW architecture and principles of operation. Section 3 presents analytical results to characterize the overall gain that could be expected from the introduction of WDM. Section 4 provides the details of the simulation, the traffic model, and the experiments used to evaluate POW's performance. Section 5 presents the results of the evaluation. Section 6 offers conclusions to be drawn from the study.

2. POW ARCHITECTURE

A starting point for this work is to consider a wide-area backbone network that would be based upon advanced optical technology. In today's Internet a user's organization (business concern, educational institute, government agency, etc.) operates an enterprise network that attaches to an Internet service provider (ISP). A packet going from one customer to another then traverses the sending customer's enterprise network, one or more ISPs, and — finally — the receiving customer's enterprise network. More frequently the user's ISP provides wide-area transit of packets over its own backbone network; this ISP will typically hand off the packet to the receiving customer's ISP (also likely to be a wide-area backbone operator). A packet thus suffers a significant part of its IP-forwarding hops in the backbone network. It is not uncommon for a packet that travels coast-to-coast across North America to experience more than a dozen IP-forwarding hops. IP forwarding is expensive, because it is normally a software-controlled process. The dominant costs of forwarding come from matching the packet's destination IP address prefix to an entry in a routing table and accessing the packet's next hop from the table, which in a backbone today can exceed 60,000 entries. Although promising techniques for rapid lookup of addresses have been proposed [4, 11, 20] and are under consideration by router manufacturers, they have not been demonstrated widely in actual networks. Even if fast lookup is employed, there is still a significant store-and-forward delay associated with each hop when the forwarding path is used; this store-and-forward penalty is avoided in the switched mode, because switching is normally cut-through, allowing the head of the packet to exit the switch even before its tail has entered. One subsequent goal is to reduce the number of hops incurred by a packet while traveling through a large backbone network.

The introduction of WDM into the telecommunications network offers ISPs the opportunity to achieve greater performance and to scale their networks in speed and size. Consider an ISP-operated backbone that consists of routers connected by optical fibers that support WDM. Further assume that wavelength-selective optical crossconnect switches are available to channel wavelengths from incoming optical fibers to outgoing fibers [17]. A functional depiction of a wavelength-selective optical crossconnect switch (also known as a wavelength router) is shown in Fig. 1. This switch is a wavelength-selective optical crossconnect device that is capable of routing a specific wavelength of an incoming fiber to an outgoing fiber. The path is entirely optical and free from buffering or other delays. The wavelength routings are independent of each other, so that wavelength 1 arriving from incoming fiber 1 may be switched to outgoing fiber 1, while wavelength 2 arriving from incoming fiber 1 may be switched independently and simultaneously to outgoing fiber 2. The optical crossconnect switch is not a rapidly switching device; it is configured on time scales of microseconds to milliseconds and typically is left in a specific configuration for an extended period of time (e.g. the lifetime of an IP flow, typically tens to hundreds of seconds).

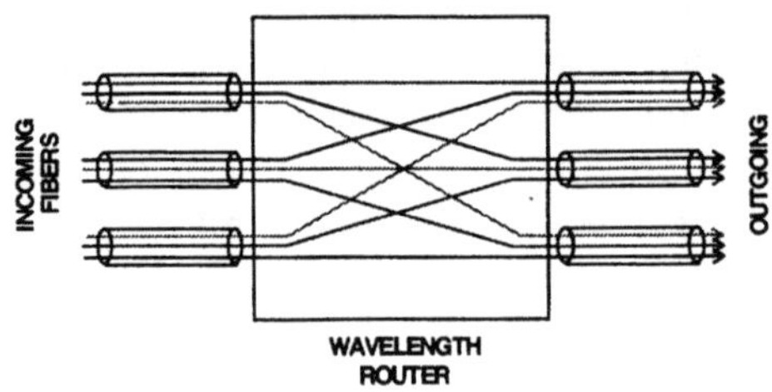

Figure 1 Optical Crossconnect Switch

The combination of an optical crossconnect switch and an IP router is employed in the POW switch–router to implement a node that is able to reassign an IP flow from the IP-forwarding process directly to a wavelength. An IP flow is can be defined as a sequence of packets that travel together along a subset of the same route in the network before exiting the network. This is a generalization of the more-common, narrow definition which identifies a flow as a sequence of packets with the same source and destination IP addresses and transport port numbers. POW's definition can focus on aggregated flows of greater intensity than narrowly defined flows.

By default, all packets flow initially through an IP router, which runs a process that detects and classifies flows of sufficient intensity and duration to merit fast-path switching. Each incoming fiber uses a special wavelength for the default traffic. When a flow is recognized, the router's control software attempts to shunt the flow straight through on its own wavelength. Shunting requires that the optical crossconnect switch be configured to support a wavelength that is routed from the flow's incoming fiber to its outgoing fiber. Suppose that a strong flow (call it flow 9) has been detected coming in on the default wavelength of fiber 1 and exiting on the default wavelength of fiber 3. The control software would seek to identify an unused wavelength on both incoming fiber 1 and outgoing fiber 3. If wavelength 2 is unused on both these fibers, then the router would signal the upstream router on the other end of incoming fiber 1 that it should bind all flow-9 packets to wavelength 2 going out on fiber 1. Similar actions are coordinated with the downstream router at the other of fiber 3 that flow-9 packets will be coming in over wavelength 2. In this way flow 9 will be carried from its ingress router to its egress router in the network. This sequence of steps is shown in Fig. 2.

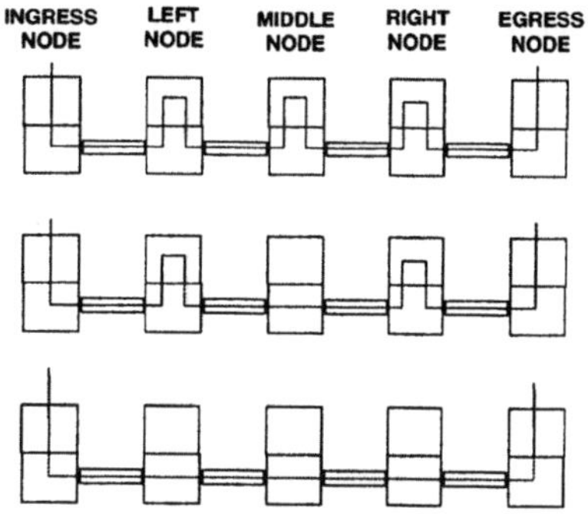

Figure 2 Assigning Wavelengths to Flows

Network architects have long recognized the desirability of assigning an IP flow to a wavelength so that the packets of the flow move along an all-optical path (sometimes called a lightpath or lightpipe) the network. The earliest attempts at this sought to create an overlay on top of a physical WDM-based network of a specific virtual topology optimized for the predicted traffic patterns [1, 13]. These attempts relied on a central controller that processed the network's long-term traffic statistics and preformed an optimization to identify the wavelength assignment (virtual topology) that maximized a chosen performance metric under the network's prevailing traffic conditions. The process is essentially static. It is computationally challenging, attempting a large-scale global optimization. Finally, it is subject to a single point of failure. These approaches implicitly assume that whichever controller identified the best virtual topology would be responsible for reconfiguring the network to realize the desired topology. It is questionable whether an operational network could implement this without imposing severe penalties on users. The assignment of flows to wavelengths in the backbone must be done dynamically, adapting to short-term traffic fluctuations and not dependent on a central point of control or requiring large-scale interruptions of service.

Signaling Protocol

The POW signaling protocol — called the flow-management protocol (FMP) — is built under the assumption of reliable message delivery, thus reducing the complexity of the signaling protocol. This assumption is enforced by running the protocol on top of a reliable transport protocol, e.g. the transmission control protocol (TCP). The POW flow analyzer recognizes three granularities of flows: fine-, medium-, and coarse-grain flows. A fine-grain flow is a sequence of packets with the same source and destination IP addresses, and the same source and destination TCP or UDP ports, i.e., a flow defined by a session between two applications. A medium-grain flow is an aggregation of fine-grain flows with the same source and destination IP addresses, i.e. a flow defined as the stream of information between two hosts. A coarse-grain flow is an aggregation of medium-grain flows that pass through the same ingress and egress nodes, i.e., a flow defined by the stream of packets that enter and exit the backbone at two given points of presence. The three granularities of flows are illustrated in Fig. 3.

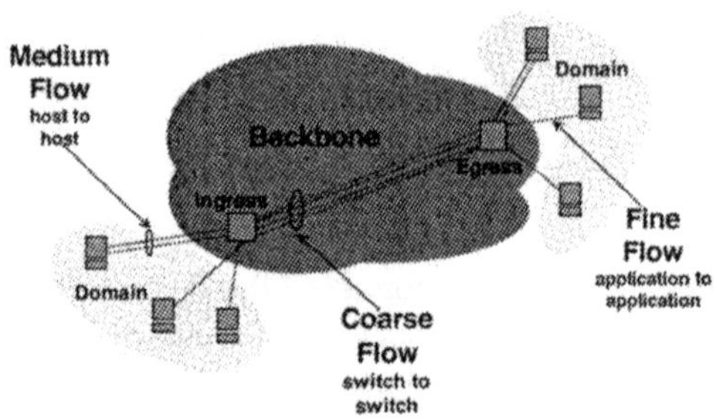

Figure 3 Flow Granularity

A flow is detected by means of the common *X/Y* flow classifier [12], in which a flow is declared eligible for switching whenever the switch–router observes *X* packets of a flow within a time period of *Y* seconds or less. Once a node detects a flow of the targeted granularity, it uses FMP to bind the flow to a wavelength that traverses the network.

Immediately after the detection of a suitable flow, FMP initiates messages to agree upon the existence of a set of free wavelengths along the route taken by the flow and to choose one wavelength common to each hop, thereby establishing a contiguous lightpath for the flow. FMP's strategy is to construct lightpaths from the egress node back towards the ingress node. The lightpath lasts as long as there is sufficient momentum in the flow to justify its assignment to a dedicated wavelength. A weakened flow causes a hop to disengage and propagates teardown messages along the lightpath.

Routing Requirements

The POW architecture depends on the ability of nodes to monitor and classify flows of packets. Because packets transit an optical network at very high rates, it is essential to monitor the network in real time and with little or no interference. Given such a feat, it is necessary to identify a flow on the basis of its routing. Although a challenging performance problem, recognizing a fine- or medium-grain flow from source and destination IP addresses poses no fundamental difficulties, because these addresses part of the IP headers of the packets that comprise the flow.

More problematic is that coarse-grain flows are the aggregations of packets that might not have common IP addresses. Their commonality stems from sharing the same ingress or egress nodes of the backbone network. However, ingress and egress points are not usually expressed explicitly in packets, unless they happen to be source-routed (as is possible — but not widely supported — in IP). It is critical for POW to be able to deduce at least the ingress and egress nodes of a packet by examining only the header of the packet. Happily, this requirement is supported easily by the most-commonly encountered backbone routing protocols. For example, the IS–IS (intermediate system to intermediate system) routing protocol, which is used by many of the largest backbone operators, provides the entire path specification of all routes through its network [5]. Such information is easily incorporated into the routing table, and it can be henceforth assumed that the POW router node software can lookup the next-hop, ingress, and egress nodes of a packet.

Routes used by the IP protocol may change in response to network conditions. Most commonly, a new route is computed whenever there is a failure in the network. Less commonly, a new route might be computed to optimize a specific performance or cost metric. POW lives comfortably with route updates, which are typically on time scales of seconds. POW might not function well where routes changing dynamically and more frequently. Fortunately, routes in today's Internet backbones are extremely stable, with average route lifetimes lasting several days [9].

Node Design

A functional diagram of the POW node is shown in Fig. 4. The router is a general-purpose computing platform such as a PC used as a forwarding engine. It includes software for monitoring packet flows, FMP signaling software, as well as software to control the associated optical crossconnect switch. The router supports the backbone network's chosen interior routing protocol, which identifies the egress router of a packet in transit.

The POW node is connected to other POW nodes by high-bandwidth optical fibers that employ WDM to carry several channels of information. The link protocol should be transparent to the optical crossconnect switch, its implementation residing principally in the router. The exact link protocol is at the discretion of the router operator, and it might differ from node to node (except where interoperability is needed). SONET, gigabit ethernet, or the point-to-point protocol (PPP) are likely candidates. This study does not assume the use any specific link protocol in the simulation model.

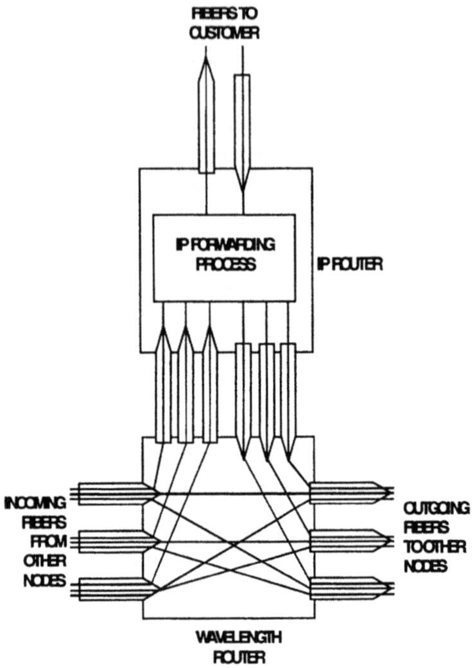

Figure 4 POW Node Architecture

The optical crossconnect switch is connected to the IP router by high-bandwidth optical fibers. These intranode fibers support only a single wavelength, which is the default channel over which all IP-forwarded traffic and signaling packets move. The IP router is the interface to the customer(s), with which it shares one or more links of a chosen technology (optical, electronic, etc.). The IP router is thus a standard router with a specially designed interface to the optical crossconnect switch.

Wavelength Merging

The reuse of precious wavelengths is supported by aggregating tributary flows by merging packets from several streams. The optical crossconnect component of the POW node requires enhanced capabilities to perform this merging function. The design and implementation of a wavelength-selective optical cross-connect with merge capabilities are being pursued as part of the

POW project [2]. The device can route the same wavelength from different incoming fibers into a single outgoing fiber. It requires that contention between bits on the wavelength must be resolved before they are multiplexed into the common outgoing fiber.

Using the merge function for traffic grooming is not a new concept in the telecommunications arena [21]. It is possible to use spare capacity on an already allocated wavelength to compensate for the scarcity of flows. The optical crossconnect switch can be integrated with a contention-resolution subsystem that time-multiplexes simultaneously arriving packets from a common wavelength but different input fibers onto the same wavelength on the same output fiber [18]. The contention resolver uses a combination of compression, subcarrier multiplexing, and time-shifting.

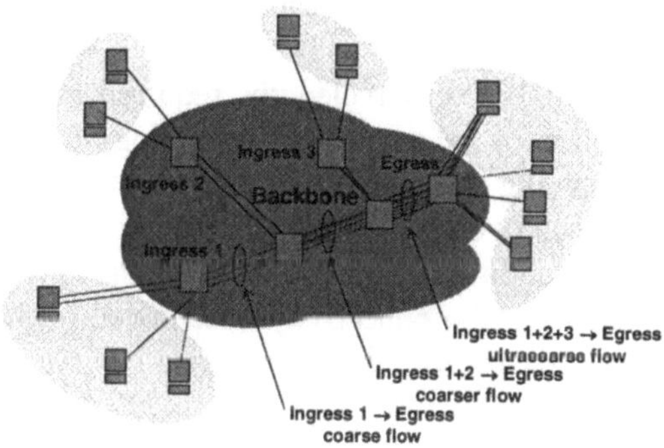

Figure 5 Wavelength Merging

Wavelength merges allow several ingress nodes to feed their flows to a single egress node, as depicted in Fig. 5. The signaling protocol must be modified a bit to allow for the allocation of wavelengths to "light-trees" rather than lightpaths, and it is also possible to merge wavelengths after they have been assigned.

3. THEORETICAL LIMITS OF WDM

As an abstract representation of a WDM backbone, consider a network of N nodes and the links that interconnect them. Suppose that the links can carry information on separate channels, one may ask how many channels are required to create a virtual overlay on the physical network that interconnects all nodes by exactly one hop. The goal of using WDM in an IP backbone is to put each pair of routers in the backbone within a single hop of each other, so that switching is favored over forwarding. It is therefore instructive to explore how many wavelengths are needed to realize a fully connected virtual topology in an arbitrary graph.

Although it is difficult to answer this question for all graphs, it may be answered for specific graphs that represents extremes of physical connectivity. Consider first the graph K in which each pair of nodes is connected by two links; K represents the idealized physical topology with maximal connectivity. Next consider the graph R in which all nodes are arranged in a ring, the links of which are all unidirectional; R is the idealized physical topology with the poorest connectivity (subject to the constraint that all nodes are connected by at least one path). How many wavelengths are needed in K and R to connect every pair of nodes by one hop?

It is clear that only one wavelength is needed in K to realize a single-hop topology, since the underlying physical topology is already single-hop. The number of wavelengths required to create a single-hop virtual topology in the ring R is much larger and depends on N.

Let f_N be the number of wavelengths required to overlay a single-hop virtual topology on top of the ring physical topology R. f_{N+1} can be computed inductively by observing that a new (N+1)-node ring can be created by inserting a node between two specific neighboring nodes of R. Using the original f_N wavelengths in addition to N new wavelengths to connect the new node to the original N nodes, full connectivity is achieved in the (N+1)-node ring. This yields a simple recurrence relation

$$f_{N+1} = f_N + N$$

It is clear that f_1=0, since a single-node degenerate network requires no wavelengths. Take the z-transform of the recurrence relation to obtain

$$\sum_{k=0}^{\infty} f_{k+1} z^{-k} = \sum_{k=0}^{\infty} f_k z^{-k} + \sum_{k=0}^{\infty} k z^{-k}$$

After algebraic manipulation of this last equation, the z-transform $F(z)$ of f_N is seen to be

$$F(z) = \frac{1}{(z-1)^3}$$

That this function is the z-transform of the sequence

$$f_N = N(N-1)/2$$

may be verified by consulting a table of common z-transform pairs [8].

To summarize, in a richly connected physical topology (K, the bidirectional complete graph) one wavelength per link is required to create a single-hop virtual topology, whereas in a poorly connected physical topology (R, the N-node unidirectional ring) $N(N-1)/2$ wavelengths per link are required to create a single-hop virtual topology.

If the volume of traffic between each pair of nodes is uniformly γ, then the throughput per node in the fully connected network K is

$$T_K = 2(N-1)\gamma$$

where the factor of 2 accounts for traffic both originating from and destined to the node. On the other hand, the throughput of a router in the ring under uniform traffic is

$$T_R = (N-1)(N+2)\gamma/2$$

since $(N-1)\gamma$, units of traffic are sourced by the router, $(N-1)\gamma$ units of traffic are sinked by the router, and $\sum_{k=1}^{N-2} k\gamma = (N-2)(N-1)\gamma/2$ units of traffic are transited by the router. If the N-node ring is provisioned with $N(N-1)/2$ wavelengths, then the amount of traffic that flows through a node in packet-forwarding mode can be reduced by as much as

$$T_R - T_K = (N-1)(N-2)\gamma/2$$

which is a substantial fraction of the total load offered to the ring.

The discussion above bounds the limits of performance that can be achieved by employing WDM in the network. In a poorly connected physical topology, routers can be unburdened of a large portion of their load (up to a factor that grows quadratically in the number of nodes N). The price paid for this is an increase in the number of wavelengths required per link (up to a factor that varies as the square of N). When dealing with real networks that have arbitrary physical topologies and nonuniform traffic demands, fewer than $O(N^2)$ wavelengths are expected to be used. In the next section simulations of actual networks under realistic traffic conditions will expose the practical tradeoffs between performance improvements and the number of usable wavelengths.

4. SIMULATION AND TRAFFIC MODELS

To evaluate POW a detailed simulation has been constructed for the purpose of running experiments. The goal of these experiments is to estimate the fraction of packets that could be switched (vs. forwarded) in a realistic network of POW nodes. To this end an actual topology and real traffic traces were used to drive a model built in the virtual Internet testbed network simulator (VINT/ns).

While earlier simulations focused on assessing performance in a single switch [14, 12], this study focuses in overall performance in a wavelength-limited environment. Such performance is presumably influenced by the competition for wavelengths by different nodes. It is imperative to simulate an entire multinode network rather than a single node.

VINT/ns Simulation Model

The VINT/ns tool is a popular simulation package used for evaluating protocols in large-scale networks [10]. VINT/ns performs packet-level simulation according to specified set of protocols. It has extensive facilities for the purposes of gathering data and testing functionality, and a large library of existing protocols. Most importantly for this work, it accepts as inputs log files of real packet traces.

Essential components of the simulation model include the flow classifier, which is constructed as an *X/Y* classifier with *X* set to 10 packets and *Y* set to 20 seconds, the forwarding functions, and the high-speed transmission links. The model implements the FMP signaling system (described above) for establishing lightpipes upon recognition of candidate flows. FMP is implemented on a hop-by-hop basis above TCP, which VINT/ns provides as a library protocol. The internode WDM links operate at OC-48 speeds (2.5 Gb/s), while the intranode links operate at OC-12 speeds (622 Mb/s). The node model does not use a routing protocol, but instead relies upon static routes that are preloaded in the nodes.

The nodes are interconnected in VINT/ns according to the vBNS (very high bandwidth network service) backbone topology, which is shown in Fig. 6. The vBNS network matches well the type of environment that POW would be used in: vBNS provides IP service on top of an asynchronous transfer mode network. However, the vBNS establishes a complete mesh of permanent virtual circuits among all nodes; POW would establish "circuits" (or wavelengths) dynamically in accordance with the amount of flow to be carried from one node to another.

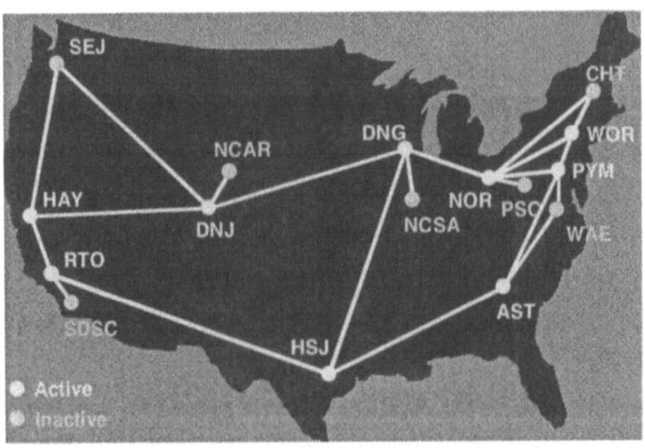

Figure 6 vBNS Backbone Topology

Each POW node is connected to its neighbors by an optical fiber that carries *W* WDM channels. In addition to these *W* channels, there is always one WDM channel reserved exclusively for routed traffic and signaling between any pair of neighboring nodes. The model of POW simulates its wavelength-management functions as well as the interactions of nodes through the FMP signaling protocol.

The simulation model is instrumented to measure several quantities. The principal metrics computed are the number of packets switched vs. the number of packets routed, the number of FMP packets exchanged as overhead, the transit delay of packets, and the number of wavelengths utilized.

Traffic Model

The simulation is based on an actual topology and real traffic traces. The vBNS backbone consists of 16 nodes, of which nine were passing traffic on September 18, 1998, when our traffic measurements were taken. These measurements are collected by the National Laboratory for Advanced Network Research and represent the average of five-minute samples taken hourly over the entire day. This data was used to compute a traffic matrix, an entry of which is the probability that a node's packet would exit the vBNS via another specified node. Thus, entry (i, j) of the traffic matrix represents the probability that a packet from node i is destined for node j. Traffic on the vBNS is relatively light, loading none of its links by more than 10% of capacity. However, it is the traffic pattern that interests us, rather than the actual loading. The matrix is displayed in Table 1.

Table 1 vBNS Traffic Matrix

	AST	DNG	DNJ	HAY	HSJ	NOR	PYM	RTO	WOR
AST	0.00000	0.56745	0.03781	0.00515	0.06092	0.09476	0.21693	0.00617	0.01081
DNG	0.08101	0.00000	0.11513	0.00379	0.61243	0.08101	0.08362	0.03870	0.01543
DNJ	0.03311	0.18448	0.00000	0.03595	0.34106	0.01441	0.08419	0.30353	0.00326
HAY	0.15571	0.00263	0.13758	0.00000	0.15903	0.08540	0.35294	0.07668	0.03004
HSJ	0.04519	0.00009	0.78623	0.00666	0.00000	0.03361	0.10832	0.01152	0.00839
NOR	0.01889	0.04205	0.01987	0.61550	0.01504	0.00000	0.11273	0.00149	0.17443
PYM	0.40164	0.00026	0.14268	0.01756	0.12685	0.17532	0.00000	0.04646	0.08924
RTO	0.01402	0.00025	0.89763	0.00399	0.01936	0.00807	0.05224	0.00000	0.00444
WOR	0.01372	0.84503	0.00483	0.00075	0.00740	0.02611	0.09917	0.00298	0.00000

The traffic matrix represents the averages of millions of packets. It is not feasible either to collect or simulate such a large sampling of traffic. A real trace of about one hour's worth of traffic was thus used. The packets were collected in tcpdump format from a router at the Lawrence Berkeley National Laboratory in 1994. The packet trace — known as LBL-PKT-5 — has "sanitized" IP addresses to protect the privacy of users whose packets were traced. The IP addresses in the trace are nonsense (and do not correspond to real hosts), except that a single value is used to replace a real traced address. Because the IP addresses refer to hosts that reside on customer networks that might or might not be attached to the backbone, it was necessary to devise a rule to assign a sanitized address to an egress router. When a packet is injected into the VINT/ns model, its address is read and randomly assigned an egress node in accordance with the probabilities in the traffic matrix. This indicates that the address is found on a network on the "other side" of the egress point. The assignment of an egress node to an IP address is consistent across a single node, but one IP address injected at different points will not necessarily exit the network from the same point.

This simulation model does not completely capture the dynamics of the end-to-end protocols. Because actual traces are used as inputs to the routers at POW points of presence, TCP behavior may not be modeled with total accuracy. The tcpdump traces that make up LBL-PKT-5 already reflect time-dependent end-to-end behavior that is governed by TCP's congestion-avoidance and flow-control mechanisms. As traffic loads fluctuate, TCP end-to-end throughput is expected to change adaptively. The packet timestamps should also change. Short of developing a complete simulation that includes thousands of hosts, it is not feasible to model the detailed behavior of TCP flows, so static traces are used to approximate the steady-state network flow.

5. PERFORMANCE EVALUATION

In partial response to the question "how many wavelengths are really needed," POW was simulated over a range of from four to 64 wavelengths (in addition to the default wavelength) deployed in the vBNS physical topology, using the traffic traces described above to drive the model. The principal performance metric is the switching gain, measured as the ratio of the number of packets that travel along an allocated lightpath (as opposed to a default wavelength) to the total number of packets submitted to the network. Also of interest is the signaling overhead, measured as the ratio of the number of FMP packets to the total number of packets submitted to the network.

As a performance metric, switching gain is an indirect reflection of throughput and delay. It relates directly to the goals of label switching, to maximize traffic over switching paths rather than routing paths.

The graph of Fig. 7 shows how much traffic can be switched as the wavelength count is increased, progressively aggregating flows. As expected, the switching gain grows steadily when the wavelength count is increased from four to 64. Less intuitive is the dramatic rise in switching gain as traffic is aggregated: when POW defines a flow according to the coarsest granularity, it can carry more that 98.59% of its traffic over dedicated lightpaths using a few as four wavelengths. When aggregation is weak (as in variants of POW that use medium- and fine-grain flows), switching gain is low, reaching about 84.56% and 65.94%, respectively, for medium- and fine-grain flows when 64 wavelengths are available. These latter figures hint at the high cost of operating POW without sufficient aggregation of traffic.

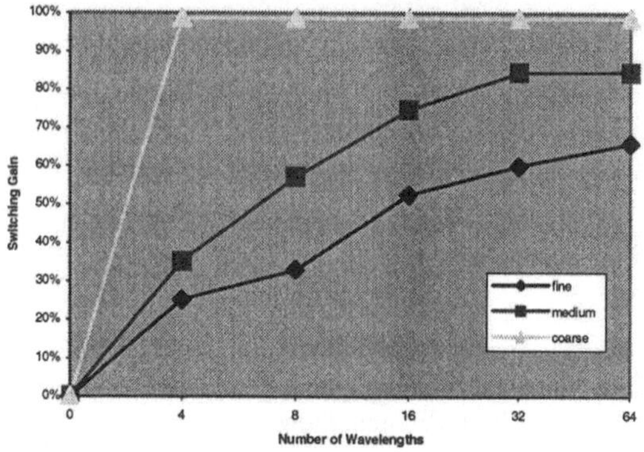

Figure 7 Switching Gain vs. Number of Wavelengths for Different Flow Granularities

Being software-based, the aggregation of traffic in a POW node does not come for free. Packet addresses must be matched, looked up, and tallied according to affinities with other addresses. Some of this dovetails easily with packet forwarding, but there is extra effort in aggregation. The wavelength-merging technology being developed for POW is a natural way to aggregate traffic by joining flows at intermediate nodes. When the fine-grain flows in POW are simulated with and without wavelength merging, an improvement in the switching gain is seen for all wavelength counts. As shown in Fig. 8, the improvement ranges from 21% to over 52%. At low wavelength counts the amount of switched traffic remains low. Given the excellent switching gain achieved with coarse-grain flows, it is unclear whether introducing wavelength-merging technology in POW will ultimately pay off.

The signaling protocol FMP imposes a penalty on the network by introducing overhead traffic that competes with user traffic for bandwidth and processing cycles. Although FMP's traffic is restricted to the default wavelength, its presence on that link still deprives other unswitched traffic of bandwidth. If the overhead of FMP is kept low as a percentage of overall traffic, then improvements in switching gain are clearly achieved. If FMP overhead is high, then one must weigh any improvements in switching gain against the cost of this overhead.

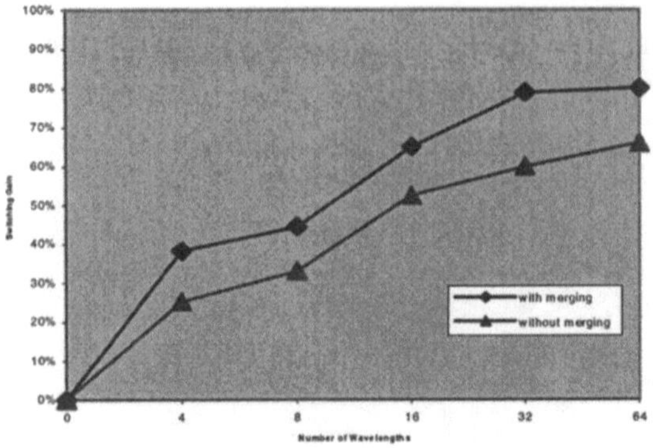

Figure 8 Switching Gain vs. Number of Wavelengths with and without Wavelength Merging for Fine-Grain Flows

Table 2 shows an account of the signaling overhead as a function of flow granularity and wavelength count for POW networks without wavelength merging. Signalling overhead remains low over most of the operating regimes of POW. The exception is when the granularity is fine and the wavelength count is high, where FMP is obliged to search the wavelength space for an available WDM channel. This search is exacerbated by temporarily locking wavelengths while FMP probes the entire path. FMP thus places significant additional traffic in the network in some circumstances. Note that signaling overhead is calculated as a fraction of all offered traffic. In the 64-wavelength, fine-grain POW configuration, the 8.60% of the offered traffic that is associated with FMP is comparable to the 34.06% of offered traffic that is not switched (see Fig. 7). In the case of coarse flows, the overhead is steady regardless of the number of wavelengths available, because four wavelengths are adequate to switch most eligible traffic, and the addition of wavelengths has no impact at all on the operation of FMP.

Table 2 Signaling Overhead

Granularity	Wavelength Count				
	4	8	16	32	64
Fine	0.18%	0.39%	0.94%	5.00%	8.60%
Medium	0.14%	0.37%	0.88%	1.41%	1.46%
Coarse	0.02%	0.02%	0.02%	0.02%	0.02%

6. CONCLUSION

This study considered the question of how many wavelengths are needed to achieve good performance for a packet-over-wavelength architecture for providing high-speed Internet service in an optical backbone network. Focusing on an existing backbone topology (vBNS) and using real traffic traces, simulation was used to evaluate the switching gain achievable as a function of wavelength count and traffic aggregation. The central conclusion is that very high switching gain (on the order of 98% of offered traffic is switched) can be achieved when traffic is coarsely aggregated according to its ingress and egress nodes, even for low wavelength counts. It is reasonable to expect that a network comparable to vBNS could benefit from POW with as few as four wavelengths.

Introducing wavelength-merging technology into POW improves the switching gain with fine-grain flows by as much as 52%. However, overall switching gain is low, even when wavelength merging is employed with fine-grain flows, reaching only 80.14% with 64 wavelengths.

The signaling overhead that is imposed by POW is generally low, except when traffic is finely aggregated. In the case of fine-grain flows with a high wavelength count, overhead amounts to more that 8.60% of the offered traffic. Because the overhead is carried entirely on links shared by unswitched traffic, it can negatively impact the network's performance.

In summary, four wavelengths are sufficient to achieve very high performance when traffic is aggregated according to its ingress and egress nodes. The conclusions drawn from this study apply to one relatively small backbone, using a traffic model based on data collected from older packet traces and traffic patterns on a lightly loaded backbone. Evaluating POW more effectively would require larger, topologically diverse backbones and packet traces that are more representative of a high-performance network. Completely ignored in this study are the issues of stability and transient response when traffic patterns change abruptly and new wavelength assignments are effected; however, such concerns would probably be among the most critical in the view of a backbone operator and its customers.

REFERENCES

[1] J. Bannister, L. Fratta, and M. Gerla, "Topological Design of the Wavelength-Division Optical Network," *Proc. IEEE INFOCOM '90,*" San Francisco, pp. 1005–1013, Apr. 1990.

[2] J. Bannister *et al.*, "How Many Wavelengths Do We Really Need? A Study of Packets Over Wavelengths," presented at GBN '99, New York, Mar. 1999.

[3] D. Blumenthal *et al.*, "WDM Optical IP Tag Switching with Packet-Rate Wavelength Conversion and Subcarrier Multiplexed Addressing," *Proc. OFC '99*, San Diego, Feb. 1999.

[4] A. Brodnik *et al.*, "Small Forwarding Tables for Fast Routing Lookups," *Proc. ACM Sigcomm '97*, Cannes, pp. 3–14, Sept. 1997.

[5] R. Callon, "Use of OSI IS–IS for Routing in TCP/IP and Dual Environments," IETF RFC 1195, Dec. 1990.

[6] R. Callon *et al.*, "A Framework for Multiprotocol Label Switching (MPLS)," (work in progress), Nov. 1997.

[7] "WDM Equipment Buyer's Guide," *Data Communications Magazine*, http://www.data.com, Apr. 1999.

[8] R. Dorf, ed., *The Electrical Engineering Handbook*, CRC Press, Boca Raton, Fla., 1993.

[9] R. Govindan and A. Reddy, "An Analysis of Inter-Domain Topology and Route Stability," *Proc. IEEE INFOCOM '97*, Kobe, pp. 850–857 Apr. 1997.

[10] P. Huang, D. Estrin, and J. Heidemann, "Enabling Large-scale Simulations: Selective Abstraction Approach to the Study of Multicast Protocols," *Proc. IEEE MASCOTS '98*, Montreal, pp. 241–248, Jul. 1998.

[11] B. Lampson, V. Srinivasan, and G. Varghese, "IP Lookup Using Multiway and Multicolumn Binary Search," *Proc. IEEE INFOCOM '98*, San Francisco, pp. 1248–1256, Apr. 1998.

[12] S. Lin and N. McKeown, "A Simulation Study of IP Switching," *Proc. ACM Sigcomm '97*, Cannes, pp. 15–24, Sept. 1997.

[13] B. Mukherjee *et al.*, "Some Principles for Designing a Wide-Area Optical Network," *Proc. IEEE INFOCOM '94*, Toronto, pp. 110–119, Jun. 1994.

[14] P. Newman *et al.*, "IP Switching — ATM Under IP," *IEEE/ACM Trans. Networking*, vol. 6, no. 2, pp. 117–129, Apr. 1998.

[15] C. Qiao and M. Yoo, "Optical Burst Switching — A New Paradigm," *J. High Speed Networks*, to appear.

[16] Y. Rekhter *et al.*, "Cisco Systems' Tag Switching Architecture Overview," IETF RFC 2105, Feb. 1997.

[17] R. Schmidt and R. Alferness, "Directional Coupler Switches, Modulators, and Filters Using Alternating δβ Techniques," in *Photonic Switching*, H. Hinton and J. Midwinter, eds., IEEE Press, New York, 1990.

[18] W. Shieh, E. Park, and A. Willner, "Demonstration of Output-Port Contention Resolution in a WDM Switching Node Based on All-Optical Wavelength Shifting and Subcarrier-Multiplexed Routing Control Headers," *IEEE Photonics Tech. Lett.*, vol. 9, pp. 1023–1025, 1997.

[19] J. Turner, "Terabit Burst Switching," Tech. Rep. WUCS-9817, Washington Univ., Dept. of Comp. Sci., Jul. 1998.

[20] M. Waldvogel *et al.*, "Scalable High Speed IP Lookups," *Proc. ACM Sigcomm '97*, Cannes, pp. 25–36, Sept. 1997.

[21] X. Zhang and C. Qiao, "An Effective and Comprehensive Solution to Traffic Grooming and Wavelength Assignment in SONET/WDM Rings," *Proc. SPIE Conf. on All-Optical Networking*, vol. 3531, pp. 221–223, Nov. 1998.

PART 3

OS AND MIDDLEWARE

SCHEDULING TCP IN THE NEMESIS OPERATING SYSTEM*

Thiemo Voigt and Bengt Ahlgren
Swedish Institute of Computer Science
Box 1263, SE-164 29 Kista, Sweden
thiemo@sics.se, bengta@sics.se

Abstract

The Nemesis operating system is designed to provide Quality of Service to applications. Nemesis also allows applications to reserve CPU time and transmit bandwidth on network interfaces. We have implemented a TCP for Nemesis that makes use of these guarantees.

We show that the Nemesis transmit scheduler rate-controls TCP traffic and thus leads to predictable traffic behavior when applications choose not to utilize non-allocated bandwidth. Applications that want to make use of the non-allocated transmit bandwidth receive the guaranteed bandwidth plus a share of the non-allocated bandwidth.

We also study the impact of the guaranteed fraction of CPU time on the throughput that networked applications achieve. We measure the amount of CPU time applications have to reserve in order to run the TCP protocol stack and send data at a particular speed. We show that these values hold even when several applications strive for CPU time and transmit bandwidth.

1 INTRODUCTION

Providing a deterministic service quality from a distributed application involves ensuring service quality in a whole chain of systems. Both the communication network and the computer platform on which the application is implemented have to provide service guarantees. In this paper we assume that the network provides the necessary service quality and focus on the mechanisms needed in the end-system computer platform to make it deliver the network

*This work is supported in part by the CEC DG III Esprit LTR project 21917 Pegasus II.

quality of service to the application. These mechanisms include providing service guarantees to the software implementing the communication protocols, i.e., guaranteed CPU time, and the allocation of transmit bandwidth on the network interface. In this paper we study CPU scheduling of a TCP/IP implementation, the scheduling of network interface transmit bandwidth and their interdependence in the context of the Nemesis operating system.

The Nemesis operating system [6] is designed to provide guaranteed quality of service (QoS) to applications. In order to provide guarantees it is necessary that all resources used by or on behalf of an application are accounted for correctly. In this respect, shared servers are a problem since they make it hard to charge the correct application for the resources used. In Nemesis the use of shared servers is instead reduced to a minimum. This leads to the *vertical structure* of Nemesis. Besides CPU time and disk I/O bandwidth, Nemesis regards transmit bandwidth on network interfaces as a resource that can be reserved.

We present a set of experiments which demonstrate the ability of Nemesis to provide the appropriate end-system communication guarantees for the application. First we show that the scheduling of transmit bandwidth can both be used as a rate limiter and to provide guaranteed transmit bandwidth. We measure the amount of CPU time an application needs in order to be able run the TCP/IP protocol stack and send data at a particular speed. Our experiments show that the CPU time to run the protocol stack increases linearly with the amount of data sent for a given packet size. We also show that the measured values hold even when several applications strive for CPU time and transmit bandwidth.

A possible usage of our scheme is an Internet service provider running one Nemesis host with several web servers for a number of customers with different performance requirements. Also other applications that need reliable data transfer can be run concurrently with guaranteed progress according to their reservations.

The contribution made in this paper is showing that the TCP/IP implementation in Nemesis can utilize the scheduling of CPU time and transmit bandwidth to provide the application with a guaranteed communication service. The scheduling of transmit bandwidth allows to rate-control TCP which can be useful for not exceeding a given traffic contract. We believe that this is difficult to achieve with traditional operating systems.

In the next section we briefly describe the features of Nemesis relevant for our work. In section three we give an overview on the design and implementation of the Nemesis TCP. Section four presents results and performance figures. In section five we discuss related work while section six concludes the paper.

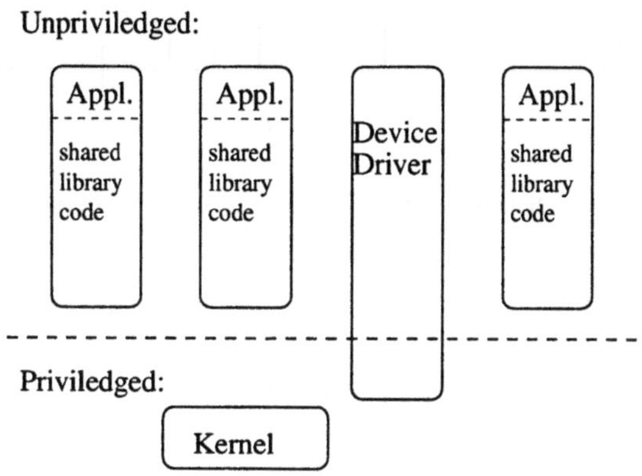

Figure 1 The Nemesis structure.

2 NEMESIS

The *vertical structure* of the Nemesis operating system is shown in Figure 1. Applications use shared library code to perform functionality usually associated with the operating system.

The Nemesis kernel is very small, consisting of the scheduler and activations of domains, the interrupt and trap handlers, support for inter-domain communication as well as some processor control. There are no kernel threads. A *domain* is similar to a Unix process. Trusted domains, such as device drivers, can register interrupt handlers and affect the processor mode. Despite having extra rights, trusted domains are scheduled like all other domains.

Nemesis has a single virtual address space which makes it easy to share data. Each domain still has its own memory protection on this address space, making lightweight inter-domain communication possible. Shared memory is used to transport the marshalled arguments and event counts synchronize the shared buffers.

Shared libraries export one or more strongly-typed *interfaces* which are specified in an interface description language called MIDDL. Interface descriptions comprise types, exceptions and methods. Having acquired a so-called binding or *interface reference* [6], domains can call methods of interfaces exported by other domains.

QoS Guarantees and Scheduling

Applications can request a share of the CPU time. Application requests consist of a tuple containing a period p, a time slice s and a flag x denoting

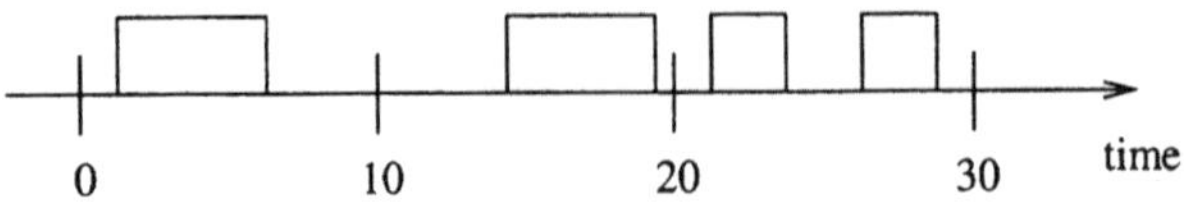

Figure 2 Scheduling of an application over three periods

whether the application wants to use *extra time*, i.e., a fair share of the non-allocated CPU time. If the reservation succeeds, the application is guaranteed a portion of s time units in each period of length p. The application is not guaranteed an atomic slice. The slice may be split up into several smaller parts.

An example is shown in Figure 2. An application has specified a period p of 10 time units, a slice time s of 5 units and the extra time flag x is set to `false`. In the first two periods the application receives one slice of 5 time units with the slice starting at different times. In the third period the application receives its slice time split up into two parts.

The scheduling is done using the Atropos scheduler [6] which internally uses an Earliest Deadline First algorithm. The deadlines are not specified by the applications but computed from the applications' specifications.

A similar scheme is used for the reservation of transmit bandwidth. Applications specify their reservations using the same tuple as described above, i.e., the reservations are expressed as transmission time and not as bandwidth. As for CPU time, the deadlines are not specified by the applications but computed from the applications' specifications. Setting the extra flag x to `true` means that the application wants a fair share of the non-allocated part of the transmit bandwidth.

Rbufs and I/0 Channels

Nemesis deploys a mechanism called *Rbufs* [3] for the inter-domain transport of bulk I/O through so-called I/O channels. Packets are formed using a data structure called I/O Record or *iorec*. An `iorec` consists of a header and a sequence of base pointer and length pairs similar to the `iovec` structure in Unix, with the header denoting how many pairs belong to the `iorec`. The base pointer points into a contiguous region of virtual address space called *Rbuf Data Area*, which is always backed by physical memory.

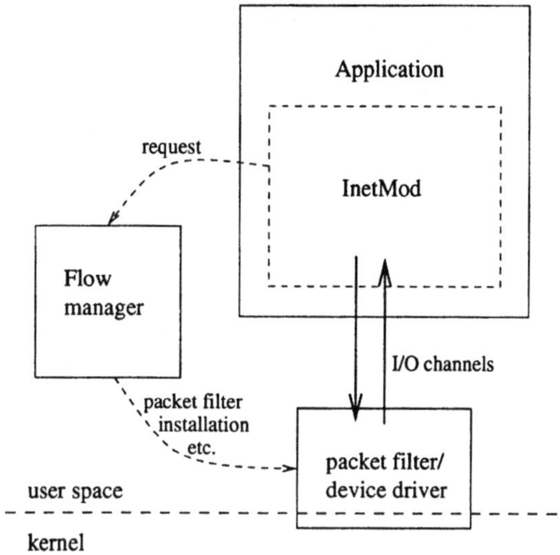

Figure 3 Architectural overview

3 TCP DESIGN AND IMPLEMENTATION

In this section we briefly describe the design and implementation of the Nemesis TCP, including some implementation problems that occurred due to the buffer handling scheme.

Overview

The Nemesis TCP implementation is partitioned between a shared library (*InetMod*) executed in the application domain and a trusted domain called the *flow manager*. The latter is responsible for both the synchronization of global resources, such as TCP port numbers, and for various control tasks like installing and removing packet filters. The main task of the packet filters is to demultiplex incoming packets to the right application at the lowest possible level. The packet filter is part of the device driver domain (see Figure 3).

Our implementation is based on the TCP/IP implementation of BSD [15]. As is done in BSD Unix, applications call TCP functions indirectly via a socket interface. For native Nemesis networking we provide two socket abstractions, namely `Socket` and `ServerSocket`.

As other TCP user-space implementations, such as Thekkat et. al. [13], our implementation uses threads, three for each connection. The *receiver thread* receives and processes incoming packets. Packets that should be delivered to the application are queued in a FIFO queue (*to_app*) containing pointers to `iorecs`. The *timer thread*'s task is to trigger delayed acknowledgements, to force retransmissions, window and keepalive probes and to drop connections when the peer does not respond. The timer thread also prevents that the connection stays in the `FIN_WAIT_2` state forever and handles the deletion of the control block in the `TIME_WAIT` state.

The third thread is the application's thread. When the application wants to transmit data its thread also places the data into the send-queue and executes `tcp_output()` as well as `ip_output()` and the link-level output function. When the application asks to receive packets, the first packet(s) from the *to_app* queue are returned. If there are no packets, the thread blocks if so specified.

Buffer Handling

The buffer handling scheme in Nemesis is different from kernel-space TCP implementations. Applications need to supply the device drivers with empty buffers to receive data in. They must also reclaim buffers from the device driver when the corresponding packet has been sent.

Supplying the Device Driver with Empty Receive Buffers

On the arrival of a packet on a network interface, the packet filter determines the receiving application and the device driver copies the packet into receive buffers provided by the application. Thus, applications must *prime* the device driver, i.e., applications have to supply the device driver with empty receive buffers. In our TCP implementation, the receiver thread allocates receive buffers for header and payload of incoming packets and sends them to the device driver. The receive buffers are allocated from shared memory between the application and the device driver.

The application returns receive buffers to `InetMod` via an *extended* I/O channel. We call this I/O channel extended because it is an intra-domain extension of the I/O channel between the device driver and `InetMod` to the application program. `InetMod` then supplies the device driver with these receive buffers.

The number of empty receive buffers at the device driver limits the number of packets that a TCP connection can receive immediately. Thus, if the application or `InetMod` return the receive buffers slowly the device driver will run out of empty receive buffers and has to drop incoming packets. In our TCP implementation this situation is avoided by basing the calculation of the window advertisement on the number of empty receive buffers at the device driver and the number of empty slots in the *to_app* queue between `InetMod` and the receiving application.

Reclaiming Used Transmit Buffers

After a packet has been transmitted, Nemesis applications must reclaim the corresponding transmit buffers from the network interface. When transmitting data, applications only allocate the memory for the payload. The memory for the header is allocated by `InetMod`. Thus, when applications reclaim used transmit buffers, `InetMod` only returns the payload buffer. Of course, `InetMod` cannot return a transmit buffer to the application before the corresponding packet has been acknowledged by the peer, in case the packet gets lost and has to be retransmitted. When an application reclaims transmit buffers and there are no transmit buffers available, the application's thread is blocked if so specified.

`InetMod` itself needs to reclaim the transmit buffers from the device driver. To achieve good performance it is important to do that at the right time. A naive solution is that `tcp_output()` reclaims the transmit buffers from the device driver after having called `ip_output()`. But this leads to bad performance since the device driver cannot return the transmit buffers before the packet has been put on the wire. Thus, it is advantageous to postpone this task until the device driver can return the transmit buffers without blocking.

Transmit Scheduling

The transmit scheduling is not part of `InetMod` but part of the device driver domain. It is implemented by a thread, the *TX thread*. The scheduled entities are the I/O channels to the device driver. The reservations are made by applications for each of their I/O channels by a method call.

The TX thread runs in an endless loop. It calls the Atropos scheduler to determine the next I/O channel to be served. The scheduler chooses an I/O channel based on the reservations. If this I/O channel has nothing to send, the scheduler searches for another suitable I/O channel. Thus, the call to the Atropos scheduler will return an I/O channel if there is an I/O channel that has pending packets and that has either a non-zero slice left in its current period or the extra flag set to `true`.

Thereafter the TX thread takes one packet out of the scheduled I/O channel, transmits the packet and charges the I/O channel for the transmission.

4 EXPERIMENTS

The experiments in the first part of this section deal with scheduling of interface transmission bandwidth only. In these experiments the applications have sufficient CPU time to produce data and process outgoing and incoming packets. Under heavier CPU load, however, solely reserving transmit bandwidth is not enough. If an application needs to send at a particular bandwidth, a sufficient part of the CPU time has to be reserved as well. Otherwise the application might not be able to produce data and run the protocol stacks fast enough. This is addressed in the experiments in the next part of this section that deals with the reservation of transmit bandwidth and CPU time. In the final part of this section we present performance results that show that the Nemesis TCP achieves good throughput.

Reserving Transmit Bandwidth

In this section we present two experiments. In the first experiment, we show how the choice of the period and slice time impacts TCP performance. The second experiment includes several transmitters that strive for transmit bandwidth. In this experiment we can also see the effect of the extra flag on the throughput that connections receive.

We have implemented a TCP sender application that sends MTU-sized packets as fast as possible to the peer. We have varied the QoS parameters for the transmit network bandwidth. The transmitter was a Pentium 200 running Nemesis with a 10 Mb/s 3c509 Ethernet card. The transmission of one MTU-sized packet (1500 bytes including TCP/IP headers) on a 10 Mb/s Ethernet takes about 1.2 ms. Setting the slice time to, e.g., twice this time allows the application to send two packets in every period.

One Transmitter

In our first experiment, the Nemesis box sends to a SPARCstation running SunOS. Figure 4 shows a section of a TCP connection with the slice time set to 2.4 ms (which allows to send up to two MTU-sized packets in one period)[1] and the period set to 50 ms. The extra time flag x is set to `false` in order to rate control TCP. The small lines with arrows represent the packets that are sent. The dotted line under the packets is the highest sequence number that has

[1]When we set the slice time to e.g. 3 ms (which allows to send "2.5" MTU-sized packets in every period), we will get periods with two mixed with periods with three packets sent. The value 2.4 ms is thus chosen to get a very regular traffic pattern.

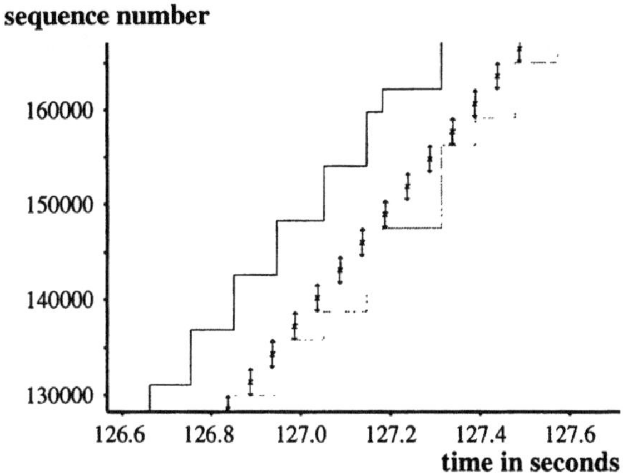

Figure 4 QoS TCP transmitting (tcpdump plot)

been acknowledged by the peer. The solid line above the packets is the window offered by the receiver. We can see that the sender transmits two packets, pauses almost 50 ms until the next two packets are sent and so on. Note that the transmission of packets is not triggered by the arrival of the acknowledgements but by the start of a new period.

From the period, slice time and the number of bytes to be sent per period we can compute the throughput for a connection. We have measured the throughput for a period of 200 ms and various slice times and compared the results with the theoretical values. For slice times up to 9.6 ms (maximum 8 MTU-sized packets per period) there are almost no discrepancies. However, for slice times that are larger than 9.6 ms, we do get very varying results. The explanation is that the receiver's window fills when the transmitter sends many packets during some periods and then the window offered by the peer varies depending on how fast the receiver acknowledges data. This prevents the transmitter from utilizing the guaranteed transmit bandwidth. However, the aim of rate-control is to set upper limits.

When transmitting over long distances or low-bandwidth connections, TCP flow control determines the overall traffic pattern. However, when the peer acknowledges several TCP segments, the Nemesis TCP does not reply by transmitting immediately a bulk of data until the receiver's window is filled again, but spreads out the packets depending on the chosen period and slice time.

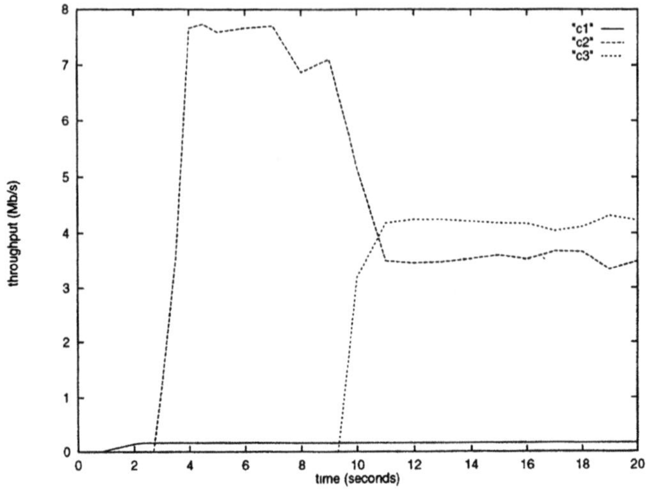

Figure 5 Time-throughput graph for 3 connections

Several Transmitters

In our second experiment, the Nemesis machine sends to a SPARCstation called *kay* and another SPARCstation (called *garuda*) running NetBSD. *Garuda* is equipped with a 10 Mb/s Ethernet card and sits on the same LAN as the Nemesis machine. The result is shown in Figure 5. First we start a TCP connection (*c1*) to *kay* with a period of 200 ms, a slice time of 3.6 ms and the extra flag set to `false`. This connection consistently receives the same bandwidth (about 0.17 Mb/s) which conforms to its guarantees.

About three seconds later, we start a second TCP transmitter (*c2*) to *garuda* with a period of 10 ms, a slice time of 1.2 ms and the extra time flag set to `true`. This means that *c2* wants to make use of the non-allocated part of the transmit bandwidth but also has some guaranteed transmit bandwidth. Since *c1* only consumes a small part of the available bandwidth, *c2* initially receives a throughput of about 7.5 Mb/s, with some variation due to how fast the receiver acknowledges the data. Some seconds later the third connection (*c3*), also to *garuda*, is started. It specifies a period of 10 ms, a slice time of 6 ms and the extra flag is set to `false`. The large slice time is chosen to reserve a large fraction of the available transmit bandwidth. As soon as *c3* has started, the non-allocated part of the transmit bandwidth decreases, and *c2* therefore receives much less transmit bandwidth (about 3.5 Mb/s).

Unfortunately, *c3* does not receive the guaranteed bandwidth of 5.6 Mb/s but only 4.2 Mb/s. The reason for this lower than expected throughput is that, quite often, the sender is not allowed to transmit since the receiver's window is closed. This happens because the acknowledgements that the receiver sends are often delayed and arrive in bursts instead of arriving regularly (we saw a similar behavior when we ran Linux on both the sender and a receiver on the same LAN and transmitted as fast as possible). The delay is most likely caused by contention for the Ethernet media. We use a 10 Mb/s hub and have two fast connections. Under these conditions the shared Ethernet becomes a bottleneck. On the other hand, since *c2* has the extra flag set, the overall throughput does not decrease because *c2* makes use of the bandwidth that *c3* cannot utilize due to the closed window.

Reserving Transmit Bandwidth and CPU Time

In this section we present experiments that show the impact of CPU reservations on the achieved bandwidth of TCP applications. All connections are on a LAN with both transmitter and receiver running de4x5 100 Mb/s Ethernet cards. The transmitter is a Nemesis machine while the receiver runs Linux. In the following experiments we run a TCP application called *tcp_send* that transmits MTU-sized packets as fast as possible. We also run an application called *carnage*. This application has the property that it makes use of all its reservations. If it is guaranteed a certain fraction of the CPU time, it will make use of this fraction.

Impact of CPU Time on Achieved Throughput

In this experiment *tcp_send* reserves a large fraction of the network transmit bandwidth and has the extra time flag *x* set to `true`. Since *tcp_send* is the only transmitting application it will receive almost all the available transmit bandwidth. The CPU reservation request of *tcp_send* specifies a period of 10 ms, a slice time of 2 ms and the extra time flag is set to `true`. Thus *tcp_send* will receive a fraction of about 20 % of the CPU time and a fair share of the CPU time not used by other applications. *carnage* has specified a period of 20 ms, the extra flag is set to `false` and we vary the slice time to control the fraction of the CPU time that *carnage* receives. The more CPU time *carnage* receives the less CPU time is left for *tcp_send*. *tcp_send* will receive its slice time every period but the non-allocated part of the CPU time will decrease when *carnage's* slice time increases.

Figure 6 shows how the decreasing fraction of the CPU impacts the throughput that *tcp_send* achieves. Since *tcp_send* reserves 20 % of the CPU time, we

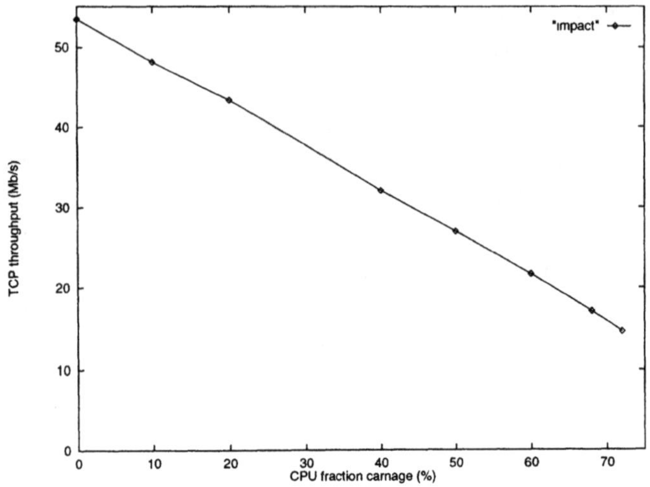

Figure 6 Impact of *carnage* application on TCP bandwidth

set the maximum reservation for *carnage* to 72 %. We do not make a reservation of 80 % for *carnage* since there are also other domains running such as the flow manager and several device drivers. In particular the Ethernet driver consumes a non-negligible part of the CPU time in the experiments in this section.

When only *tcp_send* is running, it achieves a throughput of about 53 Mb/s. The figure shows that the throughput decreases proportionally to the fraction of CPU time used by *carnage*.

Reserving CPU Time to Achieve Throughput

In this experiment we assume that we have an application that wants to transmit data with a desired throughput. The goal is to determine the fraction of the CPU time an application needs in order to produce data and run the protocol stack fast enough to be able to transmit the desired amount of data. This can be important when you have reserved network bandwidth and you want to make sure that your application really achieves the bandwidth you pay for but you still want to have your text editor and other applications running.

The application *tcp_send* reserves the desired transmit bandwidth on the network interface. When the desired throughput is e.g. 10 Mb/s, *tcp_send* specifies a period of 1 ms, a slice time of 110 μs and sets the extra flag to `false`. The transmission of one MTU-sized packet (1500 bytes including TCP/IP headers) takes about 120 μs on a 100 Mb/s Ethernet. Since we need to send slightly less than one packet per millisecond to achieve a throughput of

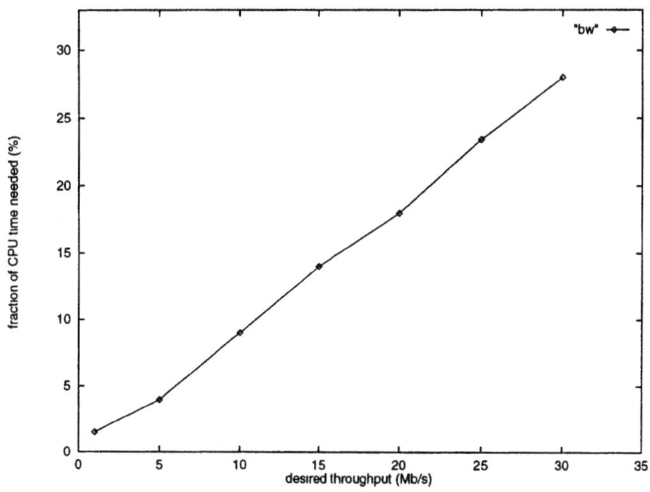

Figure 7 Fraction of CPU necessary to send particular amount of data

10 Mb/s, setting the slice time to 110 μs seems to be reasonable. This has been confirmed by measurements.

In Figure 7 we show the fraction of the CPU time the application *tcp_send* needs to reserve to be able to transmit the desired amount of data. Since *tcp_send* does not do any data processing and mainly sends and retrieves buffers this can be seen as a minimum CPU fraction necessary to run the TCP protocol stack. However, the exact fraction of the CPU time needed depends on the packet length, the CPU, the network adapter and other system components.

Figure 7 shows that the CPU fraction needed increases linearly with the amount of data sent.

Several Applications Reserving Transmit Bandwidth and CPU Time

In the next experiment we run three *tcp_send* applications (*s1*, *s2* and *s3*). *s1* and *s2* both want to transmit data at a speed of 10 Mb/s and *s3* at a speed of 5 Mb/s. The applications set the corresponding QoS-parameters (see Table 1) using the tuple (period, slice time, extra flag).

The fractions of the CPU share are the ones we determined in the previous experiment (see Figure 7), i.e., 10 % for *s1* and *s2* (*s1* and *s2* have different period and slice times but reserve the same fraction of CPU time and transmit bandwidth) and 5 % for *s3*. We also run a *carnage* application that has the extra flag set to `true` and thus consumes all the non-allocated CPU time.

Table 1 also shows that all applications receive their desired throughput.

Table 1 Experiment with three transmitting applications

app.	aim	TX QoS	CPU QoS	Throughput
s1	10 Mb/s	1 ms, 110 μs, F	10 ms, 1 ms, F	10.1 Mb/s
s2	10 Mb/s	2 ms, 220 μs, F	20 ms, 2 ms, F	10.1 Mb/s
s3	5 Mb/s	2 ms, 110 μs, F	20 ms, 1 ms, F	5.1 Mb/s

Performance

Nemesis and its network architecture are primarily designed to support QoS. Raw throughput performance is secondary. We nevertheless think that the throughput we achieved with the TCP is reasonable. We have run *tcp_send* between a Pentium 200 Nemesis machine and another Pentium 200 machine running Linux. Both machines are equipped with 100 Mb/s de4x5 Ethernet cards. We received a throughput of more than 58 Mb/s. This is lower than the 81 Mb/s we received when running Linux on both machines but we still think this is reasonable considering the primary goal with Nemesis. We believe that it is possible to optimize the Nemesis TCP a lot more. A problem in our architecture is that the transmitting application and the device driver run as different domains and are thus scheduled separately. The deployment of a *path* mechanism as in Scout [10] would probably increase throughput performance.

5 RELATED WORK

Satyavolu *et. al.* [12] have investigated in methods for controlling the rate of TCP applications. Our work deals with the end system, whereas their techniques can be applied in ATM edge devices and Internet routers. Crowcroft and Oechslin [4] do not rate control TCP traffic but limit the throughput of TCP connections by decreasing the size of the receive buffer in order to achieve weighted proportional fairness. Black *et. al.* [2] have used Nemesis and the Atropos scheduler for UDP. In contrast to TCP, UDP does not have schemes for, e.g., congestion and flow control which can prevent a transmitter from sending although there are packets ready for transmission. Stride scheduling [14] has been used for both CPU and device driver scheduling but the authors do not report on any results of an integrated use.

Other architectures than Nemesis for providing QoS in an end system have been proposed. Yau and Lam [16] propose an end system architecture that supports networking with quality of service guarantees. They also use scheduling for both CPU and network interface access by deploying an adaptive rate-controlled (ARC) scheduler. The AQUA framework of Lakshman and Yavatkar [8] is used to manage CPU and network I/O resources in an integrated fashion. Their scheme is adaptive while we use reservations to provide QoS. Both Yau's and Lakshman's architectures have been implemented in Solaris whereas we use the Nemesis operating system which is designed from scratch to support quality of service. Gopalakrishnan and Parulkar [5] have implemented an efficient user-space protocol that supports QoS using real-time upcalls (RTU's). They achieve impressive performance running TCP/IP over ATM. Their mechanisms also allow to minimize delay or maximize throughput. The architecture the authors present in their paper deals with protocol processing only. In our scheme, the binding between an application and the underlying protocol processing unit is more explicit because protocol processing is performed by the application itself using shared libraries. Rajkumar et. al. [9] aim for predictable communication protocol processing in Real-Time Mach by using *processor reserves.* As in Nemesis, library code in the application implements protocol processing. In contrast to Nemesis, their scheme relies on processor reservations only. Thus, it is possible that an application that is able to produce data faster can achieve higher throughput than an application that has higher processor reserves but needs more time to produce the data that it transmits. Another difference is that processor reserves are made per thread and the real-time socket library comprises at least four threads.

The Rialto operating system [7] supports coexisting independent real-time and non-real-time programs by sharing the limited physical resources available to them. In one of their experiments, the authors study the influence of CPU reservations over video rendering fidelity. Due to the interdependency between frames there is no linear relationship between the CPU reservation and the frames not rendered.

A different way of providing quality of service in an end-system are feedback-based approaches such as G. Beaton's [1]. One of the goals of this approach is to avoid the complexity of other architectures like Nahrstedt's and Smith's QoS Broker [11].

6 CONCLUSIONS

We have designed and implemented a TCP for Nemesis, a vertically integrated operating system that can guarantee resources such as CPU time, disk I/O bandwidth and transmit network bandwidth to applications. Our experiments show that the Nemesis transmit scheduler rate-controls TCP traffic when applications choose not to utilize non-allocated bandwidth. Applications that want to make use of the non-allocated transmit bandwidth receive the guaranteed bandwidth plus a share of the non-allocated bandwidth. We show that the CPU time needed to run the protocol stack increases linearly with the amount of data sent for a given packet size. When networked applications reserve enough CPU time and transmit bandwidth they receive sufficient resources even when several applications strive for both CPU time and transmit bandwidth.

Thus, Nemesis allows us to run several applications, which require both CPU time and transmit bandwidth, concurrently, making sure each of them receives the guaranteed resources. Possible applications include concurrently running web servers with different performance requirements as well as other applications requiring reliable data transfer.

7 FUTURE WORK

After having optimized the Nemesis TCP we plan to investigate how Nemesis can be extended to perform as an end-host in a differentiated services platform. We believe that we might benefit from the Nemesis architecture here. An obvious advantage is that applications that have reserved enough resources can produce their data in time, independent of other applications.

8 ACKNOWLEDGEMENTS

Many people have contributed to Nemesis during the last years. Without their work we could not have written this paper. In particular Austin Donnelly's work has been of importance to us.

The authors would also like to thank Per Gunningberg for valuable comments on an earlier draft of this paper.

References

[1] Gordon Beaton. A feedback-based quality of service management scheme. In *Third International Workshop on High Performance Protocol Architectures (HIPPARCH '97)*, Uppsala, Sweden, June 12–13 1997.

[2] Richard Black, Paul Barham, Austin Donnelly, and Neil Stratford. Protocol implementation in a vertically structured operating system. In *IEEE 22nd Annual Conference on Computer Networks (LCN)*, pages 179–188, November 2–5 1997.

[3] R.J. Black. Explicit network scheduling. Technical Report 361, University of Cambridge Computer Laboratory, December 1994. Ph.D. Dissertation.

[4] J. Crowcroft and P. Oechslin. Differentiated end-to-end internet services using a weighted proportional fair sharing tcp. *ACM SIGCOMM Computer Communication Review*, 28(3):53–69, July 1998.

[5] R. Gopalakrishnan and G. M. Parulkar. Efficient user space protocol implementations with qos guarantees using real-time upcalls. *IEEE/ACM Transactions on Networking*, 6(4):374–388, August 1998.

[6] I.M.Leslie, D.McAuley, R.Black, T.Roscoe, P.Barham, D.Evers, R.Fairbanks, and E.Hyden. The design and implementation of an operating system to support distributed multimedia applications. *IEEE Journal on Selected Areas in Communications*, 14(7):1280–1297, September 1996.

[7] M. B. Jones, J. S. Barrera III, A. Forin, P. J. Leach, D. Rosu, and M. Rosu. An overview of the rialto real-time architecture. In *Seventh ACM SIGOPS European Workshop*, pages 249–256, Connemara, Ireland, September 1996.

[8] K. Lakshman, R. Yavatkar, and R. Finkel. Integrated cpu and network-i/o qos management in an endsystem. In *Int. Workshop on Quality of Service (IWQoS)*, pages 167–178, 1997.

[9] C. Lee, K. Yoshida, C. Mercer, and R. Rajkumar. Predictable communication protocol processing in real-time mach. In *Proceedings of the Real-Time Technology and Application Symposium*, pages 115–123, June 1996.

[10] D. Mosberger and L. L. Peterson. Making paths explicit in the scout operating system. In *Symposium on Operating Systems Design and Implementation*, pages 153–167, October 1996.

[11] K. Nahrstedt and J. Smith. The qos broker. *IEEE Multimedia*, 2(1):53–67, 1995.

[12] Ramakrishna Satyavolu, Ketan Duvedi, and Shivkumar Kalyanaraman. Explicit rate control of tcp applications. ATM Forum Document, February 1999. ATM Forum Document Number: ATM_Forum/98-0152R1.

[13] Chandramohan A. Thekkath, Thu D. Nguyen, Evelyn Moy, and Edward D. Lazowska. Implementing network protocols at user level. *IEEE/ACM Transactions on Networking*, 1(5):554–565, October 1993.

[14] C.A. Waldspurger and W.E. Weihl. Stride scheduling: Deterministic proportional-share resource management. Technical report, MIT Laboratory for Computer Science, 1995.

[15] G.R. Wright and W.R. Stevens. *TCP/IP Illustrated, Volume 2*. Addison-Wesley Publishing Company, 1995. ISBN 0-201-63354-X.

[16] David K.Y. Yau and Simon S. Lam. Migrating sockets - end system support for networking with quality of service guarantees. *IEEE/ACM Transactions on Networking*, 6(6):700–716, December 1998.

[illegible]

[illegible] June 1995.

[6] I. M. Leslie, D. McAuley, R. Black, T. Roscoe, P. Barham, D. Evers, R. Fairbairns, and E. Hyden. The design and implementation of an operating system to support distributed multimedia applications. *IEEE Journal on Selected Areas in Communications*, 14(7):1280–1297, September 1996.

[illegible]

THE DESIGN AND PERFORMANCE OF A PLUGGABLE PROTOCOLS FRAMEWORK FOR CORBA MIDDLEWARE

Fred Kuhns, Carlos O'Ryan, Douglas C. Schmidt, Ossama Othman, and Jeff Parsons
Department of Computer Science, Washington University St. Louis, MO 63130, USA
{fredk,coryan,schmidt,othman,parsons}@cs.wustl.edu

Abstract

To be an effective platform for performance-sensitive real-time and embedded applications, off-the-shelf CORBA middleware must preserve communication layer quality of service (QoS) properties to applications end-to-end. However, the standard CORBA's GIOP/IIOP interoperability protocols are not well suited for applications that cannot tolerate the message footprint size, latency, and jitter associated with general-purpose messaging and transport protocols. It is essential, therefore, to develop standard pluggable protocols frameworks that allow custom messaging and transport protocols to be configured flexibly and used transparently by applications.

This paper provides three contributions to research on pluggable protocols frameworks for performance-sensitive communication middleware. First, we outline the key design challenges faced by pluggable protocols developers. Second, we describe how TAO, our high-performance, real-time CORBA-compliant ORB, addresses these challenges in its pluggable protocols framework. Third, we present the results of benchmarks that pinpoint the impact of TAO's OO design on its end-to-end efficiency, predictability, and scalability.

Our results demonstrate how applying strategic optimizations to communication middleware can yield highly flexible/reusable designs and highly efficient/predictable implementations. In particular, the overall round-trip latency of a TAO two-way method invocation is $\sim$125 μsecs using the standard CORBA inter-ORB protocol on a commercial, off-the-self Pentium II Xeon 400 MHz workstation running in loopback mode. The ORB middleware accounts for $\sim$60 μsecs of the total round-trip latency. These results illustrate that (1) communication middleware performance is largely an implementation detail and (2) the next-generation of optimized, standards-based CORBA middleware can replace ad hoc and proprietary solutions.

1. INTRODUCTION

Communication middleware resides between client and server applications in distributed systems. It simplifies application development by providing a uniform view of heterogeneous networks, protocols, and OS layers. At the heart of communication middleware are *Object Request Brokers* (ORBs), such as CORBA [6], which eliminate many of tedious, error-prone, and non-portable aspects of developing and maintaining distributed applications programmed using low-level mechanisms like sockets. However, the general lack of support in this off-the-shelf communication middleware for QoS specification and enforcement features, integration with high-speed networking technology, and performance, predictability, and scalability optimizations optimizations, has limited the rate at which applications have been developed to leverage advances in communication middleware.

To address the shortcomings of communication middleware we have developed *The ACE ORB* (TAO). TAO is open-source, standards-based, high-performance, real-time ORB endsystem communication middleware that supports applications with deterministic and statistical QoS requirements, as well as "best-effort" requirements. TAO is the first ORB to support end-to-end QoS guarantees over ATM/IP networks [3]. The source code for TAO is available at `www.cs.wustl.edu/~schmidt/TAO.html`.

We have used TAO to research many dimensions of high-performance and real-time ORB endsystems, including static and dynamic scheduling, request demultiplexing, event processing, ORB Core connection and concurrency architectures, IDL compiler stub/skeleton optimizations, systematic benchmarking of multiple ORBs, I/O subsystem integration, and patterns for ORB extensibility. This paper focuses on a previously unexamined dimension in the high-performance and real-time ORB endsystem design space: *the design and performance of a pluggable protocols framework* that supports high-speed protocols and networks, real-time embedded system interconnects, and standard TCP/IP protocols over the Internet.

The remainder of this paper is organized as follows: Section 2 outlines the CORBA protocol interoperability architecture; Section 3 motivates the need for a CORBA pluggable protocols framework and describes how TAO's pluggable protocols framework is designed; Section 4 illustrates the performance characteristics of TAO's pluggable protocols framework; Section 5 compares TAO with related work; and Section 6 presents concluding remarks.

2. OVERVIEW OF THE CORBA PROTOCOL INTEROPERABILITY ARCHITECTURE

The CORBA specification [6] defines an architecture for ORB interoperability. Although a complete description of the model is beyond the scope of this paper, this section outlines the portions of the CORBA specification that are relevant to our present topic, *i.e.*, object addressing and inter-ORB protocols.

Object addressing synopsis: To identify objects, CORBA defines a generic format called the Interoperable Object Reference (IOR). An object reference identifies one instance of an object and associates one or more paths or routes by which that object can be accessed.

The same object may be located by different object references, *e.g.*, if a server is re-started on a new port or migrated to another host. Likewise, multiple server locations can be referenced by one IOR, *e.g.*, if a server has multiple network interfaces connecting it to distinct networks, there may be multiple network addresses.

References to server locations are called *profiles*. A profile provides an opaque, protocol-specific representation of an object location. Profiles can be used to annotate the server location with QoS information, such as the priority of the thread serving each endpoint or redundant addresses to enhance fault-tolerance.

Protocol model synopsis: CORBA Inter-ORB Protocols (IOP)s define interoperability between ORB endsystems. IOPs provide data representation formats and ORB messaging protocol specifications that can be mapped onto standard and/or customized transport protocols. Regardless of the choice of ORB messaging or transport protocol, however, the standard CORBA programming model is exposed to the application developers. Figure 1 shows the relationships between these various components and layers.

In the CORBA protocol interoperability architecture, the standard *General Inter-ORB Protocol* (GIOP) is defined by the CORBA specification [6]. In addition, CORBA defines a TCP/IP mapping of GIOP, which is called the *Internet Inter-ORB Protocol* (IIOP). ORBs must support IIOP to be "interoperability compliant." Other mappings of GIOP onto different transport protocols are allowed by the specification, as are different inter-ORB protocols, which are known as *Environment Specific Inter-ORB Protocols* (ESIOP)s.

Regardless of whether GIOP or an ESIOP is used, a CORBA IOP must define a data representation, an ORB message format, an ORB transport protocol or transport protocol adapter, and an object addressing format. Below, we outline how GIOP defines each of these IOP elements.

GIOP synopsis: The GIOP specification consists of the following elements:

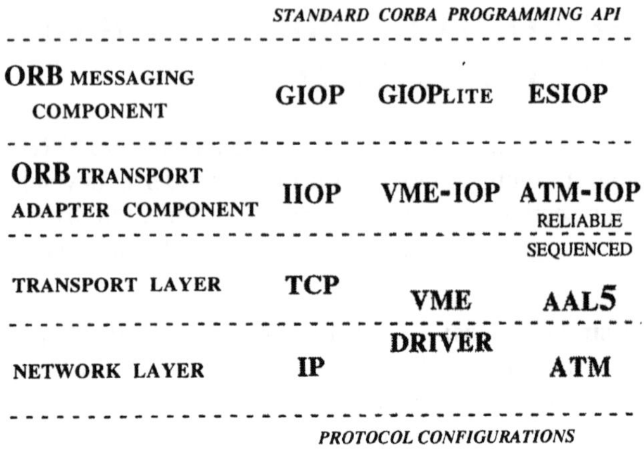

Figure 1 Relationship Between Inter-ORB Protocols and Transport-specific Mappings

• **A Common Data Representation (CDR) definition:** CDR is a transfer syntax that maps IDL types from their native host format into a low-level *bi-canonical* representation, which supports both little-endian and big-endian formats. CDR-encoded messages are used to transmit CORBA requests and server responses across a network. All IDL data types are marshaled using the CDR syntax into an *encapsulation*, which is an octet stream that holds marshaled data.

• **GIOP message formats:** The GIOP specification defines seven types of messages that send requests, receive replies, locate objects, and manage communication channels.

• **GIOP transport adapter:** The GIOP specification describes the features of an ORB transport protocol that can carry GIOP messages. Such protocols must be reliable and connection-oriented. In addition, GIOP defines a connection management protocol and a set of constraints for GIOP message ordering.

• **Object addressing:** An Interoperable Object Reference (IOR) is a sequence of opaque *profiles*, each representing a protocol-specific representation of an object's location. For example, an IIOP profile includes the IP address and port number where the server accepts connections, as well as the object key that identifies an object within a particular server. There may be multiple paths or routes to an object. Therefore, the same IOR can contain multiple IIOP profiles, along with profiles for other protocols, such as GIOP over ATM or non-GIOP protocols.

ESIOP synopsis: In addition to the standard GIOP and IIOP protocols, the CORBA specification allows ORB implementors to define Environment Specific Inter-ORB Protocols (ESIOP)s. ESIOPs can define unique data representation formats, ORB messaging protocols, ORB transport protocols or transport protocol adapters, and object addressing formats. These protocols can exploit the QoS features and guarantees provided in certain domains, such as telecommunications or avionics, to satisfy performance-sensitive applications that have stringent bandwidth, latency, and jitter requirements.

3. A PLUGGABLE PROTOCOLS FRAMEWORK FOR CORBA

The CORBA specification provides a standard for general-purpose communication middleware. Within the scope of this specification, however, ORB implementors are free to optimize internal data structures and algorithms. Moreover, ORBs may use specialized inter-ORB protocols and ORB services and still comply with the CORBA specification. However, an ORB *must* implement GIOP/IIOP, to be interoperability-compliant. This section identifies the limitations of current ORBs with respect to their protocol support, describes how TAO's pluggable protocols framework is designed to overcome these limitations, and then describes how TAO can be applied to develop middleware for high-performance multimedia applications.

Protocol Limitations of Conventional ORBs

CORBA's standard GIOP/IIOP protocols are well suited for traditional request/response applications with best-effort QoS requirements. They are not well suited, however, for high-performance, real-time, and/or embedded applications that cannot tolerate the message footprint size of GIOP or the latency, overhead, and jitter of the TCP/IP-based IIOP transport protocol. For instance, TCP functionality, such as adaptive retransmissions, deferred transmissions, and delayed acknowledgments, can cause excessive overhead and latency for real-time applications. Likewise, networking protocols, such as IPv4, lack the functionality of packet admission policies and rate control, which can lead to excessive congestion and missed deadlines in networks and endsystems.

Therefore, applications with more stringent QoS requirements need optimized protocol implementations, QoS-aware interfaces, custom presentations layers, specialized memory management (*e.g.*, shared memory between ORB and I/O subsystem), and alternative transport programming APIs (*e.g.*, sockets vs. TLI). Domains where highly optimized ORB messaging and transport protocols are particularly important include (1) multimedia applications running over high-speed networks, such as Gigabit Ethernet or ATM, and (2) real-time applications running over embedded system interconnects, such as VME or CompactPCI.

Conventional CORBA implementations have the following limitations that make it hard for them to support performance-sensitive applications effectively:

1. Static protocol configurations: Many ORBs support a limited number of statically configured protocols, typically only GIOP/IIOP over TCP/IP.

2. Lack of protocol control interfaces: Many ORBs do not allow applications to configure key protocol policies and properties, such as peak virtual circuit bandwidth or cell pacing rate.

3. Single protocol support: Many ORBs do not support simultaneous use of multiple inter-ORB messaging or transport protocols.

4. Lack of real-time protocol support: Many ORBs have limited or no support for specifying and enforcing real-time protocol requirements across a backplane, network, or Internet end-to-end.

Overview of TAO's Pluggable Protocols Framework

To overcome the limitations described in Section 3, we identified logical communication component layers within TAO, factored out common features, defined general framework interfaces, and implemented components to support different concrete inter-ORB protocols. Higher-level services in the ORB, such as stubs, skeletons, and standard CORBA pseudo-objects, are decoupled from the implementation details of particular protocols, as shown in Figure 2. This decoupling is essential to resolve several limitations of conven-

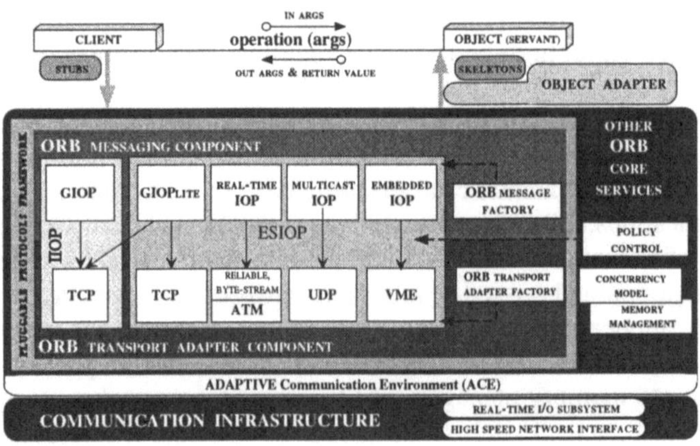

Figure 2 TAO's Pluggable Protocols Framework Architecture

tional ORBs outlined in Section 3.

In general, the higher-level components and services of TAO use a facade [2] interface to access the mechanisms provided by its pluggable protocols framework. Thus, applications can (re)configure custom protocols without requiring global changes to the ORB. Moreover, because applications typically access only the standard CORBA APIs, TAO's pluggable protocols framework can be entirely transparent to CORBA application developers.

Figure 2 also illustrates the key components in TAO's pluggable protocols framework: (1) the ORB messaging component, (2) the ORB transport adapter component, and (3) the ORB policy control component, which are outlined below.

ORB Messaging Component

This component is responsible for implementing ORB messaging protocols, such as the standard CORBA GIOP ORB messaging protocol, as well as custom ESIOPs. As described in Section 2, ORB messaging protocols should define a data representation, an ORB message format, an ORB transport protocol or transport adapter, and an object addressing format. Within this framework, ORB protocol developers are free to implement optimized Inter-ORB protocols and enhanced transport adaptors, as long as the ORB interfaces are respected.

Each ORB messaging protocol implementation inherits from a common base class that defines a uniform interface. This interface can be extended to include new capabilities needed by special protocol-aware policies. For example, ORB end-to-end resource reservation or priority negotiation can be implemented in an ORB messaging component. TAO's pluggable protocols framework ensures consistent operational characteristics and enforces general IOP syntax and semantic constraints, such as error handling.

ORB Transport Adapter Component

This component maps a specific ORB messaging protocol, such as GIOP or DCE-CIOP, onto a specific instance of an underlying transport protocol, such as TCP or ATM. Figure 2 shows an example in which TAO's transport adapter maps the GIOP messaging protocol onto TCP (this standard mapping is called IIOP). In this case, the ORB transport adapter combined with TCP corresponds to the transport layer in the Internet reference model. However, if ORBs are communicating over an embedded interconnect, such as a VME bus, the bus driver and DMA controller provide the "transport layer" in the communication infrastructure.

TAO's ORB transport component accepts a byte stream from the ORB messaging component, provides any additional processing required, and passes the resulting data unit to the underlying communication infrastructure. Additional processing that can be implemented by protocol developers includes (1) concurrency strategies, (2) endsystem/network resource reservation protocols, (3) high-performance techniques, such as zero-copy I/O, shared memory pools, periodic I/O, and interface pooling, (4) enhancement of underlying communications protocols, *e.g.*, provision of a reliable byte stream protocol over ATM, and (5) tight coupling between the ORB and efficient user-space protocol implementations, such as Fast Messages [4].

ORB Policy Control Component

This component allows applications to control the QoS attributes of configured ORB transport protocols explicitly. It is not possible to determine *a priori* all attributes defined by all protocols. Therefore, TAO's pluggable protocols framework provides an extensible *policy control* component, which implements the QoS framework defined in the CORBA Messaging [5] and Real-time CORBA [7] specifications.

The CORBA QoS framework allows applications to specify various *policies* to control the QoS attributes in the ORB. The CORBA specification uses policies to define semantic properties of ORB features precisely without (1) over-constraining ORB implementations or (2) increasing interface complexity for common use cases. Example policies relevant for pluggable protocols include buffer pre-allocations, fragmentation, bandwidth reservation, and maximum transport queue sizes.

Policies in CORBA can be set at the ORB, thread, or object level. Thus, application developers can set global policies that take effect for any request issued in a particular ORB. Moreover, these global settings can be overridden on a per-thread basis, a per-object basis, or even before a particular request. In general, CORBA's Policy framework provides very fine-grained control over the ORB behavior, while providing simplicity for the common case.

A Pluggable Protocol Scenario

To illustrate how TAO's pluggable protocols framework can be applied in practice, we now describe a scenario where pluggable protocols can be used to support performance-sensitive and real-time CORBA applications. This scenario is based on our experience developing high-bandwidth, low-latency audio/video streaming applications and avionics mission computing systems. In previous work [3], we addressed the network interface and I/O system and how to achieve predictable, real-time performance. In the discussion below, we focus on ORB support for alternate protocols.

Low-latency, high-bandwidth multimedia streaming: Multimedia applications running over high-speed networks require optimizations to utilize available link bandwidth, while still meeting application deadlines. For example, consider Figure 3, where network interfaces supporting 1.2 Mbps or

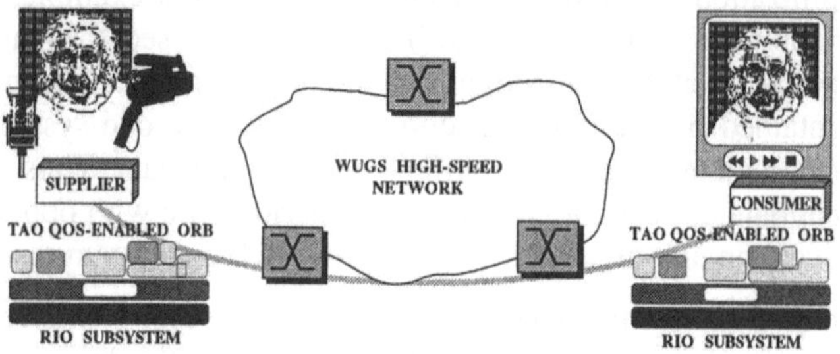

Figure 3 Example CORBA-based Audio/Video (A/V) Application

2.4 Mbps link speeds are used for a CORBA-based studio quality audio/video (A/V) application.

In this example, we can use TAO's pluggable protocols framework to replace GIOP/IIOP with a custom ORB messaging and transport protocol that transmits A/V frames using TAO's real-time I/O (RIO) subsystem [3]. At the core of RIO is the high-speed ATM port interconnect controller (APIC) [1]. APIC is a high-performance ATM interface card that supports standard ATM host interface features, such as AAL5 (SAR). In addition, the APIC supports (1) shared memory pools between user and kernel space, (2) per-VC pacing, (3) two levels of priority queues, and (4) interrupt disabling on a per-VC bases.

We are leveraging the APIC features and the underlying ATM network to support end-to-end QoS guarantees for TAO middleware. In particular, pluggable ORB message and transport protocols can be created to provide QoS services to applications, while the ORB middleware encapsulates the actual resource allocation and QoS enforcement mechanisms. Leveraging the underlying APIC hardware requires the resolution of the following two design challenges:

1. Custom protocols: The first challenge is to create custom ORB messaging and transport protocols that can exploit high-speed network interface hardware. A careful examination of the system requirements along with the hardware and communication infrastructure is required in order to determine both the set of optimizations required and the best partitioning of the solution into ORB messaging, transport and policy components.

The A/V streaming application is primarily concerned with pushing data to clients (i.e., one-way method invocations) and with meeting a specific set of latency and jitter requirements. Considering this, a simple frame sequencing protocol can be used as the ORB's ESIOP. Moreover, because multimedia data has diminishing value over time, a reliable protocol, such as TCP, is not required. Thus, the overhead of GIOP is not required, nor are the underlying assumptions that require a transport protocol with the semantics of TCP.

The ORB messaging protocol can be mapped onto an ORB transport protocol using AAL5. The transport adapter is then responsible for exploiting any local optimizations to hardware or the endsystem. For example, conventional ORBs copy user parameters into internal buffers used for marshaling. These buffers may be allocated from global memory or possibly from a memory pool maintained by the ORB. In either case, at least one system call is required to obtain mutexes, allocate buffers, and copy the data. Thus, not only is an additional data copy incurred, but this scenario is rife with opportunities for priority inversion and jitter while waiting for ORB endsystem resources.

2. Optimized protocol implementations: The second challenge is to produce an optimized pluggable protocol that implements the design described above. For example, memory can be shared throughout the ORB endsystem, *i.e.*, between the application, ORB middleware, OS kernel, and network interface, by allocating memory from a common buffer pool [1]. This optimization eliminates memory copies between user- and kernel-space when data is sent or received. Moreover, the ORB endsystem can manage this memory, thereby relieving application developers from this responsibility. In addition, the ORB endsystem can manage the APIC interface driver, interrupt rates, and pacing parameters, as outlined in [3].

4. THE PERFORMANCE OF TAO'S PLUGGABLE PROTOCOLS FRAMEWORK

Despite the growing demand for off-the-shelf middleware in many application domains, a widespread belief persists that OO techniques are not suitable for real-time systems due to performance penalties attributed to the OO paradigm. In particular, the dynamic binding properties of OO programming languages and the indirection implied in OO designs seem antithetical to real-time systems, which require low latency and jitter. The results presented in this section are significant, therefore, because they illustrate empirically how the choice of implementation strategies and optimization principles makes it possible to implement very predictable, efficient, and scalable middleware *without* compromising non-functional requirements, such as portability, flexibility, reusability, and maintainability, offered by CORBA.

To quantify the benefits and costs of TAO's pluggable protocols framework, we conducted several benchmarks using two different ORB messaging protocols, GIOP and GIOPlite, and two different transport protocols, POSIX local IPC (also known as UNIX-domain sockets) and TCP/IP. These benchmarks are based on our experience developing communication middleware for avionics mission computing applications and multimedia applications.

POSIX local IPC is not a traditional high-performance networking environment. However, it does provide the opportunity to obtain an accurate measure of ORB and pluggable protocols framework overhead. Based on these measurements, we have isolated the overhead associated with each component, which provides a baseline for future work in high-performance protocol development and experimentation.

Hardware/Software Benchmarking Platform

All benchmarks in this section were run on a Quad-CPU Intel Pentium II Xeon 400 MHz workstation, with one gigabyte of RAM. The operating system used for the benchmarking was Debian GNU/Linux "potato" (glibc 2.1) with Linux kernel version 2.2.10. GNU/Linux is an open-source operating system that supports true multi-tasking, multi-threading, and symmetric multiprocessing.

Our benchmarks were run using the standard GIOP ORB messaging protocol, as well as TAO's GIOPlite messaging protocol, described in Section 3. For the TCP/IP tests, the GIOP and GIOPLite ORB messaging protocols were run using the standard CORBA IIOP transport adapter along with the Linux TCP/IP socket library and the loopback interface. For the local IPC tests, GIOP and GIOPLite were used along with the optimized local IPC transport adapter. This resulted in four different Inter-ORB Protocols: GIOP over TCP (IIOP), GIOPLite over TCP, GIOP over local IPC (UIOP) and GIOPLite over local IPC. No changes were required to our standard CORBA benchmarking tool, called `IDL_Cubit` [9], for either of the ORB messaging and transport protocol implementations.

Blackbox Benchmarks

Blackbox benchmarks measure the end-to-end performance of a system from an external application perspective. In our experiments, we used blackbox benchmarks to compute the average two-way response time incurred by clients sending various types of data using the four different Inter-ORB transport protocols.

Measurement technique: A single-threaded client is used in the `IDL_Cubit` benchmark to issue two-way IDL operations at the fastest possible rate. The server performs the operation, which cubes each parameter in the request. For two-way calls, the client thread waits for the response and checks that it is correct. Interprocess communication is performed over selected IOPs, as described above.

We measure throughput for operations using a variety of IDL data types, including `void`, `sequence`, and `struct` types. The `void` data type instructs the server not to perform any processing other than that necessary to prepare and send the response, *i.e.*, it does not cube any input parameters. The `sequence` and `struct` data types exercise TAO's (de)marshaling engine. The `struct` contains an `octet`, a `long`, and a `short`, along with padding necessary to align those fields. We also measure throughput using long and short sequences of the `long` and `octet` types. The `long` sequences contain 4,096 bytes (1,024 four byte `longs` or 4,096 `octets`) and the short sequences are 4 bytes (one four byte `long` or four `octets`).

Blackbox results: The blackbox benchmark results are shown in Figure 4. All blackbox benchmarks were averaged over 100,000 two-way operation calls for each data type, as depicted by the bars in Figure 4.

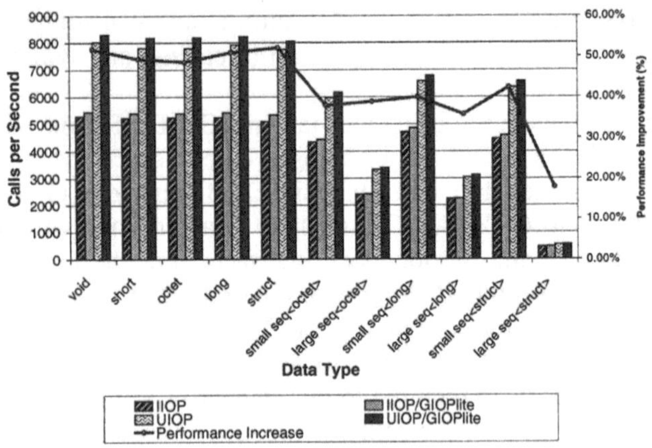

Figure 4 TAO's Pluggable Protocols Framework Performance Over Local IPC and TCP/IP

UIOP performance surpassed IIOP performance for all data types. The benchmarks show UIOP improves performance from 20% to 50% depending on the data type and size. For smaller data sizes and basic types, such as `octet` and `long`, the performance improvement is approximately 50%. However, for larger data payload sizes and more complex data types, the performance improvements are reduced. This is a direct result of the increasing cost of both the data copies associated with performing I/O and increasing complexity of marshaling structures other than the basic data types.

For certain data types, additional improvements are obtained by reducing the number of data copies required. Such a situation exists when marshaling and demarshaling data of type `octet` and `long`. For complicated data types, such as a large `sequence` of `structs`, ORB overhead is particularly prevalent. Large ORB overhead implies lower efficiency, which accounts for the smaller performance improvement gained by UIOP over IIOP for complex data types.

GIOPlite outperformed GIOP by a small margin. For IIOP, GIOPlite performance increases over GIOP ranged from 0.36% to 4.74%, with an average performance increase of 2.74%. GIOPlite performance improvements were slightly better over UIOP due to the fact that UIOP is more efficient than IIOP. GIOPlite over UIOP provided improvements ranging from 0.37% to 5.29%, with an average of 3.26%.

Our blackbox results suggest that more substantial changes to the GIOP message protocol are required to achieve significant performance improvements. However, these results also illustrate that the GIOP message footprint has a relatively minor performance impact over high-speed networks and embedded interconnects. Naturally, the impact of the GIOP message footprint for lower-speed links, such as second-generation wireless systems or low-speed modems, is more significant.

Whitebox Benchmarks

Whitebox benchmarks measure the performance of specific components or layers in a system from an internal perspective. In our experiments, we used whitebox benchmarks to pinpoint the time spent in key components in TAO's client and server ORBs. The ORB logical layers, or components, are shown in Figure 5 along with the timeprobe locations used for these benchmarks.

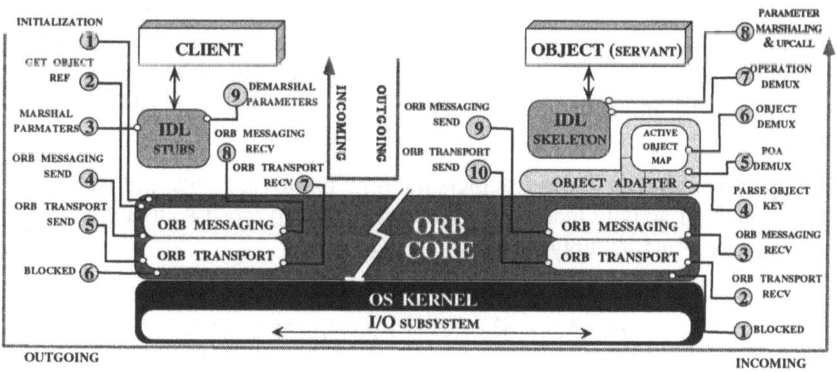

Figure 5 Timeprobe Locations for Whitebox Experiment

Measurement Techniques

One way to measure performance overhead of operations in complex communication middleware is to use a profiling tool like Quantify. Quantify instruments an application's binary instructions and then analyzes performance bottlenecks by identifying sections of code that dominate execution time. Quantify is useful because it can measure the overhead of system calls and third-party libraries without requiring source code access.

Unfortunately, Quantify is not available for Linux kernel-based operating systems for which whitebox measurement of TAO's performance is needed.

Moreover, Quantify modifies the binary code to collect timing information. Therefore, it is most useful for measuring *relative* overhead of different operations in a system, rather than measuring *absolute* run-time performance.

To avoid the limitations of Quantify, we therefore used a lightweight timeprobe mechanism provided by TAO to precisely pinpoint the amount of time spent in various ORB components and layers. The TAO timeprobe mechanism provides highly accurate, low-cost timestamps that record the time spent between regions of code in a software system. These timeprobes have minimal performance impact, *e.g.*, 1-2 μsec overhead per timeprobe, and no binary code instrumentation is required.

Depending on the underlying platform, TAO's timeprobes are implemented either by high-resolution OS timers or by high-precision timing hardware. An example of the latter is the VMEtro board, which is a VME bus monitor. VMEtro writes unique TAO timeprobe values to an otherwise unused VME address. These values record the duration between timeprobe markers across multiple processors using a single clock. This enables TAO to collect synchronized timestamps and accurately measure communication delays end-to-end across distributed CPUs.

Below, we examine the client and server whitebox performance in detail.

Whitebox Results

Figure 5 shows the points in a two-way operation request path where timeprobes were inserted. Each labeled number in the figure corresponds to an entry in Table 1 and Table 2 below. The results presented in the tables and figures which follow where averaged over 1,000 samples.

Client performance: Table 1 depicts the time in microseconds (μs) spent in each sequential activity that a TAO client performs to process an outgoing operation request and its reply.

Table 1 μseconds Spent in Each Client Processing Step

Direction	Client Activities	Absolute Time (μs)
Outgoing	1. *Initialization*	6.30
	2. *Get object reference*	15.6
	3. *Parameter marshal*	0.74 (param. dependent)
	4. *ORB messaging send*	7.78
	5. *ORB transport send*	1.02
	6. *I/O*	8.70 (op. dependent)
	7. *ORB transport recv*	50.7
	8. *ORB messaging recv*	9.25
	9. *Parameter demarshal*	op. dependent

Server performance: Table 2 depicts the time in microseconds (μs) spent in each activity as a TAO server processes a request.

Table 2 μseconds Spent in Each Server Processing Step

Direction	Server Activities	Absolute Time (μs)
Incoming	1. *I/O*	7.0 (op. dependent)
	2. *ORB transport recv*	24.8
	3. *ORB messaging recv*	4.5
	4. *Parsing object key*	4.6
	5. *POA demux*	1.39
	6. *Servant demux*	4.6
	7. *Operation demux*	4.52
	8. *User upcall*	3.84 (op. dependent)
Outgoing	9. *ORB messaging send*	4.56
	10. *ORB transport send*	93.6

Depending on the type and number of operation parameters, the *ORB transport recv* step typically requires the most ORB processing time. This time is dominated by the required data copies. By using a transport adapter which implements a shared buffer strategy these costs can be reduced significantly.

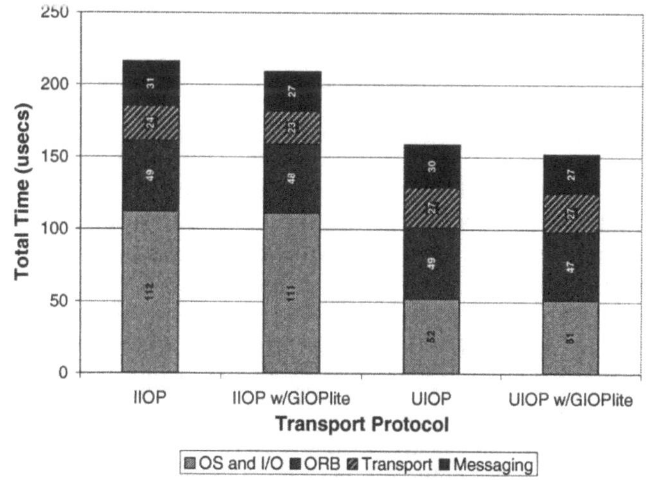

Figure 6 Comparison of ORB and Transport/OS Overhead Using Timeprobes

Component costs: Figure 6 compares the relative overhead attributable to the ORB messaging component, transport adaptor, ORB and OS for two-way

IDL_Cubit calls to the cube_void operation for each possible protocol combination. This figure shows that when using IIOP the I/O and OS overhead accounts for just over 50% of the total round trip latency.

It also shows that the difference in performance between IIOP and UIOP is primarily due to the larger OS and I/O overhead that TCP/IP has, as compared to local IPC.

The only overhead that depends on size is *(de)marshaling*, which depends on the type complexity, number, and size of operation parameters, and *data copying*, which depends on the size of the data. In our whitebox experiment, only the parameter size changes, *i.e.*, the sequences vary in length. Moreover, TAO's (de)marshaling optimizations incur minimal overhead when running between homogeneous ORB endsystems.

In Figure 7, the parameter size is varied and the above test is repeated. It shows that as the size of the operation parameters increases, I/O overhead

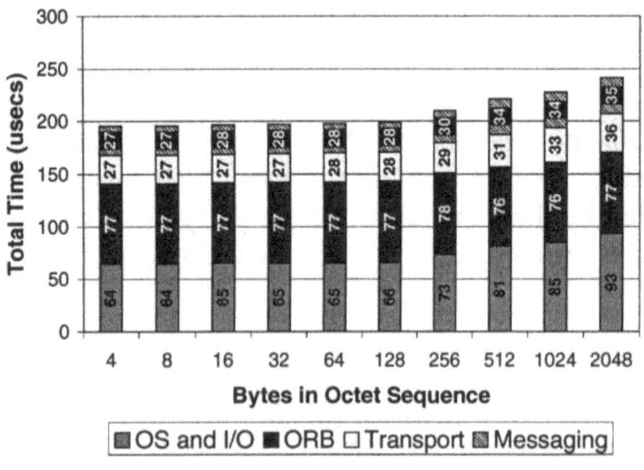

Figure 7 ORB and Transport/OS Overhead Versus Parameter Size

grows faster than the overall ORB overhead (including messaging and transport). This result illustrates that the overall ORB overhead is largely independent of the request size. In particular, demultiplexing a request, creating message headers, and invoking an operation upcall are not affected by the size of the request.

TAO employs standard buffer size and data copy tradeoff optimizations. This optimization is demonstrated in Figure 7 by the fact that there is a slight increase in the time spent both in the transport component and in the ORB itself when the sequence size is greater than 256 bytes. The data copy tradeoff optimization is fully configurable via run-time command line options, so it is possible to configure TAO to further improve performance above the 256 byte data copy threshold.

For the operations tested in the IDL_Cubit benchmark, the overhead of the ORB is dominated by memory bandwidth limitations. Both the loopback driver and local IPC driver copy data within the same host. Therefore, memory bandwidth limitations should essentially be the same for both IIOP and UIOP. This result is illustrated in Figure 6 by the fact that the time spent in the ORB is generally constant for the four protocol combinations shown.

In general, the use of UIOP demonstrates the advantages of this framework and how optimized, domain-specific protocols can be deployed.

5. RELATED WORK

The design of TAO's pluggable protocols framework is influenced by prior research on the design and optimization of protocol frameworks for communication subsystems. This section outlines this research and compares it with our work.

The architecture of TAO's pluggable protocols framework is based on Open Communications Interface (OCI) [8]. The OCI framework provides a flexible, intuitive, and portable interface for pluggable protocols. The framework interfaces are defined in IDL, with a few special rules to map critical types, such as data buffers.

Defining pluggable protocol interfaces with IDL permits developers to familiarize themselves with a single programming model that can be used to implement protocols in different languages. In addition, the use of IDL makes it possible to write pluggable protocols that are portable among different ORB implementations and platforms.

Though the OCI pluggable protocols framework is useful for many applications and ORBs, TAO implements a highly optimized pluggable protocol framework that is tuned for high-performance and real-time application requirements. For example, TAO's pluggable protocols framework can be integrated with zero-copy high-speed network interfaces [1, 3].

However, TAO's pluggable protocols framework does not preclude the use of more general frameworks like the ORBacus OCI. In fact, we plan to implement OCI as a pluggable protocol into TAO, thereby allowing application developers to test and use OCI pluggable protocols. If applications have very stringent performance requirements, developers can use the internal TAO pluggable protocol framework to obtain the higher performance and greater predictability.

6. CONCLUDING REMARKS

To be an effective development platform for performance-sensitive applications, OO middleware must preserve communication layer QoS properties of applications end-to-end. It is essential, therefore, to define a pluggable protocols framework that allows custom inter-ORB messaging and transport protocols to be configured flexibly and transparently by CORBA applications.

This paper identifies the protocol-related limitations of current ORBs and describes a CORBA-based pluggable protocols framework we developed and integrated with TAO to address these limitations. Benchmarking results are also presented which demonstrate that applying appropriate optimizations to communication middleware can yield highly efficient and predictable implementations, without sacrificing flexibility or reuse.

REFERENCES

[1] Zubin D. Dittia, Guru M. Parulkar, and Jerome R. Cox, Jr. The APIC Approach to High Performance Network Interface Design: Protected DMA and Other Techniques. In *Proceedings of INFOCOM '97*, pages 179–187, Kobe, Japan, April 1997. IEEE.

[2] Erich Gamma, Richard Helm, Ralph Johnson, and John Vlissides. *Design Patterns: Elements of Reusable Object-Oriented Software*. Addison-Wesley, Reading, MA, 1995.

[3] Fred Kuhns, Douglas C. Schmidt, and David L. Levine. The Design and Performance of a Real-time I/O Subsystem. In *Proceedings of the* 5th *IEEE Real-Time Technology and Applications Symposium*, pages 154–163, Vancouver, British Columbia, Canada, June 1999. IEEE.

[4] M. Lauria, S. Pakin, and A. Chien. Efficient Layering for High Speed Communication: Fast Messages 2.x. In *Proceedings of the 7th High Performance Distributed Computing (HPDC7) conference*, Chicago, Illinois, July 1998.

[5] Object Management Group. *CORBA Messaging Specification*, OMG Document orbos/98-05-05 edition, May 1998.

[6] Object Management Group. *The Common Object Request Broker: Architecture and Specification*, 2.2 edition, February 1998.

[7] Object Management Group. *Realtime CORBA Joint Revised Submission*, OMG Document orbos/99-02-12 edition, March 1999.

[8] Inc. Object-Oriented Concepts. ORBacus User Manual - Version 3.1.2. www.ooc.com/ob, 1999.

[9] Douglas C. Schmidt, Sumedh Mungee, Sergio Flores-Gaitan, and Aniruddha Gokhale. Software Architectures for Reducing Priority Inversion and Non-determinism in Real-time Object Request Brokers. *Journal of Real-time Systems*, To appear 1999.

PART 4

QUALITY OF SERVICE

PACKET SCHEDULING FOR HETEROGENEOUS MULTICAST TRANSMISSIONS

Vincent Roca
Université Pierre et Marie Curie
LIP6 - CNRS, thème Réseaux et Performances
8, rue capitaine Scott; 75015 Paris; FRANCE
phone: (+33) 1.44.27.75.14; fax: (+33) 1.44.27.87.32
vincent.roca@lip6.fr; http://www-rp.lip6.fr/~roca

Abstract

Multicast transmissions naturally raise the problem of the heterogeneity of receivers in terms of networking possibilities, host performances and user desires. Several solutions have been introduced but none suits all the situations. This paper describes a scheduling algorithm that unifies some of these solutions, in particular in case of continuous data flows, and which is suited to a broad range of applications. An implementation of this algorithm is used to illustrate its behavior.

1 INTRODUCTION: THE NEEDS

Multicast transmissions naturally raise the problem of the heterogeneity of receivers. Several levels of heterogeneity can be identified: (1) the intrinsic performance of various parts of the network can be largely different; (2) the network performance can vary over the time because of congestion problems, of external factors (e.g. weather conditions in case of wireless communications), or a change of communication technology (e.g. switching from WaveLAN to GSM); (3) some privileged networks can take advantage of improved transmission services (e.g. using differentiated services); while other ones will be at the mercy of router congestions. (4) some hosts can be limited by their processing power (e.g. palmtop); and (5) some users can be content with a medium quality data flow, while other ones will insist to have the highest possible quality.

We believe that a large group will include several (all?) kinds of heterogeneity. Traditionally one restricts oneself to homogeneous multicast transmissions, sending data at a rate determined by the slowest receiver.

It implies defining a maximum rate either statically (compilation or application parameter) or dynamically [8]. Our proposal intends to fill this gap by providing a general purpose heterogeneous multicast scheme, i.e. the possibility to send *any data flow* to a group where each receiver chooses a reception rate according to its network quality, workstation power, and desires.

This paper is organized as follows: section 2 introduces several approaches to support heterogeneous multicast transmissions. Our proposal is detailed in section 3. Section 4 introduces some experimental results. Section 5 discusses additional properties, then we conclude.

2 Limitations of Current Solutions

Several directions have been proposed to address heterogeneity. Some of them rely on packet scheduling schemes (DSS/MMG/MCM), others on coding (e.g. the hierarchical coding of a video stream [5]), on transcoding (the information is tailored, e.g. an image definition is reduced, according to the needs of a particular client [9]), or on filtering [11] [19]. This section focuses on the scheduling schemes.

Destination Set Splitting (DSS)

This solution, also called Simulcast, achieves heterogeneity by using multiple uncoordinated streams at different rates on several multicast groups [1][2]. A receiver chooses the desired throughput and subscribes to the associated group. Here each receiver gets a copy of all the data.

This solution has several limitations:

- because data is sent on all the groups, it leads to a high load of the sender's network where traffic is concentrated.
- a receiver that wants to change of group (e.g. if the selected throughput turns out to be too high) may loose many packets if it unsubscribes to the old group and then subscribes to the new one. If it does the contrary (i.e. subscribing before unsubscribing), the presence of two data flows in the meanwhile can also lead to losses.

But this solution avoids any packet duplication at the receiver side (we'll see that it is not the case of our GMMG scheduling), and can be used with data flows generated on-the-fly.

Multiple Multicast Groups (MMG)

The MMG [3] scheme is based on a cumulative layered scheduling. The idea is to let each multicast group take advantage of the previous groups. Here also everyone receives everything at a pace that depends on its possibilities.

Let us consider a sender S that uses three multicast groups (figure 1). Data is first divided into four equal parts. On group 1, S sends parts 1 to 4 at a rate compatible with that of the slowest receiver. On group 2 S sends parts 2 and 4, which enables a receiver having subscribed to both groups to receive data twice as fast, etc.

```
G1:  part_1  part_3  part_2  part_4
G2:  part_2  part_4
G3:  part_3
     part_4
```

Figure 1: Scheduling in case of the MMG approach.

We see several limitations to the MMG approach as proposed in [3]:

- the sender is supposed to know in advance the amount of data to send in order to partition it. This hypothesis is rather restrictive.
- the sender is supposed to know in advance the available throughput of each receiver in order to define the features of each group. This is usually impossible since group membership is by nature dynamic and the network features highly variable.
- our personal experience implementing our proposal suggests that the packet ordering within each group should be kept increasing.

Multiple-Channel Multicast (MCM)

This class of solutions is also based on a cumulative layered scheduling. It includes the Partition Organization channel scheduling (PO) [7] and the Session Organization (SO) channel scheduling [16]. Like MMG, these solutions require that the data stream is known in advance (in order to partition it) which restricts their use. On the other hand, an advantage of this hypothesis is that asynchronous starts are possible since packets are cyclically transmitted on each multicast group.

Discussion

The previous analysis has highlighted that many hypotheses on the data flow nature are made. For instance hierarchical coding is restricted to data flows that can be organized in cumulative layers. It typically concerns video streams. The MMG and MCM schemes require to know in advance the amount of data to send in order to find the optimal scheduling. A typical example is a file transfer application.

Unfortunately a broad range of applications that generate *on-the-fly data flows* are not satisfied. A white board (e.g. `wb` [18]) or an application sharing environment (e.g. doing X11 message multiplexing like `XTV` [20]) are two typical examples. The amount of data exchanged can be rather low during a certain span of time and then, because of a participant action (e.g. he launches a new X Windows application under `XTV`'s control), the tool generates "on the fly" large amounts of data. If the DSS approach can handle these applications, it has limitations as explained before.

3 The GMMG (Generalized MMG) Approach

This section introduces a hybrid solution that mixes some of the previous approaches. To be as general as possible, we consider that data is submitted by the application as a *collection of messages, called ADU* (Application Data Units) to the sending control layer. We make no hypothesis on the nature of the ADU and whether or not the application follows the ALF paradigm [4]. Unlike MGM, we do not consider the possibility of receivers starting reception asynchronously. This feature is handled at user level with the kind of applications considered.

The Case of an Isolated ADU

We first consider an isolated ADU. GMMG is then *very close to MMG*. The ADU of figure 2 is first segmented into sixteen 512 byte packets (i.e. small enough to avoid IP fragmentation). Each ADU is identified by its constituting packets, noted as a range of packet sequence numbers (e.g. [1; 16] identifies the first ADU which is segmented in 16 packets). A little vertical arrow indicates that the application submits a new ADU to the control layer. In figure 2 the sender S uses four transmission layers and schedules packets in a cumulative way, so that a receiver subscribing to an additional layer experiences a reception rate two times higher[1]. Therefore on layer i we transmit the packets of all the previous layers delimited by the upper half of the packets sent on layer i-1 (dashed areas of figure 2).

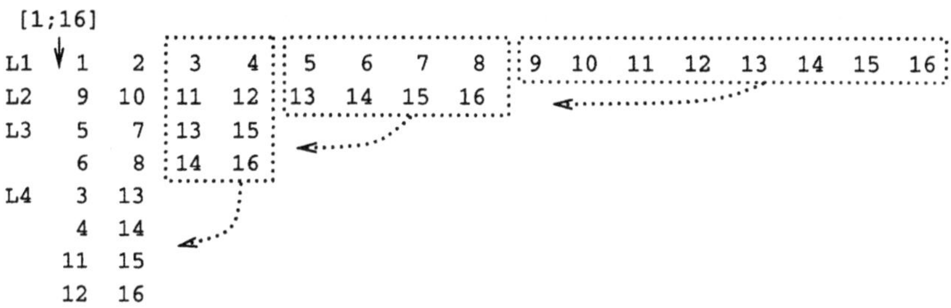

Figure 2: GMMG scheduling of an isolated ADU.

Because transmissions on each layer occur at a regular rate determined by layer 1, we use this rate as a virtual time scale. As we neglect the transmission and propagation times, it is regarded either as the sending or receiving time scale. At time 1, S sends successively packet 1 on layer 1, packet 9 on layer 2, packets 5 and 6 on layer 3, etc. Then it waits. At time 2, S sends all the packets scheduled for time 2 and so on.

Several evaluation criteria are considered:

total reception time: Time required to receive all the packets of all the ADUs, expressed in terms of layer 1 packet times ("virtual time"). For instance, in figure 2, subscribing to layers 1 and 2 allows the reception of all packets in 8 virtual time slots.

spreading of the ADU reception times: The regular arrival of ADUs (i.e. the reception of all the packets of each ADU) enables the receiver to process them regularly, as soon as possible, and limits buffer use. This spreading is represented by the list of reception times of each ADU.

total number of packets transmitted: Number of packets transmitted over all layers subscribed. In spite of the cumulative aspect of transmissions, certain packets are transmitted several times. Obviously, the fewer, the better. This metric is also expressed as the ratio of the number of packets sent for a given number of layers to the number of packets sent on layer 1 (i.e. non-duplicated packets).

[1]For simplicity we only consider ratios of 2. This is not compulsory as explained in section 5

cumulative throughput ratio: The total transmission rate on the sender's network increases with the number of transmission layers. The tables give the ratio of the maximum throughput when subscribing a given number of layers to the throughput of layer 1.

number of multicast groups: using a multicast group is costly, so the fewer the better. So far we have supposed that each layer corresponds to a multicast group. Section 5 discusses this assumption.

Table 1: Evaluation of the example of figure 2.

layers	end	spreading	nb of pkts/ratio	throughput ratio
L1 only	16	16	16 / 1.0 ratio	1.0 ratio
L1+2	8	8	24 / 1.5 ratio	2.0 ratio
L1+2+3	4	4	32 / 2.0 ratio	4.0 ratio
L1+2+3+4	2	2	40 / 2.5 ratio	8.0 ratio

Table 1 applies these criteria to figure 2. Compared to layer 1, the presence of layers 2 and 3 reduces by a factor 4 the end of reception, at the expense of a maximum total throughput 4 times higher, but with only twice as many packets sent. With layer 4, data is received 8 times faster with only 2.5 as many packets sent.

The Case of Close ADU Submissions

We now consider the case of close ADU submissions. The transmission control layer does not know in advance the amount of data to send. Therefore, it must continuously decide when to send each packet, and whether or not to reconsider the planned transmissions when a new ADU arrives. Three strategies are possible: the first one consists in sending ADUs independently to one another. Another one, more drastic, consists in reconsidering the whole transmission planning each time a new ADU is received. None of these solutions is recommended as explained in annex A. Therefore we focus on the third intermediate solution.

Description of the GMMG algorithm

This solution takes into account a new ADU as soon as it is available without modifying the transmissions already planned. When the application submits the new ADU, some packets from previous ADUs (possibly 0) wait to be sent on each level. Let call them rem_1, rem_2 and rem_3. We have: $rem_1 >= rem_2 >= rem_3 >= 0$. Let $part_1$, $part_2$ and $part_3$

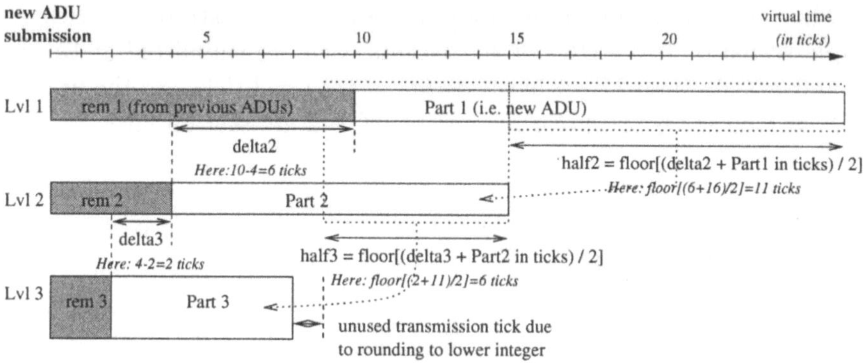

Figure 3: GMMG scheduling algorithm.

be the various packets belonging to the new ADU sent respectively on layer 1, 2 and 3. By definition, $part_1$ includes all the packets of the new ADU. $part_2$ is built as follows. We first calculate:

$$delta_2(in\ ticks) = tick_2(rem_2) - tick_1(rem_1)$$

where the $tick_i()$ function gives the number of ticks required to transmit the given number of packets on layer i[2]. $part_2$ includes all the packets of $part_1$ contained in the upper half, of duration $half_2$ ticks, of the set $delta_2 \cup part_1$. Therefore[3]:

$$half_2(in\ ticks) = floor[(delta_2 + tick_1(part_1))/2]$$

$$part_2 = \{upper\ half_2\ packets\ of\ part_1\}$$

Likewise $part_3$ includes the packets of $part_1 \cup part_2$ delimited by the upper half, of duration $half_3$, of the set $delta_3 \cup part_2$ (area within the dashed box of figure 3). $part_3$ is bounded by the times $start_3$ and end_3:

$$delta_3(in\ ticks) = tick_3(rem_3) - tick_2(rem_2)$$

$$half_3(in\ ticks) = floor[(delta_3 + tick_2(part_2))/2]$$

$$end_3\ (in\ ticks) = tick_2(rem_2 \cup part_2)$$

$$start_3\ (in\ ticks) = end_3 - half_3$$

$$part_3 = \{pkts\ of\ new\ ADU\ sent\ between\ start_3\ and\ end_3\ on\ L1 \cup L2\}$$

[2] $tick_i(l\ bytes) = l/number\ of\ bytes\ sent\ per\ tick\ on\ layer\ i$

[3] The $floor()$ function returns the largest integral value not greater than x

This algorithm can be generalized. Figure 4 illustrates it with a simple scenario: two ADUs of six packets each are submitted at times 0.5 and 2.5. At time 2.5 we have: $delta_2 = 4 - 1 = 3$ ticks. So the upper $half_2 = floor((3+6)/2) = 4$ packets of ADU 2 are sent on layer 2.

```
  [1;6]     [7;12]
    |         |
L1  V 1    2  V 3    4    5    6 | 7    8    9   10   11   12
L2    4    5    6 |  9   10   11   12      |
```

Figure 4: GMMG scheduling applied to a simple scenario.

Table 2: Evaluation of the example of figure 4.

layers	end	spreading	nb of pkts/ratio	throughput ratio
L1 only	12	6, 12	12 / 1.0 ratio	1.0 ratio
L1+2	8	3, 8	19 / 1.6 ratio	2.0 ratio

Compared to the two other solutions of annex A, this solution (1) improves the spreading of the end of ADU reception, and (2) reduces the total reception time for L1+L2. This is made possible by the precise knowledge of remaining packets on the various layers.

A Necessary Improvement: the Notion of Credit

This algorithm has limitations. Suppose we are building $part_i$. On the previous levels (i.e. 1 to $i-1$), between $start_i$ and end_i there can be packets that do not belong to the new ADU. These packets are ignored and the corresponding number of transmission slots of $part_i$ are lost. This is the *"lost cycle phenomenon"*. It happens in figure 3 when building $part_3$. A transmission slot is lost because the first packet of layer 1 within the dashed area (time 9) belongs to rem_1, not to $Part_1$.

If ADUs are submitted too rapidly, packets progressively accumulate on the lowest levels and "lost cycles" are more and more numerous. Higher layers are seriously affected and may even become useless. To avoid it we consider that each lost cycle creates *"credit"*. Let *tot_credit* be the sum of these credits for all layers. We calculate the possible anticipation:

$$anticipation\ (in\_ticks) = floor(tick_i(tot\_credit)/2);$$

that we subtract to the $start_i$ variable:

$$start_i = start_i - anticipation$$

By extending the area considered when building $part_i$, we make up for the lost cycles. Note that the implementation of GMMG described in [15] completely avoids this problem.

One Step Further: the Case of Continuous Data Flows

In the previous section we considered close ADU submissions. We now go further and consider the case of continuous data flows. This is (partially) illustrated in figure 5.

```
[1;12][13;16][17;28]
    |    |    |
 L1 V 1  V 2  V 3   4    5    6    7    8    9   10   11   12| 13   14   15   16| 17   18 ...
 L2   7    8    9  10   11   12| 13   14   15   16| 20   21   22   23   25   26   27   28|
 L3   4    6   11| 13   15| 17   19   21   23   25   27|
      5   10   12| 14   16| 18   20   22   24   26   28|
 L4   3|  13|  17  21   25|
      9|  14|  18  22   26|
     11|  15|  19  23   27|
     12|  16|  20  24   28|
```

Figure 5: Continuous data flows (extract).

If the ADU submission rate is superior to the packet transmission rate of level 1, then $delta_i$ and $half_i$ increase. It means that $part_i$ tends to be identical to $part_1$. If the end of reception time of the ADUs is still improved, this is to the detriment of the total number of packets sent, and GMMG tends to DSS where data is sent on each layer. *Our approach is thus a balance between the MMG (sparse ADU submission) and the simulcast (continuous ADU submission) flow controls.*

Because data cannot indefinitely accumulate at the sender waiting to be transmitted on the lower layers, the application will eventually be blocked. Lower layers will take advantage of this pause to keep up with higher layers. Therefore, a limitation not solved by this approach is that the *transmission of truly continuous data flows, on the long range, take place at the rhythm of the lowest transmission level* because of limited buffer capabilities. A partial solution is introduced in section 5.

Defining Several Transmission Subflows

Up to now we have supposed that ADUs had to be sent to all the receivers. In fact an application may identify several subflows and leave each receiver choose what to receive (as with a hierarchical coding).

```
     [1;16] subflow 1
     [a;l]  subflow 2
       |
L1   V 1   2   3   4   5   6   7   8   9  10  11  12  13  14  15  16
L2     9  10  11  12  13  14  15  16
L3     a   b   c   d   e   f   g   h   i   j   k   l
L4     g   h   i   j   k   l
```

Figure 6: Scheduling of two ADUs belonging to two subflows.

In figure 6 we consider the subflow 1 sent to everybody, and the subflow 2 providing optional details. For each subflow we offer the possibility to receive data at different rates. A receiver now has two complementary levels of choice: (1) *what detail* he needs (i.e. how many subflows), and (2) *how fast* data should be received (i.e. how many layers for each subflow). Depending on the application some combinations can be meaningless, but this is an application decision that does not concern the transmission control layer.

4 Preliminary Simulation Results

We have implemented this algorithm as a C library and linked it to a traffic generator. This section illustrates the algorithm behavior with a data stream that we believe is significant of that of a white-board (for a detailed performance evaluation see [15]). There is no packet loss. The scenario consists of three bursts separated by inactivity periods:

step 1: send two ADUs of ten packets each ([1;10] and [11;20]), at one time tick interval (i.e. at times 1 and 2)

step 2: wait 10 ticks

step 3: send again two more ADUs ([21;30] and [31;40]), at one tick interval (i.e. at times 12 and 13)

step 4: wait 28 ticks (so that level 1 finishes to send all the packets left)

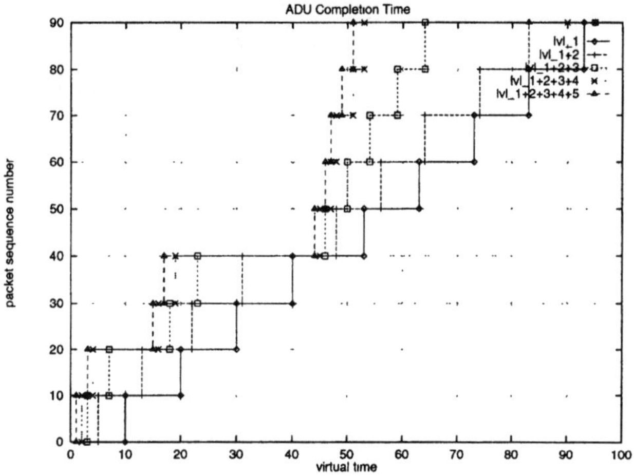

Figure 7: End of ADU reception while varying the number of layers.

step 5: send five ADUs ([41;50] to [81;90]) at one time tick interval (i.e. at times 41 to 46). Wait until the sender has received all of them, even if the ADU has already been completed[4].

Figure 7 shows the ADU reception times according to the number of layers subscribed, and figure 8 the packets sent on each layer. The horizontal steps in figure 7 at sequence numbers 20, 40 and 90 indicate that all the ADUs of steps 1, 3, and 5 respectively have been received. Subscribing to more layers leads to a faster reception of ADUs. Yet the gains are not always a power of two. This is due to the delay experienced on lower levels. For instance, during step 5, packet scheduling on layer 2 can only take advantage of layer 1 transmissions for the ADU [41; 50]. Then ADUs are received at the same rhythm no matter whether one has subscribed to layer 1 only or to both layers. This is different with layers 3 to 5. Their higher transmission rate is sufficient to process the packet burst of step 5 and each level takes advantage of transmissions on (some of) the previous levels.

The final duplication ratio is given in table 3. If this ratio is 3.6 when receiving all the layers, the five ADUs of step 5 have been received in 8 time ticks instead of 47, namely 5.8 times faster! These experiments show that our cumulative transmission organization can handle bursty

[4] It means that extra duplicated packets will be received. Another possibility would be for the receiver to close the socket once all the ADUs have been received. In that case the duplication ratio would be largely improved.

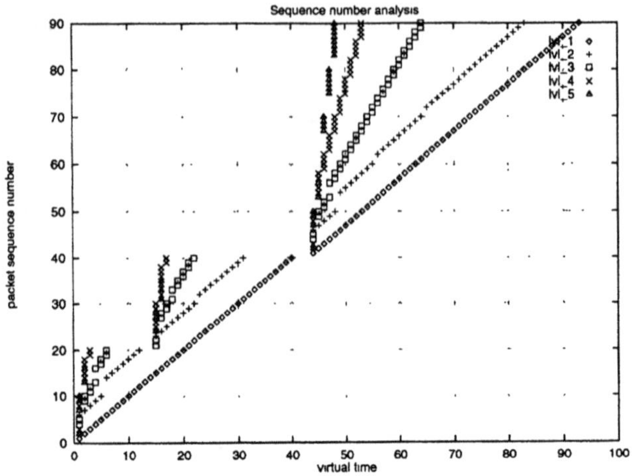

Figure 8: Packet sent on each layer when subscribing all of them.

Table 3: Duplication ratio while varying the number of levels.

Level 1	Levels 1+2	Levels 1+2+3	Levels 1+2+3+4	Levels 1+2+3+4+5
1.0	1.7	2.5	3.2	3.6

data flows efficiently while minimizing the number of packets sent.

5 Additional Aspects And Related Work

We now discuss some additional aspects related to the use of our scheduling algorithm. Many items (e.g. congestion control, reliability, how many layers to use, etc.) are not covered by this paper even if they are required.

Storing ADUs on the Disk to Limit the Continuous Data Flow Problem

The problem with (pseudo) continuous data flows is not so serious because our transmission scheme is implemented as a user-level library [15]. The process image (code+data) is naturally swappable and using a large transmission buffer will only result in a large area in the swapping partition. The sender can cope with "reasonably long" continuous data flows since data is in fact stored on the disk rather than in physical memory[5].

[5]A common rule of thumb is to define a swapping area 2 to 3 times larger than the available physical memory.

If not sufficient, it is possible to go further and to *explicitly store data on the disk* rather than in memory buffers. The scheduling module only keeps a small memory buffer which is used as a cache to store data read from the disk archive. Because transmissions are planned in advance, the disk access latency can be easily hidden. This technique enables very large transmission archives without competing with other processes.

This approach is more general than just its application to our scheduling algorithm. In particular it could be of benefits for reliable multicast transmissions. Data buffering is a problem because the sender must be able to cope with any delayed retransmission request, (even in case of a receiver-initiated approach [13]) which requires to keep data in memory for long (infinite?) periods.

Non Bijective "Transmission Level" to "Multicast Group" Mapping

GMMG (like other layered schemes) uses several transmission levels (or levels), and for simplicity we considered so far that they were mapped to several multicast groups. But several problems arise:

- resources are kept by multicast routers for each group,
- DVMRP [14] leads to periodical flooding and pruning stages for each group, and finally
- several multicast addresses must be allocated and announced.

A first way to limit the problems consists in mapping several transmission levels on a multicast group. For instance group 1 can be used for level 1 which provides an elementary transmission service. Group 2 can be used both for levels 2 and 3 for an intermediate transmission service. Finally group 3 can be used for levels 4 and 5, providing a high throughput service.

Another approach to provide a large range of throughputs with a limited number of multicast groups is to define a throughput scale that is not necessarily a power of 2 [3]. This is also possible with GMMG using the efficient implementation described in [15]. This latter accommodates *any scale of throughputs* since the number of packets sent on each level at each time tick can be freely set.

6 Conclusions

We have introduced a new scheduling algorithm (GMMG) for heterogeneous multicast transmissions unifying the MMG and DSS approaches. This algorithm can be used with a broad range of applications like CSCW ("Computer Supported Collaborative Work") tools that generate on-the-fly data flows. It has also been implemented in a general purpose library which is freely distributed (with source code) in the author's home page. A companion paper [15] discusses the design of this library and compares various scheduling algorithms including GMMG.

Acknowledgments

The author thanks S. Fdida, his colleagues from LIP6 and the anonymous reviewers who contributed to improve the quality of this paper.

References

[1] M. Ammar, L. Wu, "Improving the Performance of Point to Multi-Point ARQ Protocols through Destination Set Splitting", *Proceedings of IEEE INFOCOM'92, May 1992.*

[2] M. Ammar, D. Towsley, "Flow control for multicast applications", *Multicast tutorial during SIGCOMM'97, September 1997.*

[3] S. Bhattacharyya, J. Kurose, D. Towsley, R. Nagarajan, "Efficient multicast flow control using multiple multicast groups", *Proceedings of IEEE INFOCOM'98, February 1998.*

[4] D. Clark, D. Tennenhouse, "Architectural considerations for a new generation of protocols", *Proc. ACM SIGCOMM'90, September 1990.*

[5] J. Bolot, T. Turletti, "Scalable feedback control for multicast video distribution in the Internet", *Proceedings SIGCOMM'94, September 1994.*

[6] C. Diot, W. Dabbous, J. Crowcroft, "Multipoint communication: a survey of protocols, functions, and mechanisms", *IEEE Journal on Selected Areas in Communications, Vol. 15, No. 3, April 1997.*

[7] M. Donahoo, M. Ammar, E. Zegura, "Multiple-Channel Multicast scheduling for scalable bulk-data transport", *Proceedings of IEEE INFOCOM'99, March 1999.*

[8] S. Floyd, V. Jacobson, S. McCanne, C. Liu, L. Zhang, "A reliable multicast framework for light-weight sessions and application level framing", *Proceedings ACM SIGCOMM'95, 1995.*

[9] A. Fox, S. Gribble, Y. Chawathe, E. Brewer, "Adapting to network and client variation using infrastructural proxies: lessons and perspective", *IEEE Personal Communications, Vol. 5 No. 4, August 1998.*

[10] B. Levine, JJ. Garcia-Luna-Aceves, "Improving Internet multicast with routing labels", *Proceeding of IEEE ICNP'97, October 1997.*

[11] M. Luby, L. Vicisano, T. Speakman, "Heterogeneous multicast congestion control based on router packet filtering", *Work in progress, presented at RMRG meeting, June 1999.*

[12] S. McCanne, V. Jacobson, M. Vetterli, "Receiver-driven layered multicast", *Proceedings ACM SIGCOMM'96, October 1996.*

[13] S. Pingali, D. Towsley, J.F. Kurose, "A comparison of sender-initiated and receiver-initiated reliable multicast protocol", *IEEE Journal on Selected Areas in Communications, April 1997.*

[14] T. Pusateri, "Distance Vector Multicast Routing Protocol", *Internet Draft <draft-ietf-idmr-dvmrp-v3-06.txt>, March 1998.*

[15] V. Roca, "Design of a library for the heterogeneous multicast distribution of data flows generated on the fly", *Submitted, July 1999.*

[16] L. Vicisano, "Notes on a cumulative layered organisation of data packets across multiple streams with different rates", *Work in progress, May 1998.*

[17] L. Vicisano, L. Rizzo, J. Crowcroft, "TCP-like congestion control for layered multicast data transfer", *Proceedings of IEEE INFOCOM'98, February 1998.*

[18] "wb - LBNL Whiteboard Tool", *available at URL http://www-nrg.ee.lbl.gov/wb/*

[19] R. Wittmann, M. Zitterbart, "Active multicasting for heterogeneous groups", *Proceeding of 4th IFIP Broadband Communications, BC'98, April 1998.*

[20] Hussein Abdel-Wahab, Mark Feit, "XTV: A Framework for Sharing X Window Clients in Remote Synchronous Collaboration", *Proceedings, IEEE TriComm '91: Communications for Distributed Applications and Systems, April 1991.*

A Two Suboptimal Algorithms

This section explains why the first two algorithms mentioned in section 3 have not be selected.

Send ADUs Independently to One Another

```
      [1;6]      [7;12]
        |          |
L1    V 1    2   V 3    4    5    6 |  7    8    9   10   11   12
L2      4    5      6 | 10   11   12 |
```

Figure 9: Scheduling with ADUs sent independently to one another.

Figure 9 illustrates the first strategy using a simple scenario: two ADUs, each of them segmented into six packets, are submitted at times 0.5 and 2.5. Here, S sends the packets 1 to 6 (first ADU) without taking into account the availability of packets 7 to 12 (second ADU). Then S send the upper half of the packets of the second ADU on level 2 as if it was an isolated ADU. Because transmissions are performed blindly, reception only finishes at time 9 with both layers.

Table 4: Evaluation of solution 1.

layers	end	spreading	nb of pkts/ratio	throughput ratio
L1 only	12	6, 12	12 / 1.0 ratio	1.0 ratio
L1+2	9	3, 9	18 / 1.5 ratio	2.0 ratio

Renegotiate Packet Transmission at Each ADU Submission

```
     [1;6]      [7;12]
       |          |
L1   V 1     2  V 3     4     5     6 |  7     8     9    10    11    12
L2       4   5      8   9    10    11 | 12 |
```

Figure 10: Scheduling when reconsidering transmission at each ADU.

An opposite solution is possible, taking into account the availability of the second ADU immediately (figure 10). Here, the whole transmission planning is reconsidered at time 3 and the transmission of packet 6 on layer 2 is given up. As packets 3 to 12 remain to be sent, S continues with the transmission of the upper half of the remaining packets on layer 2. It is packet: $3 + floor((12-2)/2) = 8$. The reception is faster than with solution 1, but the first ADU is only available at time 6. Besides, the total number of packets is higher because packets 4 and 5 have been sent pointlessly on layer 2. The problem is that this solution does not take the ADU boundaries into account.

Table 5: Evaluation of solution 2.

layers	end	spreading	nb of pkts/ratio	throughput ratio
L1 only	12	6, 12	12 / 1.0 ratio	1.0 ratio
L1+2	7	6,7	19 / 1.6 ratio	2.0 ratio

FAIR BANDWIDTH ALLOCATION FOR DIFFERENTIATED SERVICES

Anindya Basu and Zheng Wang
Bell Laboratories
{basu, zhwang}@research.bell-lab.com

ABSTRACT

In this paper, we present a comparative study of three proposals for differentiated services – the RIO scheme, the two-bit scheme and the User-Share Differentiation (USD) scheme. We simulate the three schemes under a number of different scenarios including mismatching of bottleneck bandwidth and profiles, short duration traffic, and non-responsive sources. Our findings show that although the simpler schemes for Differentiated Services reduce the complexity in the core, they tend to perform less well when there is a mismatch between the allocated profiles and bottleneck bandwidth, and also when the traffic sources are bursty, and non-responsive.

1. INTRODUCTION

Over the last ten years, considerable effort has been made to provide Quality-of-Services (QoS) guarantees in the Internet. Much of the work has focused on the end-to-end per-session reservation approach where an application makes an end-to-end reservation before starting a session [16]. While it makes sense to set up a reservation for a long-lasting session, this approach is not suitable for short duration, and transaction-oriented applications such as browsing the World Wide Web where the overheads and latency involved in setting up a reservation for each session could become disproportionately high. Furthermore, there are also concerns regarding the scalability of providing guarantees at the per-session level in the core of the Internet.

The above issues have led to a number of new proposals for providing differentiated services in the Internet [1]. In contrast to the per-session reservation approach, the differentiated services approach allows service providers to offer different levels of services to a few (typically, a small number such as two or three) classes of aggregated traffic flows. Examples of this approach include the RIO scheme by Clark *et al* [2] and the two-bit scheme by Nichols *et al* [11]. They advocate pushing traffic policing and admission control to the edge of the network and leave the core of the network as simple as possible.

With such an approach, Incoming traffic from a user is monitored at the edge of the network against the profile that the user has registered (and paid for) with the service provider. The packets that are out of profile are either shaped or tagged and the core routers process such tagged (or untagged) packets according to predefined policies. Such an approach has the advantage of simplicity since core routers do not need to store state for each traffic flow; instead, they can process packets using different policies for each traffic class which is determined by a small number of bits in the packet header.

A different set of proposals that is exemplified by the User-Share Differentiation (USD) scheme proposed by Wang [15] advocate putting modestly sophisticated control mechanisms in core routers to provide proportional fair sharing (PFS) of resources and per-prefix traffic isolation. The advantage of such schemes is that they do not require a priori estimation of resources that a particular user or an application expects to use. At any point in the network, the USD scheme can ensure that the bandwidth allocated to a flow is commensurate with some predefined metric, such as the price paid by the originator of the flow to the ISP. For example, it is possible to guarantee that user A who pays twice as much as user B, gets twice as much bandwidth as user B anywhere in a network. The major disadvantage of such schemes lie in the increased complexity of the routers in the network core and the concern that such complexity may not be amenable to scaling.

In this paper, we present a comparative study of the three proposals for differentiated services, namely the RIO scheme, the 2-bit scheme and the User-Share Differentiation (USD) scheme. We implement each of these schemes on a simulated network using the REAL network simulator [9] and study their performances under different network configurations. We find that the USD scheme provides a better match of performance to user expectations and is more robust with respect to short-lived flows such as web traffic, but this comes at the added cost of implementing PFS at the network core.

The rest of the paper is organized as follows: Section 2 describes the three schemes in detail. Section 3 evaluates the performance of the three schemes under different scenarios, followed by Section 4 that summarizes the results of the evaluation. We conclude the paper in Section 5 with a discussion of some of the implications of our findings.

2. THREE DIFFSERV SCHEMES

In this section, we describe in more detail the three differentiated services schemes, namely, the RIO scheme, the two-bit scheme and the USD scheme.

The RIO scheme (RIO stands for Random Early Detection with In/Out bit) uses some form of packet tagging to indicate the drop priority of the packet to the core network routers. Each user (or traffic flow, depending upon the granularity) is assigned a service profile by the ISP based on the expected bandwidth utilization by the user. At the edge of the network domain managed by the ISP (i.e., at the ingress points), user traffic is monitored by a profile meter to ensure that it stays within the profile. Any packets that are out of profile are marked as "out" while those that conform to the user profile are marked as "in". In the network core, the "in" and "out" packets are treated with different drop priorities using RED (Random Early Detection).

Since the "in" packets start being dropped only when the queue size crosses a higher threshold than in the case of "out" packets, they get dropped with a lower probability than "out" packets. This ensures that in-profile traffic has less chance of getting dropped than out-of-profile traffic, and therefore gets predictable levels of service so long as it stays within profile (even when congestion occurs). The RIO scheme also makes it possible to use statistical multiplexing to utilize any excess bandwidth that may be available since it does not prevent out-of-profile packets from entering the network.

The two-bit differentiated services architecture combines the RIO scheme with Jacobson's premium service [8] to come up with three different classes of service, namely premium, assured and best-effort. The premium service is based on explicit resource reservations and a simple priority queuing model where the premium traffic is transmitted prior to other traffic. Such a service is useful for time-critical applications that require minimum delay as well as applications that require explicit bandwidth and delay guarantees.

The premium traffic is strictly policed at the edge of the network: packets that are out of the service profile are dropped or delayed until they are within the service profile. The assured service class corresponds to the "in" traffic in the RIO scheme and has a lower drop priority than the ordinary best-effort service. When congestion occurs, the chances are high that the assured packets would receive predictable levels of service if they conform to their service profile, which is typically based on average bandwidth utilization. This service is appropriate for users who are willing to pay somewhat more in order to get better (or predictable) performance in times of congestion.

The USD scheme takes an approach that is different from that of the RIO and two-bit schemes. First, instead of taking a minimalist approach with a small number of distinguishable classes, the USD scheme allows traffic isolation on a per-customer basis. This allows more sophisticated service contracts to be supported. Second, in contrast to the RIO and two-bit schemes where the traffic policing happens at the edge of the network, the USD scheme manages bandwidth allocation directly on the bottlenecks where the congestion takes place. Finally, while both RIO and two-bit schemes primarily deal with outgoing traffic traveling from customers' networks to their ISP, the USD scheme works with traffic of both outgoing and incoming directions.

The USD scheme introduces two terms for bandwidth allocation, user and share. The *user* refers to the customer to which the bandwidth is allocated. In the USD scheme, a user can be a network, a group of networks identified by a prefix, or an individual end user. Each user is assigned a number called *share,* based on some predefined metrics, such as the amount that a user has paid for the service. The USD scheme operates with the *proportional fair sharing* (*PFS*) principle, where at any point in a network, the bandwidth allocated to the traffic from or to a user is in proportion to the user's share. In other words, the exact amount of bandwidth allocated to flow from or to a user is determined by the total bandwidth available at the bottleneck and the relative weights (or shares) of active users competing for the bottleneck resources.

The USD scheme can be implemented with a classifier capable of prefix lookup (to identify flows belonging to individual customers) and a scheduler that supports PFS. Prefix lookup has been extensively studied for route lookups and several novel algorithms have been proposed for this purpose [5]. Hardware-based route lookup implementations that can support over 1 millions entries [10] exist and the same techniques can be used in the USD for identifying which customer a packet belongs to. A large number of scheduling algorithms can support PFS. Among them, weighted fair queuing (WFQ) [12] can support PFS with the most stringent fairness guarantees. Many variations of WFQ, such as Deficit Round Robin (DRR) and Self-Clocked Fair Queuing (SCFQ), have lower implementation complexity and yet provide reasonable fairness guarantees [7,13]. For example, the PacketStar Router from Bell Labs implements a variant of WFQ with 64,000 queues at 622 Mb/s speed [10].

3. SIMULATING DIFFERENTIATED SERVICES

In this section, we present and discuss the simulation results for the three differentiated services proposals described in the previous section. While the ideal method of doing a comparative study would be to deploy each of the three schemes on the internet, we relied on simulations instead since deploying new mechanisms on a real network without a thorough understanding of the ramifications would be inappropriate. These simulations are intended to provide us with a detailed description of how the network behaves when such schemes are deployed. Through such a process, we hope to gain a deeper understanding of the strengths and weaknesses of these schemes before they are actually deployed on a real network.

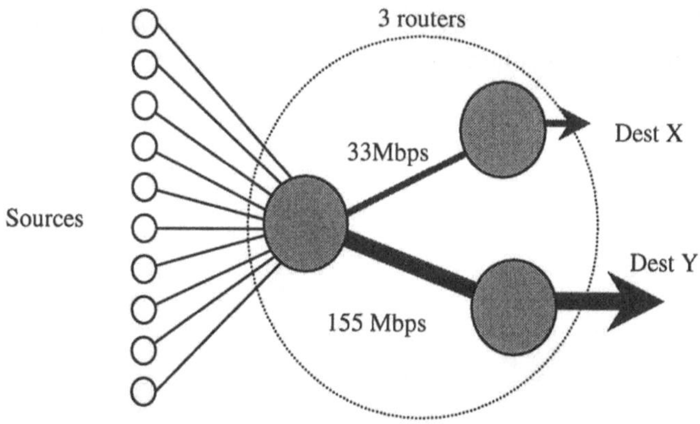

Figure 1: Simulated Network

The simulations were done with the REAL network simulator [9]. For purposes of the simulation, we used a network with the configuration shown in Figure 1. In the simulation, we have 10 sources (1 through 10 counting downwards) that communicate with one of two different destinations, X and Y. The sources are connected to destination X through a bottleneck link of capacity 33Mbps and to destination Y through a bottleneck link of capacity 155Mbps. Each of the links that connects a source to the first router in the diagram has a capacity of 30Mb/s. The one-way propagation delays (the same to both X and Y) for the sources (counting from top downwards) were set at 20, 20, 40, 40, 50, 50, 70, 70, 100, and 100 milliseconds respectively. The sources are all TCP-Reno sources (unless specified otherwise) that use a packet size of 500 bytes and each of them sends 500,000 packets to the destination.

For the RIO implementation, the routers use RED with the values of 400 packets, 800 packets, and 0.02 for *min_in, max_in,* and P_{max_in}, and 100 packets, 200 packets and 0.5 for *min_out*, *max_out*, and P_{max_out} [2] where *min_in* and *max_in* represent the upper and lower bounds for the average queue size for in profile packets when RED kicks in and P_{max_in} is the maximum drop probability for an in profile packet when the average queue size is in the [*min_in, max_in*] range. The *min_out*, *max_out* and P_{max_out} are the corresponding parameters for the out of profile packets. Note that the total queue sizes are used when calculating the drop probability for out of profile packets, as suggested in [2].

For the USD scheme, we used the weighted fair queuing (WFQ) discipline on the router to provide PFS. While it can be argued that WFQ was not the most appropriate scheme to use for this purpose which advocates use of WFQ variants with less implementation complexity and less strict guarantees), we feel that the results provide an important baseline for purposes of comparison with the other schemes.

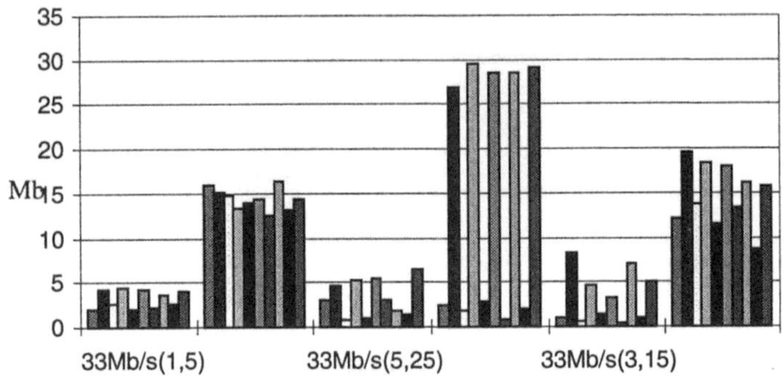

Figure 1: Bandwidth share with two different bottleneck bandwidths and 3 different expected profiles using the RIO scheme

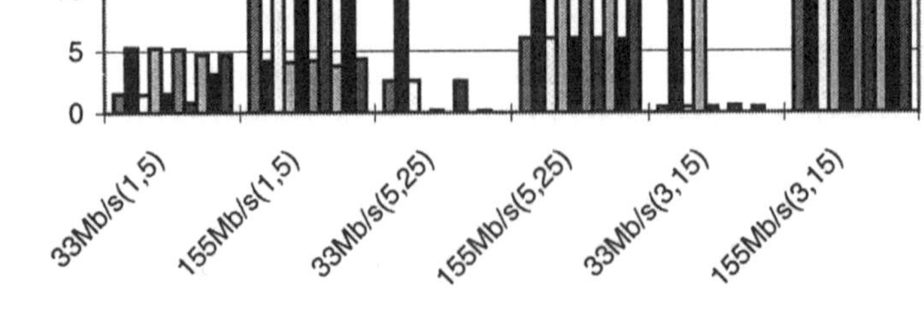

Figure 2: Bandwidth share with two different bottleneck bandwidths and 3 different expected profiles using the two-bit scheme.

Effect of Expected Bandwidth Profiles

We first evaluated the effect of expected bandwidth profiles and bottleneck bandwidths on actual bandwidth allocation. For this purpose, we ran three sets of simulations for each of the two bottleneck links (33Mb/s to destination X and 155Mb/s to destination Y). In each of the simulations, the odd numbered sources (1,3,5,7,9) had the lower expected bandwidth and the even numbered sources (2,4,6,8,10) had the higher expected bandwidth. In the first set of simulations, we set the expected lower and higher bandwidths to 1Mb/s and 5Mb/s, respectively, such that the aggregate (i.e., sum of) expected bandwidth of all the flows matched the 33Mb/s bottleneck bandwidth. In the second set, the expected bandwidths were chosen to be 5 and 25Mb/s, respectively to match the 155Mb/s bottleneck and in the third set, they were set to 3 and 15Mb/s, respectively, which is the average of expected bandwidths in the first two sets.

The performance of the RIO scheme is shown in Figure 1. The figure consists of six clusters with 10 bars in each cluster. Each cluster has a label of the form *x* Mb/s (*y*,*z*), which means that the particular cluster represents the bandwidth allocation for the 10 sources when the bottleneck bandwidth is *x* Mb/s and the higher and lower expected bandwidths are *y* and *z* Mb/s, respectively. The results indicate that if the aggregate expected bandwidth of all the flows passing through the bottleneck closely matches the bottleneck

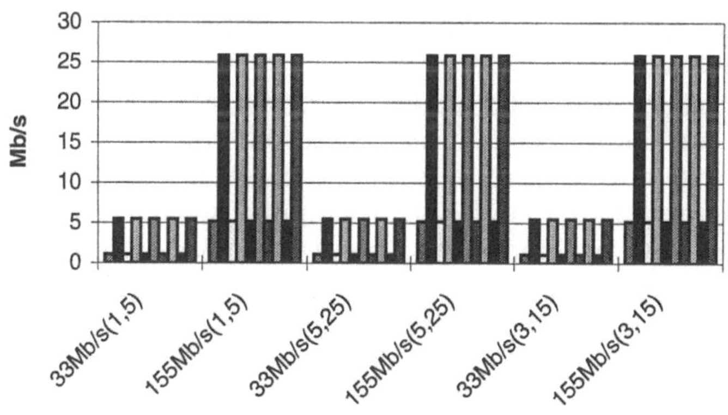

Figure 3: Bandwidth share with two different bottleneck bandwidths and 3 different expected profiles using the USD scheme

bandwidth, the RIO scheme is able to allocate bandwidth in accordance with the expected bandwidth profiles. This is clear from the graphs for the 33Mb/s (1,5) and 155Mb/s (5,25) cases. In the first case, the sources with a lower expected bandwidth are allocated a slightly higher bandwidth than their expected profiles at the expense of sources with a higher expected bandwidth and the situation is the reverse in the 155Mb/s (5,25) case. We expect that some tuning of the RED parameters is required to obtain a bandwidth allocation that is more commensurate with the expected bandwidth profiles. If the bottleneck bandwidth is in excess of the aggregated expected bandwidth, the excess bandwidth is more or less evenly allocated among all the sources. This is evident from the figures for the 155Mb/s (3,15) and the 155Mb/s (1,5) cases. In the 155Mb/s (3,15) case, the sources with the higher expected bandwidth do get more bandwidth than the others, but the relative difference is smaller than those in the 33Mb/s (1,5) and the 155Mb/s (5,25) cases where the bottleneck bandwidth matches the aggregate expected bandwidth. In the 155Mb/s (1,5) case (where the difference between the bottleneck bandwidth and the aggregated expected bandwidth is higher), the bandwidth allocation is fairly even among all the sources. This is because the excess bandwidth is only allocated to the out of profile packets, and the RED scheme for out of profile packets ensures that this excess bandwidth is allocated fairly. Finally, if the aggregated expected bandwidth is less than the bottleneck bandwidth, the RIO scheme is able (for the most part) to allocate the existing bandwidth in a manner that is commensurate with existing user expectations. There is one exception in the 33Mb/s (5,25) case, where the bandwidth allocated to source 8 is less than that allocated to sources 1 and 7 although the latter have lower expected bandwidths. In summary, the RIO scheme performs well if the bottleneck bandwidth matches or is less than the aggregate expected bandwidth of all the flows passing through the bottleneck, but is unable to allocate bandwidth in proportion to user expectations if there is excess bandwidth at the bottleneck.

To evaluate the two-bit scheme, we set the higher bandwidth traffic as the premium traffic. For example, in the 33Mb/s (1,5) case, the 5Mb/s sources were all considered premium sources with a peak sending rate of 5Mb/s. Network bandwidth for premium traffic was reserved at connection set up time. The low bandwidth sources were subjected to the RIO scheme where all the in profile packets had their A-bit set while the out of profile packets did not. The RIO parameters in this case were the same as in the previous experiment. Figure 2 shows the bandwidth allocation for the two-bit scheme. We see that the bandwidth allocation matches the expected bandwidth in the 33Mb/s (1,5) case and the 155Mb/s (5,25) case. This implies that the two-bit scheme performs well when the bottleneck bandwidth matches the aggregate expected bandwidth. However, we see that in the 155Mbit/s (1,5) and the 155Mb/s (3,15) cases, the bandwidth share allocated to the sources with the lower expected bandwidth is higher. This is because of how premium traffic is handled in the network: any out of profile premium packet is dropped by the profile meter. Consequently, all the excess bandwidth in these cases goes to the sources with lower expected bandwidth. In this respect, the bandwidth allocation done by the RIO scheme is more in keeping with user expectations. In the 33Mb/s (5,25) and 33Mb/s (3,15) cases, some of the high expected bandwidth sources do not get any bandwidth at all. This is because their connection set up calls get rejected due to unavailable bandwidth. Thus, for the two-bit scheme with premium traffic, it is important that the aggregated expected bandwidth through the bottleneck match the bottleneck bandwidth, else, some premium traffic may get denied bandwidth because the network resources have been over committed.

Finally, we simulated the USD scheme using weighted fair queuing in the network core. The bandwidth allocation is shown in Figure 3. In this case, we see that the relative bandwidth allocated to all the sources remain the same in all cases. In other words, the sources with high expected bandwidth (which presumably have paid more for such a privilege) get a higher relative share of the bandwidth than the others, independent of the bottleneck bandwidth or the absolute values of the expected bandwidth profiles.

Short Duration Traffic

A significant component of Internet traffic today is web traffic [14] that is characterized by short connection lifetimes. In order to study the effect of short connection lifetimes on the three different schemes, we ran simulations with the same settings as before except that the sources now sent only 200 packets to the destination. This corresponds to a web transfer of 100Kbytes, a moderately sized web page with embedded graphics. Figure 4 shows the performance for the 33Mb/s (1,5) (or matching bottleneck bandwidth) scenario and Figure 5 shows the performance for the 155Mb/s (1,5) (or excess bottleneck bandwidth) scenario. The numbers for the 33Mb/s (1,5) scenario show

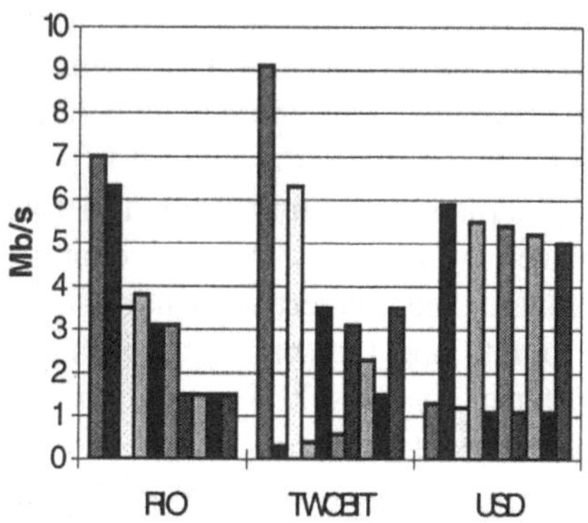

Figure 4: Short-duration traffic with 33Mb/s (1,5)

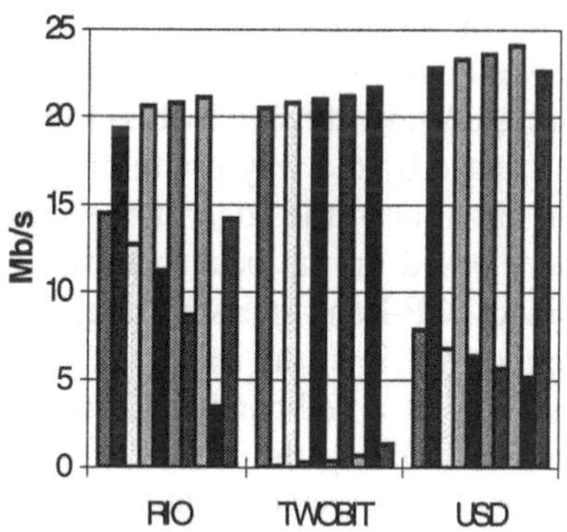

Figure 5: Short-duration traffic with 155Mb/s (1,5)

that on such short time scales, the bandwidth allocated by the RIO scheme is not commensurate with the expected bandwidth profiles. This is because the RED technique used in the routers for estimating average queue lengths (that determines when to drop a packet) and the Time Sliding Window technique used by a profile meter to estimate the sending rate for a source (that determines whether a packet is in or out of profile) depend on long term averages. In the shorter term, the Time Sliding Window technique tends to overestimate the sending rate and mark more packets as out of profile than is necessary. We have performed some experiments to test how sensitive the calculated sending rates are to the length of the time window (the results are not shown here for lack of space), and found that the closer the time windows are to the round trip time, the more accurate the estimates are. This implies that it may be difficult to estimate sending rates accurately in the absence of information about round-trip times, which is the case if the profile meter is decoupled from the sender. In the 155Mb/s (1,5) case, the bandwidth allocation is more reasonable in the sense that the higher bandwidth sources receive greater bandwidth than the lower bandwidth ones, except for source 10 that gets slightly lower bandwidth than source 1. However, the bandwidth allocations are not in proportion to the respective expected average bandwidths. We have seen earlier (section 0) that the bandwidth at the bottleneck that is in excess of the aggregate expected bandwidth is more or less evenly allocated among all the sources – in this case, where all the traffic flows are of much shorter duration, RED is unable to enforce fair sharing of the excess bandwidth. The higher bandwidth sources, in the short term, are able to grab a higher share of the excess bandwidth since their congestion windows open up faster (due to lower drop rates at the routers that implement RIO) than those of the lower bandwidth sources.

The numbers for the two-bit scheme are interesting. The even sources (i.e., those with expected bandwidths of 5Mb/s), for the most part, show a lower bandwidth allocation compared to the odd sources (i.e. those with expected bandwidths of 1Mb/s) in both the scenarios. This anomalous behavior is caused by the way premium traffic is managed under the two-bit scheme: the monitor at the edge of the network generates premium tokens at a fixed rate, based on the peak bandwidth reserved by the call set up mechanism. Since TCP-Reno starts by doubling the size of the congestion window every round trip time, the traffic generated is bursty and the sending rate can exceed the reserved bandwidth in the short term. As a result, the premium traffic, on reaching the monitor, faces an absence of premium tokens and gets dropped. This happens in the initial stages of the opening up of the congestion window (before *ssthresh* is reached) and fast recovery does not occur because there are not enough lost packets. Thus, TCP times out multiple times and causes the congestion window to open up very slowly. In the long run, this effect is absent because over longer time scales, enough premium tokens are generated to absorb such bursts. Thus, in the short term, the sources with the lower expected bandwidth are able to make use of the excess bandwidth that is freed up by a lack of premium traffic and therefore show higher bandwidth utilization. In the case of the USD scheme, the short term bandwidth allocations match the long term case: the figures in each of the two scenarios show that the bandwidth shares for the sources are in proportion to their expected bandwidth profiles. Thus, for short-lived flows such as web traffic, where end-to-end mechanisms are harder to implement because they need at least one round trip time to react, USD is an attractive option for providing differentiated services.

Non-Responsive Sources

We used two different kinds of non-responsive sources, CBR (Constant Bit Rate) sources that send at a fixed rate and malicious sources that flood the network by sending as fast as they can. None of these sources back off in the face of congestion. We first investigated the effects of CBR sources on each of the three schemes. The simulations were repeated using bottleneck links of capacity 33Mb/s and 155Mb/s. In the simulations, sources 1 and 2 were CBR sources transmitting at 5Mb/s and the other sources were TCP-Reno sources where the odd numbered sources had an expected bandwidth of 1Mb/s and the even numbered sources had an expected bandwidth of 5Mb/s. All CBR traffic was marked as out of profile.

Figure 6 shows the bandwidth allocation in each of the three schemes when the bottleneck bandwidth is 33Mb/s and Figure 7 shows the same when the bottleneck bandwidth is 155Mb/s. In both figures, the first two bars in

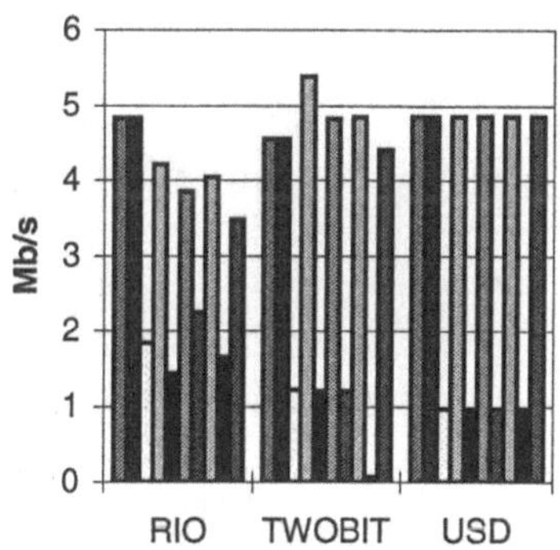

Figure 6: Effect of two non-responsive (CBR) sources with 33Mb/s (1,5)

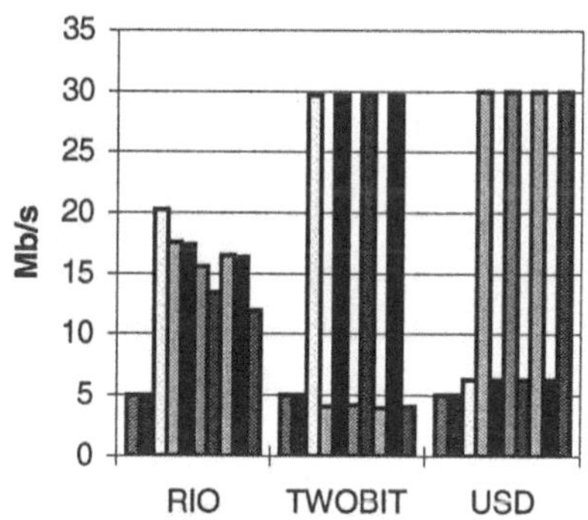

Figure 7: Effect of two non-responsive (CBR) sources with 155Mb/s (1,5)

each cluster are for the CBR sources and the rest are for the TCP-Reno sources. The numbers for the 33Mb/s (1,5) case indicate that in the case of RIO, the CBR sources are able to get close to their expected bandwidth (i.e., about 5Mb/s) despite all of their traffic being marked out of profile (i.e. lower priority). However, the TCP-Reno sources perform reasonably well, the sources with higher expected bandwidth show a bandwidth share of about 4Mb/s which is close to what the expected bandwidth profile is. The sources with a lower expected bandwidth show bandwidth shares that are higher than their expected bandwidth profiles, closer to about 2Mb/s rather than 1Mb/s. As in section 0, we expect that this can be remedied by an appropriate adjustment of the RIO parameters. In the 155Mb/s (1,5) case, the CBR sources get about 5Mb/s as in the previous case. All the other sources (that are all TCP-Reno sources) receive bandwidths that are in excess of their expected average bandwidths, and it is clear that the excess bandwidth at the bottleneck is allocated fairly evenly among the TCP sources by the RED mechanism, as was the case in Section 0.

For the two-bit scheme, the CBR sources get close to their expected bandwidth (about 4.5Mb/s) in both the scenarios. The sources with the higher expected high bandwidth, whose packets are all marked as premium traffic, also get close to 5Mb/s bandwidth (about 4.8Mb/s from the graphs). In the 33Mb/s (1, 5) case, 3 of the 4 sources that have a low expected bandwidth profile of 1Mb/s, get a slightly higher bandwidth allocation than their expected profiles. All of this comes at the expense of the fourth low bandwidth source, which gets almost close to zero bandwidth. Thus, it appears that in

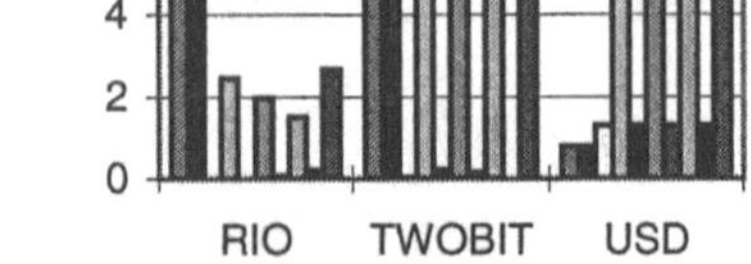

Figure 8: Two malicious sources with 33Mb/s (1,5)

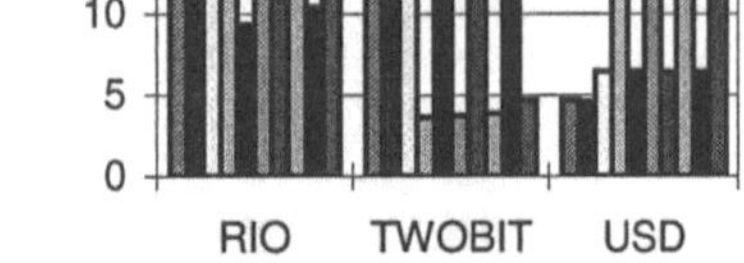

Figure 9: Two malicious sources with 155Mb/s (1,5)

the two-bit scheme, if there are non-cooperative, bandwidth hungry sources (even if all their packets are marked out of profile), other well-behaved, low priority traffic may get starved. The situation is slightly different when there is excess bandwidth at the bottleneck, i.e., the 155Mb/s (1,5) case. In this scenario, the premium bandwidth sources do not get any more than their expected bandwidths because premium traffic that is out of profile gets dropped. Consequently, the excess bandwidth at the bottleneck is shared evenly by the low bandwidth TCP-Reno sources, that now show a higher bandwidth allocation than the higher bandwidth sources. Finally, the numbers for the USD scheme show that the bandwidth allocations are commensurate with the expected bandwidth profiles, which implies that the USD scheme is effective in the presence of non co-operative CBR sources.

To investigate the effect of malicious sources, we again used bottleneck bandwidths of 33Mb/s and 155Mb/s. Sources 1 and 2 were set to be malicious sources that declare an expected bandwidth of 1Mb/s and then try to flood the network by sending as fast as they can. The other sources are TCP-Reno sources where the odd numbered sources have an expected bandwidth of 1Mb/s and the even numbered sources have an expected bandwidth of 5Mb/s. Note that these scenarios are different from the CBR cases described earlier, because in the CBR cases, the sources did not try to flood the network in addition to not responding to congestion. The purpose of simulating malicious sources here is to see if they have a negative effect on low priority traffic by filling up the queues allocated for such traffic.

The results for the 33Mb/s (1,5) scenario are shown in Figure 8. In the RIO case, the low bandwidth sources get very little bandwidth – sources 3 and 5 get nothing and sources 7 and 9 get about 0.1Mb/s. The high bandwidth sources do not do well either, none of the sources are able to get more than 2.5Mb/s. The reason for this is that the packets for the malicious sources fill up the queues on the bottleneck routers very quickly and causes packets from other sources to be dropped more often. Consequently, the TCP windows do not open up to the extent required to get the expected average bandwidth. For the two-bit scheme, the low bandwidth sources get very little bandwidth (as in the RIO case) for the same reason and the bulk of the bandwidth goes to the malicious sources. However, in this case, the malicious sources grab about 6Mb/s each as opposed to 12Mb/s each in the RIO case. The reason is that the packets from the high bandwidth sources in the two-bit scheme are enqueued in a separate, higher priority, premium traffic queue. As a result, the high bandwidth sources are able to get close to their expected bandwidths of 5Mb/s while the low bandwidth sources get very little – sources 3, 5 and 7 get less than 0.2Mb/s and source 9 gets nothing. Thus, in both RIO and two-bit schemes, a malicious source can easily deprive low priority traffic of their fair share, but the high priority traffic tends to do better in the two-bit scheme because such traffic is enqueued in a separate, high priority queue. In the case of the USD scheme, the malicious sources are penalized and actually receive slightly less than their average expected bandwidth (0.79Mb/s in place of 1Mb/s) while the other sources get slightly more than their expected bandwidth – the low bandwidth sources get 1.31Mb/s instead of 1Mb/s and the high bandwidth sources get 6.54Mb/s instead of 5Mb/s.

The results for the 155Mb/s (1,5) scenario are shown in Figure 9. In this scenario, the malicious sources for the RIO and the two-bit schemes are able to grab almost the full bandwidth of their outgoing links, which is set to 30Mb/s in the simulation. In the RIO case, the TCP-Reno sources are able to get more than their expected bandwidth profiles, but not in proportion to their expected bandwidths. Again, the reason is that the excess bandwidth (that is consumed only by out of profile packets) is more or less evenly distributed by the RED scheme among all the sources. In the two-bit case, the premium sources are able to get slightly less than their expected bandwidths (in the range 3.5 – 4Mb/s instead of 5Mb/s). This is somewhat surprising since, given that the bottleneck bandwidth in this case is 155Mb/s, and the fact that premium traffic gets higher priority than best effort traffic, one would have expected that the premium traffic would get the full 5Mb/s bandwidth. We conjecture that this is because the malicious sources constantly fill up the lower priority queues and therefore the routers spend more time in processing the lower priority queues than the higher priority ones. Consequently, the congestion windows for the higher bandwidth premium traffic does not open up fast enough to utilize the requisite expected bandwidth. The excess bottleneck bandwidth is more or less evenly allocated only among the low bandwidth sources because any premium traffic that is out of profile is dropped. This causes the low bandwidth sources to get a higher bandwidth allocation than the high bandwidth sources. Lastly, the USD scheme again penalizes the malicious sources and the allocation of bandwidth among the well behaved TCP-Reno sources is in proportion to their expected average bandwidths – the figures show that the low bandwidth sources get about 6Mb/s while the high bandwidth sources get about 30Mb/s.

4. SUMMARY

In this paper, we have evaluated the bandwidth allocation performance of the RIO, the two-bit and the USD schemes. We have shown that matching the network bottleneck bandwidth to the aggregated expected bandwidth profiles over all the traffic flows through the bottleneck is an important issue. While the RIO and the two-bit schemes perform well when there is no mismatch, such is not the case if the bottleneck bandwidth available is in excess of the aggregated expected bandwidth through the bottleneck. The RIO and two-bit schemes need to be modified in some way to react more quickly to short-lived flows. In the case of non-responsive sources, RIO performs better than the two-bit scheme when the non-responsive sources are CBR, however, malicious sources that flood the network are able to starve low priority traffic. The USD scheme is able to perform well in all scenarios.

REFERENCES

[1] D. Black, S. Blake, M. Carlson, E. Davies, Z. Wang, and W. Weiss. An Architecture for Differentiated Services, RFC 2475, May 1998.

[2] D. Clark and W. Fang. Explicit Allocation of Best Effort Packet Delivery Service, Work in progress, 1998.

[3] D. Clark, S. Shenker, and L. Zhang. Supporting Real-Time Applications in an Integrated Services Packet Network: Architecture and Mechanisms, *In Proceedings of ACM SIGCOMM'92*, August 1992.

[4] D. Clark, J. Wroclawski. An Approach to Service Allocation in the Internet, Work in progress, July 1997.

[5] M. Degermark, A. Brodnok, S. Carlsson, and S. Pink. Small Forwarding Tables for Fast Routing Lookups, *In Proceedings of ACM SIGCOMM'97*, Cannes, France, September 1997.

[6] K. Fall and S. Floyd. Promoting the Use of End-to-End Congestion Control in the Internet, Work in progress, February 1998.

[7] S. Golestani. A self-clocked fair queuing scheme for broadband applications, *In Proceedings of IEEE INFOCOM'94*, pages 636-646, April 1994.

[8] V. Jacobson. Differentiated Services Architecture, Presented at the IETF meeting at the Munich IETF, August 1997.

[9] S. Keshav. REAL 5.0 Manuals, http://www.cs.cornell.edu/skeshav/real/man.html, August 1997.

[10] V. P. Kumar, T. V. Lakshman, and D. Stiliadis. Beyond Best Effort: Router Architectures for the Differentiated Services of Tomorrow's Internet, *IEEE Communications Magazine*, May 1998.

[11] K. Nichols, V. Jacobson, and L. Zhang. A Two-bit Differentiated Services Architecture for the Internet, Work in progress, November 1997.

[12] A. K. Parekh and R. G. Gallager, "A Generalized Processor Sharing Approach to Flow Control - the Single Node Case, *In Proceedings of IEEE INFOCOM'92*, May 1992.

[13] M. Shreedhar and G. Varghese. Efficient Fair Queuing Using Deficit Round Robin, *In Proceedings of ACM SIGCOMM'95*, Cambridge, Massachusetts, August 1995.

[14] K. Thompson, G. Miller, and R. Wilder. Wide-Area Internet Traffic Patterns and Characteristics, *IEEE Network*, November 1997.

[15] Z. Wang. USD: Scalable Bandwidth Allocation for the Internet, *In Proceedings of HPN'98*, September 1998.

[16] L. Zheng, S. Deering, S. Estrin, S. Shenker, and D. Zappala. A New Resource Reservation Protocol, *IEEE Network*, September 1993.

MODELLING AND IMPROVING FLOW ESTABLISHMENT IN RSVP

Laurent Mathy, David Hutchison and Steven Simpson
Lancaster University, UK
{laurent, dh, ss}@comp.lancs.ac.uk

Abstract

RSVP has developed as a key component for the evolving Internet, and in particular for the Integrated Services Architecture. Therefore, RSVP performance is crucially important; yet this has been little studied up till now. In this paper, we target one of the most important aspects of RSVP: its ability to establish flows. We first identify the factors influencing the performance of the protocol by modelling the establishment mechanism. Then, we propose a Fast Establishment Mechanism (FEM) aimed at speeding up the set-up procedure in RSVP. We analyse FEM by means of simulation, and show that it offers improvements to the performance of RSVP over a range of likely circumstances.

1. INTRODUCTION

It is now widely recognized that to become a global telecommunication platform with integrated services—a must in the provision of information super-highways—the Internet must evolve to provide proper support for applications, such as distributed multimedia applications, that require a variety of qualities of service. In an ideal world, this evolution should depend on the evolution of the traffic mix in the network (that is the ratio best-effort and guaranteed traffic). Unfortunately, the evolution of the traffic mix is very hard to forecast.

If best-effort traffic clearly dominates, then a well provisioned network, possibly enhanced with some simple form of traffic differentiation [3], can probably satisfy the occasional requests for Quality of Service (QoS) guarantees [6]. In other words, appropriate bandwidth is the key to QoS. On the other hand, if the proportion of guaranteed traffic becomes significant, more advanced resource management mechanisms are likely to be needed to meet the level of service expected by the users. One such mechanism considered here is resource reservation.

Recent studies [14] have found that in today's Internet, which is dominated by best-effort traffic, congestion occurs mainly at the edge of the network (e.g. in ISP access networks, links from campus networks, etc.). However, it has also been shown that some backbone links (especially some trans-continental links) are saturated for a substantial part of a day. These observations suggest that to support applications — such as interactive multimedia application or real-time applications — with stringent QoS requirements, resource management mechanisms will have to be provided at the edge of the network at least. This argument is reinforced by the fact that, as such applications appear, the traffic mix in the network may shift towards traffic requiring more resource usage control.

Among resource management mechanisms, those offering the finest grain of traffic control operate on a per-flow basis. These mechanisms, however, suffer from state scalability problems as the number of flows with reservations increases. Although this rules out their use within the core of the network, per-flow provisioning can still be used at the edge of the network where the concentration of flows is rather low. In the Internet, the IntServ (Integrated Services) architecture [4] offers a framework for QoS control which relies on RSVP ("Resource ReSerVation Protocol") [5][18] as the signalling protocol. Several proposals, mainly flow aggregation techniques [11][2] and the DiffServ (Differentiated Services) architecture [3], have been put forward to overcome the state scalability problems in the core of the network.

Although RSVP was originally designed for resource reservation, several proposals have now been tabled where RSVP is used to carry other types of control information in the network [13][8][10]. Another example is the possible use of RSVP within the DiffServ architecture [1]. Therefore, we believe that, whether it is for resource reservation or other control/signalling purposes, RSVP will have to operate over routes of various lengths and to satisfy demands exhibiting a broad range of dynamics. Consequently, RSVP's ability to carry control information efficiently across the network in any circumstances will be vital to the effective operation of the Internet.

That is why, in this paper, we study some of RSVP's performance aspects. The lack of experiments in "real conditions" leads us to develop, in section 2, a mathematical model of the flow establishment phase in RSVP. The results yielded by our model clearly show the need to revise the flow establishment procedure of RSVP. The principles of a modified flow establishment mechanism are then presented in section 3. Simulation results comparing the establishment procedure currently used in RSVP with our proposal are given in section 4. Some relevant related work is discussed in section 5, and section 6 concludes our discussion.

It should be noted that the primary context of resource reservation has influenced the naming of the control messages used in RSVP and it is therefore easier to describe the operations of RSVP in this context. The reader should however bear in mind that the results presented in this paper equally apply to RSVP as a "general" signalling protocol. Moreover, in this paper, we are only concerned with performance aspects of RSVP: scalability issues are not addressed.

The work presented in this paper is part of a wider effort at Lancaster University aimed at improving the support for distributed multimedia applications in the Internet, and specifically investigating the viability of resource management mechanisms.

2. MODELLING FLOW ESTABLISHMENT

Although its core ideas appeared a few years ago [18] and both research and commercial implementations are now available, to the best of our knowledge, no large-scale experiment has been done with RSVP yet. This lack of experimentation means that we do not know how RSVP will perform when used in "real conditions", as encountered in the Internet. In this section we develop a mathematical model of the establishment phase of RSVP in order to gain some insight of its performance. We are actually interested in quantifying RSVP's ability to make a successful reservation over a route where resources are plentiful. Although such a question may at first glance seem superfluous, we think it is of paramount importance to address it in order to assess RSVP's viability in the Internet, because of the unreliable character of the delivery of RSVP messages. In other words, we are interested in RSVP's external behaviour at reservation establishment as well as in dealing with network dynamics (local repair [5] may be seen as simply establishing a new reservation on a new portion of route).

In the rest of this section, we label as *sender* an RSVP node that initiate (as opposed to forward) the first Path message on a route where no (path) state has been established for the corresponding flow yet. A sender can either be an end-system (in the case of a reservation establishment) but could also be a router detecting a change of route (in the case of a local repair). We label as *receiver* an RSVP node that initiate (as opposed to forward) the first Resv message in response to the sender's Path message, that is on a "reverse route" where no reservation has been made for the corresponding flow yet. Again, the receiver can either be an end-system or a router. Any other node treating (i.e. creating state and reservation) and forwarding the messages along the route are called RSVP routers. Although our model will be developed considering only one sender and one receiver, it is nevertheless applicable to the multicast case by applying it to the (sub-)branches of multicast trees.

We know that to establish a reservation for a flow:

1. the sender issues a Path message towards the receiver,

2. upon receipt of that Path message, the receiver issues a Resv message describing the resources required.

3. every node periodically[1] sends *its own* Path and Resv messages, that is there is no way to force a node to send copies of RSVP messages in the network. However, any control message inducing a change in the state of an RSVP node is immediately forwarded by this node.

The periodic messages (a.k.a refresh messages) serve as both error correction mechanism (there is no explicit acknowledgment in RSVP) and state/reservation management mechanism (the absence of too many consecutive refreshes result in state timeouts and removal of the corresponding states/reservations).

The central parameter in our model is p, the *per-hop success probability*, which is the probability that an RSVP message sent by an RSVP node is correctly received by the RSVP process in the next node. We therefore see that p takes into account not only transmission errors but also overflow conditions at the different levels of the protocol architecture (i.e. link, IP and RSVP layers). In a well dimensioned network, routers should be provisioned with enough resources to accommodate most of the control traffic. We therefore expect the value of p to be high (i.e. close to 1). Consequently, in our model, we will ignore state timeouts because such events occur with a probability $(1-p)^K \approx 0$ (with $K = 3$ by default [5]).

It is only when a Resv message reaches the sender that the reservation is fully established (i.e. considered successful). Furthermore, because we ignore state timeouts, if any of the RSVP messages is ever lost along the way, an equivalent message is re-emitted *from the last node where it was last correctly received* at the beginning of the next refresh period. The establishment thus appears to be "incremental": from a refresh period to the next, the number of nodes holding proper state/reservation for the flow cannot decrease. Therefore the refresh messages exchanged between nodes where the corresponding states/reservations have already been established have no influence on the rest of the establishment procedure and can thus be ignored. In other words, we always consider the control message which is "ahead" of the others. Such a message will be called "establishment message".

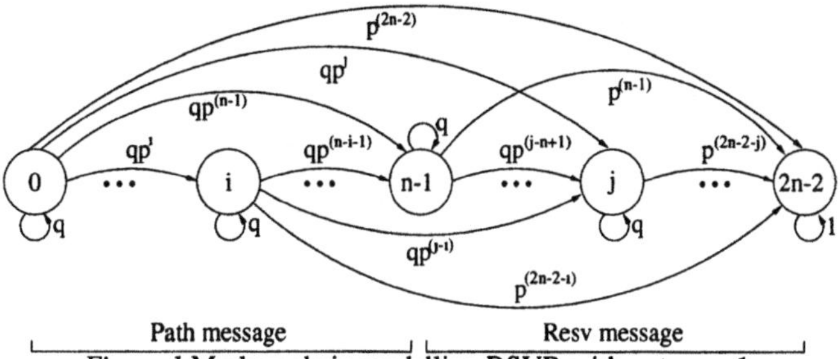

Figure 1 Markov chain modelling RSVP, with $p + q = 1$.

Another way to describe successful reservation establishment, is to note that on a route involving n RSVP nodes (including the sender and the receiver), the Path and Resv messages we consider (the establishment messages) must collectively travel $2n - 2$ hops. This is because the initial Path message is "generated" at the sender while the initial Resv message is "generated" at the receiver: these messages do not need to "travel" to reach these nodes.

At any time, the "state" of a reservation establishment can be characterised by the number of hops travelled by the establishment messages, and the residual time, in the last RSVP node that correctly received an establishment message, until the next refresh for this message. However, if we consider the state of a reservation at the instants when the residual time until refresh becomes zero (i.e. at the end of the refresh period in the last node that received an establishment message), we have a *discrete time semi-Markov process* with $2n - 2$ states (see figure 1), whose embedded Markov chain (representing the process at the instants of state transitions) has the following transition probabilities:

$$p_{i,j} = 0 \qquad 0 \leq i < 2(n-1), \quad 0 \leq j < i \tag{1}$$

$$p_{i,j} = p^{j-i}(1-p) \qquad 0 \leq i < 2(n-1), \quad i \leq j < 2(n-1) \tag{2}$$

$$p_{i,2n-2} = p^{2(n-1)-i} \qquad 0 \leq i \leq 2(n-1) \tag{3}$$

Equation (1) is the mathematical expression for the "incremental" establishment simplification. Equation (2) and (3) are based on the fact that a transition from any state of the chain to any other (including itself), is equivalent to a control message travelling a number of hops equal to the distance between the states. Equation (2) simply expresses that if the state reached is not the last one, then the control message must have been lost between two nodes. On the other hand, equation (3) states than when the Resv message reaches the sender, no more control traffic is required. Also, note that the last state of the chain is *absorbing*, stating that the establishment of the reservation is complete. The set

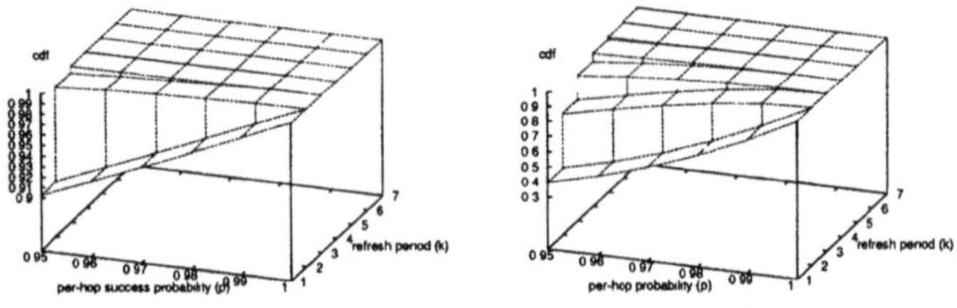

2.(a): along 2 nodes 2.(b): along 10 nodes

Figure 2 Cumulative distribution functions for the success probabilities

of equations (1)–(3) unambiguously describes the *transition probability matrix* $\boldsymbol{P}$ of the Markov chain[2].

We now express RSVP's ability to make a successful reservation. Let S be the number of periods required to establish a flow with reservation ($S \geq 1$: the first Path message sent by the sender determines the start of the first period). In the context of the model, S is the number of transitions required to reach state $2n - 2$.

Relations (1) and (3) imply that all the states but the last one are *transient*[3]. Also, because the last state of the chain is absorbing, that state is *recurrent*. In other words, the last state of the chain is eventually entered, and once it has entered it, the random process never leaves it. Consequently, the transient behaviour of $\pi_{2n-2}^{(k)}$—the probability of being in state $2n-2$ at the end of period k—can be interpreted as the probability that a reservation has been established by the end of the kth refresh period:

$$\pi_{2n-2}^{(k)} = P[S \leq k] = F_S(k). \tag{4}$$

$\pi_{2n-2}^{(k)}$ is thus the cumulative distribution function (cdf) of the success probability P_S.

Figure 2 shows the values of $F_s(k)$ for different route length (n) in terms of different per-hop success probabilities (p) and various number of periods (k).

In figure 2, it clearly appears that, even for short routes, RSVP will perform reasonably well only for very high per-hop success probabilities. Indeed, the probability of success within the first period (i.e. establishment without message loss) is in accordance with (4) and (3):

$$P_S^{(1)} = P[S = 1] = \pi_{2n-2}^{(1)} - \pi_{2n-2}^{(0)} = p^{2(n-1)}, \tag{5}$$

where $\pi^{(0)}_{2n-2}$ is 0 because the chain is always started in state 0. $P^{(1)}_S$ is an important quantity because it expresses the chances that a reservation is established without any loss of control messages.

The behaviour of equation (5) when p is in the neighbourhood of 1, is given by:

$$\lim_{p \to 1^-} \frac{\partial}{\partial p} P^{(1)}_S = 2(n-1) \tag{6}$$

and we not only see that any variation of p results in a bigger variation of $P^{(1)}_S$ but also that for routes comprising 6 nodes or more, the variation in $P^{(1)}_S$ will be an order of magnitude bigger than the variation in p.

With this model, we can also derive the average number of refresh periods needed to establish a reservation:

$$E[S] = (2n-2)\frac{1-p}{p} + 1. \tag{7}$$

The previous result allows us to obtain the average contribution of the external behaviour of RSVP to the establishment time T of a reservation, or in other words, the average establishment time when the queueing, transmission, propagation and internal processing delays are neglected. As reservation establishment occurs at any time *within* a period and the first period starts with the very first Path message from the sender, we have:

$$E[T] \approx (E[S] - 1)R = R(2n-2)\frac{1-p}{p}, \tag{8}$$

where R is the average refresh period. Both equations (7) and (8) confirm the sensitivity of RSVP to the values of the per-hop success probability.

The model presented in this section may seem a little pessimistic since we use the same value of the per-hop success probability on every link of a route. However, by extending the concept of an "RSVP node" to encompass the idea of a "lossless RSVP cloud", that is a contiguous region of the network where losses of RSVP messages do not occur or can be neglected, the model can be used to describe more realistic situations. For example, the scenario with two nodes can model a route of any length with one bottleneck, that is a route where control messages are only lost at one congested router.

As already pointed out at the beginning of this section, the value of the per-hop success probability p strongly depends on the rate of control traffic generated in the network and the associated resources needed to absorb such traffic. In RSVP, this rate of control traffic depends on both the rate at which new reservation requests are issued (either by end-systems or following route changes) and the average number of existing flows with reservations (because of the periodic refresh associated with the soft-state). Although techniques have been devised to reduce the latter type of traffic [16], the results exposed in this section strongly suggest the need for a dedicated "signalling channel[4]" in order to keep the per-hop success probability as high as possible.

This is not only true to ensure good performance at flow establishment, but also to improve resource utilization in the network. Indeed, for a resource to be released within a short delay, a teardown message must travel the path followed by a flow *without being lost* [5]. It is so because any loss of a teardown message can only be corrected when a lifetime expires, which can take several minutes (see [5]) and thus induce inefficient resource utilization. For a route with n nodes (sender and receiver included), the probability of "immediate" release of the resources of a flow is p^{n-1}. This value shows that, although the release of resources is less sensitive to the value of the per-hop success probability than the establishment (see equation (5)), this sensitivity will nonetheless become a problem over medium-length or long routes.

As a consequence, for RSVP to give acceptable results as the signalling protocol of the Internet, a carefully provisioned signalling channel will be required. Obviously, in the parts of the network where RSVP will be deployed, such a channel will be built by reserving resources for the control traffic; in non-RSVP networks (connecting "RSVP clouds" together), mechanisms such as traffic differentiation [3] or prioritization will be required.

3. IMPROVING RESERVATION SET-UP

RSVP uses periodic messages to manage its states. The lapse of time between consecutive Path or Resv messages defines the refresh period of the protocol (in a refresh period, there is one Path and one Resv message per flow on each link of the path). The default value for the refresh period R is 30 seconds. From the results of our model presented in the previous section, such a lapse of time between similar RSVP messages seems prohibitively long, since it represents the average amount of time in which the loss of a control message can be corrected at reservation establishment. It therefore seems natural to reduce the length of the refresh periods to improve RSVP's performance at establishment time.

Simply reducing the value of the refresh period is not the right approach, however. Indeed, doing so would increase the control traffic associated with every flow, thus increasing the required capacity of the signalling channel of the network while threatening to pose severe scalability problems. Consequently, reducing the refresh period *at establishment time only*[5] (including local repair conditions) is considered a better solution. In [5], it is suggested that a node could, at establishment, temporarily send control messages more often than dictated by the refresh period. However, the question of how many, as well as how often, such messages should be sent has not been addressed. This is precisely what we propose to do in this section.

In modern high speed networks, message losses are mostly due to buffer overflow. As a consequence, such losses occur in bursts [7]. We therefore see that proper "inter-spacing" is required between consecutive control messages, to prevent them from encountering the same congestion conditions along their route. This observation rules out the use of a fixed, short establishment period for the sending of consecutive RSVP messages during the establishment phase. Furthermore, in order to avoid unnecessary overhead, we must find a way to discover the end of the establishment phase, that is the moment after which the control messages related to a flow simply refresh the path states and reservations associated with that flow.

The only way to discover the end of the establishment phase of a flow is somchow to use the concept of acknowledgment. In order to keep our discussion as clear as possible and focus on principles, we present, in this section, a simple solution that only relies on the use of the Path and Resv messages, and hence does not require the introduction of explicit acknowledgment messages in RSVP.

It is clear that the role of an initial Path message is to "prepare" for a subsequent Resv message. A Resv message can therefore be considered as an acknowledgment for a Path message. This Resv message also indicates a successful reservation *to the sender of the corresponding Path message.* Therefore, any node that has forwarded a Path message, and has received a Resv message from every direct neighbour down the route followed by the corresponding flow, knows that the reservation has been successfully established *downstream.*

We still need to find a way for the receiver of a Path message to discover whether the establishment of a flow is in progress or has been completed. Because upstream nodes will use establishment periods shorter than the refresh period as long as they have not received a proper Resv message, a node can guess the status of a flow from the spacing of the Path messages it receives: if the lapse of time between consecutive Path messages is smaller than the shortest lapse of time allowed in "steady state" (that is $R/2$, see [5]) then the flow is more than likely being established and a Resv message should be forwarded as soon as possible to complete the establishment procedure (we thus see that the Resv message will be re-transmitted by the last RSVP node that correctly received the previous Resv message). On the other hand, if the time between consecutive Path messages is greater than or equal to the minimum allowed by the "classical" refresh periods then we can suspect that the Path message is simply a refresh and a Resv message should only be sent when the current refresh period expires[6]. Of course, for this technique to be robust in the event of loss of Path messages, the periods used at establishment time must be quite a lot smaller than $R/2$. To be precise, the difference between $R/2$ and any establishment period should be at least an order of magnitude larger than delay variations in the network.

It should be noted that if a node makes a wrong "guess" about consecutive Path messages, the corresponding flow does not suffer any functional damage. In the unlikely event where losses or delay variations cause two consecutively received establishment Path messages to be interpreted as refresh messages, no Resv message is sent. In such a case, FEM simply misses a chance to send a Resv message, which in the worst case, will be re-transmitted as a "classical" refresh. Furthermore, if important delay variations, or routing loops, cause refresh Path messages to be interpreted as establishment messages, a Resv message is sent. This Resv message resets the soft-state timer in the upstream node, but is not propagated any further.

If a reservation fails due to a lack of resources along the path, it may be wise to cancel FEM for the corresponding flow to prevent potentially unnecessary control traffic, although this is not an absolute necessity. The ResvErr message sent [5] may be used to cancel FEM in downstream nodes, while to cancel FEM in upstream nodes, a Resv message containing an empty reservation may be sent.

We have already ruled out the use of fixed periods at establishment. The other important point is that, if the establishment periods are too short, unnecessary RSVP messages will be sent, which increases the overhead of the protocol. Therefore, the initial establishment period (T_0) should not be smaller than the round-trip-time (RTT) for the RSVP messages, which may have to be estimated.

After sending or forwarding the initial Path message, an RSVP node will wait for a lapse of time equal to the initial establishment period (T_0). If by that time a Resv message has not been received, the node suspects a loss of control messages and retransmits the Path message (this procedure is applied by all the nodes supporting our technique, so that the copy of the Path message is generated as close as possible to where the loss of the previous RSVP message occurred). In order to be adaptive to a wide range of congestion conditions, the value of the establishment period must be backed-off: we propose to multiply it by a factor $(1 + \Delta)$ at each retransmission of a Path message. As soon as a Resv message acknowledges the establishment of the reservation, the nodes start using the refresh period R for their Path messages. A refresh period equal to R is also used if no Resv messages has been received, but the value of the establishment period has become greater than R. We therefore see that, in any case, the nodes "fall back" to the behaviour prescribed by the "classical" RSVP specification. We therefore see that FEM RSVP is backward compatible with "classical" RSVP.

With T_0 set to 3 seconds and Δ set to 0.3, this timer scheme is equivalent to the staged refresh timers described in [15]. It should be noted that for local repairs, a shorter value of T_0 would be acceptable, since we expect the new portion of the route to be fairly short. Furthermore, such a more aggressive behaviour of the protocol is justified by the fact that local repairs apply to existing flows.

The simple solution presented above requires that a receiver be able to send a Resv message immediately on receipt of a Path message. Although it will always be so in the case of local repairs, the reservation requirements might not be readily available if interaction with the end user is needed to determine these requirements. In this latter case, the solution proposed here would result in much unnecessary overhead and would fail to correct swiftly the loss of a Resv message. One way to overcome such a problem would be to define acknowledgment message for Path messages (e.g. PathAck) and Resv messages (e.g. ResvAck). An immediate Resv message would be generated at a receiver whenever possible (and FEM would be applied as presented in this section), otherwise an immediate PathAck would be sent and FEM applied on Path-PathAck pairs. As soon as the reservation requirements would be known, a Resv message would be sent and the FEM mechanisms could be applied, in the "reverse" direction, on Resv-ResvAck message pairs. Using FEM separately on Path and Resv messages would then ensure prompt recovery from losses of control messages.

In the multicast case, two strategies can be adopted for FEM. On one hand, as soon as the first Resv message is received by a node, that node forwards it upstream without delay. This has the advantage of quickly propagating reservations along the multicast tree. However, although any Resv message subsequently received by the node and that increases the reservation demands would be immediately forwarded upstream (according to the message forwarding rules of RSVP [5]), losses of such messages would not be corrected by FEM but by later refreshes. In such a case, FEM speeds up the initial establishment but cannot reduce the latency of increasing reservation demands. On the other hand, a node could hold the reservation requirements received in Resv messages either for a small lapse of time or until it has received Resv/PathAck messages on all the output ports of the multicast tree, before it forwards its own Resv message upstream. This has the advantage of establishing the final reservation at once, but has the risk of potentially increasing the overall establishment latency. Further work is needed to study and evaluate these possible strategies in the multicast case.

Finally, in order to avoid unnecessary overhead, FEM RSVP nodes should try and discover the capabilities of their neighbours (this could be done by recording the protocol version in the received messages) and refrain from using FEM when the next hop node does not support it. Furthermore, in multicast, the usual state/message merging should be applied.

4. SIMULATION RESULTS

We have simulated the external behaviour of both "classical" and FEM RSVP, in order to compare them. Our simulations consisted of repeated reservation establishments between a sender and a receiver, over routes of various lengths and under distinctly different loss conditions.

In these simulations, the loss process on each direction of a "link" is represented, independently, by a two-state model. One of the states represents congestion (i.e. loss) periods while the other one represents no-loss periods. The loss process spends an exponentially distributed time in each state, with these exponential distributions set so that the mean congestion period is 200 ms and the loss process spends a long-term proportion of time equal to the per-hop success probability in the no-loss state. Such a model was chosen because of its ability to mimic loss bursts in a simple way.

Configurations comprising respectively 2, 3, 5, 10, 15, 20 and 25 nodes (including the sender and the receiver) were considered with values of the per-hop success probability ranging from 99% to 100% inclusive. Such values for the per-hop success probability were chosen because they are likely to be encountered in a well dimensioned network. For every configuration, 1000 flows were established and no delay was introduced in nodes and links to isolate the time overhead introduced by the external (i.e. observable) operation of the protocol. Finally, the default of 30 s was used as the average value of the refresh periods in RSVP, while for FEM RSVP, T_0 and Δ have the values proposed in section 3.

The measured quantities were the mean establishment delay and the mean overhead per link (i.e. the mean number of control messages per link per reservation). For the mean establishment delay, 95% confidence intervals were computed using the method of batch means [12, p. 293] on 40 batches of 25

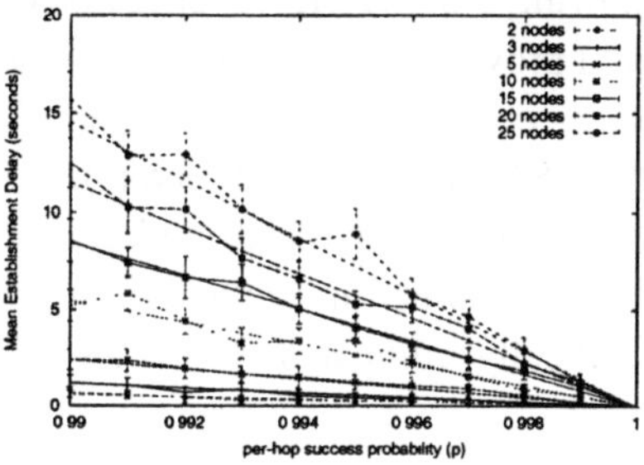

3.(a): MED with RSVP. Simulation (jagged lines) and theoretical (straight lines—eq. (8)) results.

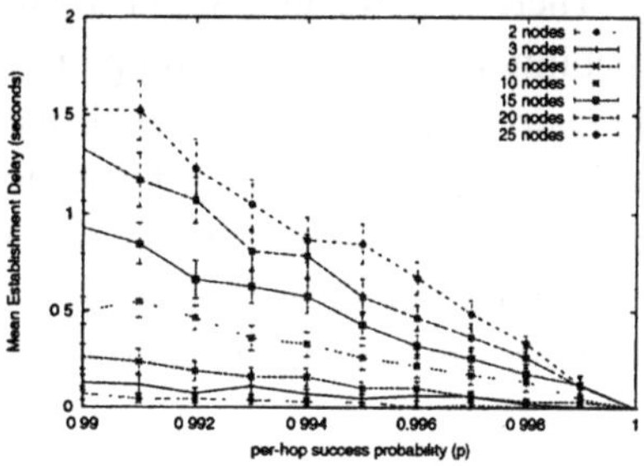

3.(b): MED with FEM RSVP.

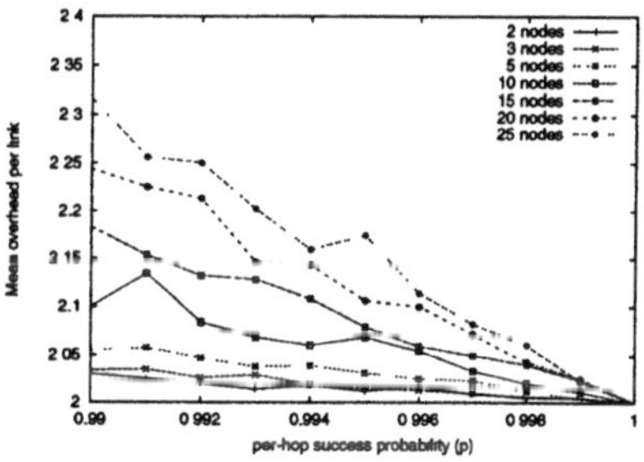

3.(c): MOPL with RSVP.

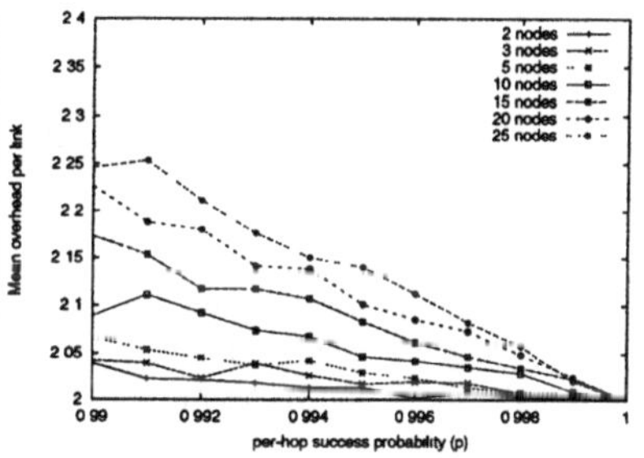

3.(d): MOPL with FEM RSVP.

Figure 3 Mean Establishment Delay (MED) and Mean Overhead Per Link (MOPL).

samples each. The results are given in figure 3. In interpreting the results in this section, special attention must be paid to the meaning of the per-hop success probability which essentially represents the chances of survival of a control message from one RSVP process to the next. Therefore, the corresponding per-hop loss probability (i.e. the probability that a control message does not reach the next RSVP process) is expected to be greater than usual packet loss probabilities, because it encompasses possible losses due to overflows of the queue holding messages awaiting to be treated by the RSVP process which usually resides in the slow path of a router.

A part from the obvious gain in performance, figure 3 also confirms the more predictable (or more stable) behaviour of FEM RSVP (the 95% confidence intervals are about an order of magnitude smaller in FEM RSVP than in RSVP). The message overhead (figures 3.(c) and 3.(d)) is fairly similar in both cases. There is however a slight trend showing a better effectiveness of FEM as reliability decreases. This property could prove very valuable in the case of local repairs, where bursts of repair messages could result in congestion of the signalling channel (including queues to the RSVP processes in routers).

Figure 3.(a) validates the predictions of our mathematical model, despite fundamental differences in the loss processes assumed in section 2 and these simulations. Figure 4, by contrast, specifically compares RSVP and FEM

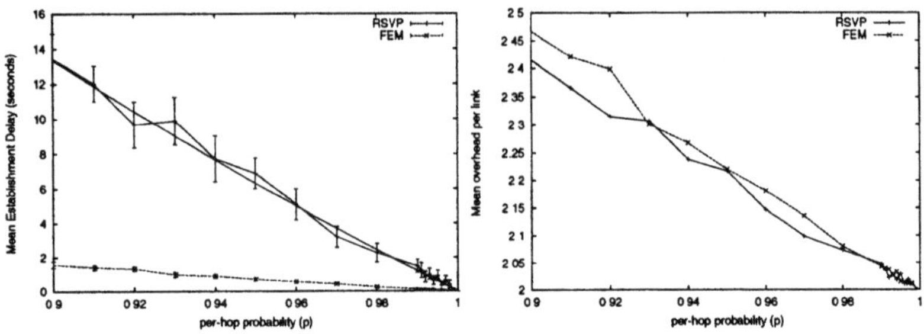

4.(a): Establishment Delay. Simulation (jagged lines) and theoretical (straight line—eq. (8)) results.

4.(b): Message Overhead.

Figure 4 Comparison of RSVP and FEM over routes of 3 nodes in a wireless scenario.

RSVP over routes of 3 nodes with per-hop success probabilities ranging from 90% to 100%. This scenario is important since it represents a case where the sender and receiver are wireless terminals, with the wired network in-between considered lossless. Again, the stability and gain in performance of FEM, with no significant increase in message overhead, are clearly demonstrated.

Another equally important scenario is the case of a route of any length with a single bottleneck. As mentioned in section 2, such a scenario is modelled as a route comprising 2 nodes connected by a lossy link. The mean establishment delay is given in figure 5, for different ranges of per-hop success probabilities. In this case, although the mean time penalty introduced by the external behaviour of RSVP is quite small and would not be considered unacceptable as long as the message loss probability does not exceed a percent. Once more, this confirms RSVP's sensitivity to the values of the per-hop success probability and their variations, even when only facing a single point of congestion.

Finally, in view of the results presented in this section, it could be argued that if the per-hop success probability was kept very close to 1, the performance of RSVP would be satisfactory, and hence the FEM extension would not

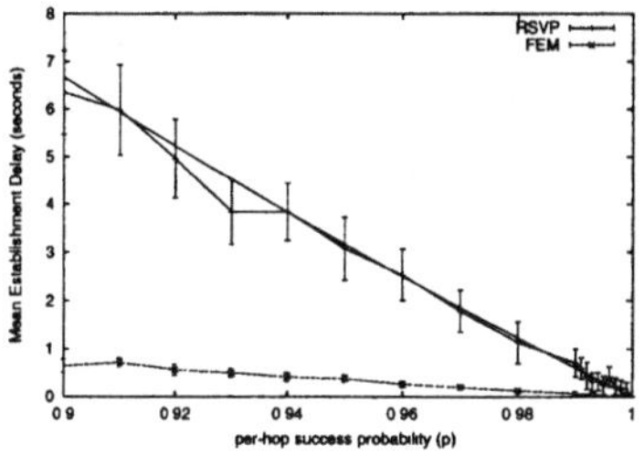

5.(a): "Low" per-hop success probabilities at bottleneck. Simulation and theoretical (eq. (8)) results.

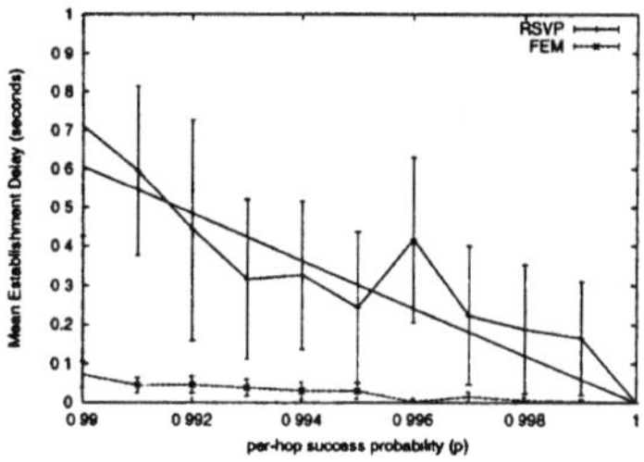

5.(b): "High" per-hop success probabilities at bottleneck. Simulation and theoretical (eq. (8)) results.

Figure 5 Comparison of RSVP and FEM over routes with a single bottleneck.

be necessary (especially over short routes). It should however be noticed that our results consist of mean values, averaged over a large number of flows and that on any particular occasion, the loss of any control message at flow establishment, is penalised by a delay of *at least* $R/2$ seconds (i.e. 15 seconds by default) with RSVP, but only by a delay of at least T_0 seconds (i.e. 3 seconds in the context of our simulations) with FEM RSVP. This fact alone probably justifies the use of FEM RSVP, even when the probability of losing a control message is extremely low. Finally, because losses of several control messages within a reservation establishment result in a set-up latency of several seconds, a signalling channel may still be necessary with FEM to ensure an acceptable establishment latency to each flow.

5. RELATED WORK

To the best of our knowledge, few other authors have reported on work closely related to our own. In [15], it is proposed to define and use explicit hop-by-hop acknowledgment messages for every control message in RSVP. To improve the responsiveness of the protocol, a procedure similar to the one described in section 3 is used for the retransmission of the control messages that have not been acknowledged. Once states or reservations have been acknowledged, it is then proposed to use long refresh periods (of the order of quarter of an hour) in order to reduce the steady state overhead.

Although this approach seems similar to ours, there is a major difference in the use of acknowledgments: the acknowledgments are used hop-by-hop. A node that has correctly received a message from one of its neighbours acknowledges it. Therefore, the semantic of these acknowledgments is weak, because the receipt of an acknowledgment does not mean that the initial message has reached, or will reach, its final destination. Finally, the long refresh periods will result in performance far worse than the one of "classical" RSVP in the following circumstances: path state instability after route changes or transient failures undetected by the routing protocol. Furthermore, because once a reservation has been established the subsequent refresh messages are not acknowledged, losses of such messages can result in a loss of state (due to soft state time-out) that will be unacceptably long to correct.

In contrast, FEM RSVP is based on end-to-end notification, which covers the conditions cited above. Furthermore, as outlined in section 3, FEM RSVP can avoid the use of explicit acknowledgment messages when reservation requirements are readily available. As this is always the case for local repairs, FEM RSVP helps in reducing the size of the message bursts that occur in those circumstances.

Compared with signalling protocols used in ATM networks [17], "RSVP-like" signalling protocols (including FEM) do not rely on underlying reliable protocols for the transfer of their messages. The design of these reliable protocols (e.g. the use of sequence numbers) is such that they not only correct losses, but can also detect node failures (e.g. when too many consecutive error correction attempts fail). As a consequence, although ATM signalling messages are acknowledged hop-by-hop, their semantics is strong. It is precisely this lack of node failure that led us to the use of end-to-end acknowledgment in FEM (as FEM does not introduce sequence numbers in RSVP).

6. CONCLUSIONS

We have modelled the resource reservation establishment mechanisms in RSVP and have shown that it is very sensitive to the values of the per-hop probability measured between RSVP processes. We have also shown that, to a lesser extent, this sensitivity affects resource release too. Consequently, there is a need for a signalling channel in the Internet, to protect as much as possible the value of the per-hop success probability experienced by RSVP messages from being adversely influenced by data traffic. Furthermore, because even the best provisioned signalling paths are never totally lossless, we have presented the principles of FEM, a Fast Establishment Mechanism that is not only more robust to the conditions in the network than the establishment mechanism currently used in RSVP, but also establishes resources faster in any circumstances.

In the case of local repairs, FEM can even achieve better performance without any increase of message overhead.

FEM introduces a slight increase in protocol state. However, we anticipate that RSVP will only be operated on a "per-flow" basis in areas of the Internet (in particular at the edges) where the concentration of flows is low. Elsewhere, RSVP will be operated in an aggregation context which greatly reduces the state scalability problem. Consequently, the small state increase in FEM RSVP should be of little consequence.

Finally, the underlying principles of FEM are very simple. The resulting modest increase of protocol complexity is negligible compared with the achieved gains in performance.

REFERENCES

[1] Y. Bernet, J. Binder, S. Blake, M. Carlson, E. Davies, B. Ohlman, D. Verma, Z. Wang, and W. Weiss. A Framework for Differentiated Services. Internet Draft draft-ietf-diffser-framework-00, IETF, May 1998. Work in Progress.

[2] S. Berson and S. Vincent. Aggregation of Internet Integrated Services State. Internet Draft draft-berson-rsvp-aggregation-00, IETF, Aug 1998.

[3] D. Black, S. Blake, M. Carlson, E. Davies, Z. Wang, and W. Weiss. An Architecture for Differentiated Services. Internet Draft draft-ietf-diffserv-arch-00, IETF, May 1998. Work in Progress.

[4] R. Braden, D. Clark, and S. Shenker. Integrated Services in the Internet Architecture: an Overview. RFC 1633, IETF, Jun 1994.

[5] R. Braden, L. Zhang, S. Berson, S. Herzog, and S. Jamin. Resource ReSerVation Protocol (RSVP)—Version 1 Functional Specification. RFC 2205, IETF, Sep 1997.

[6] L. Breslau and S. Shenker. Best-effort versus Reservations: a Simple Comparative Analysis. *ACM Comp. Comm. Reviews*, 28(4):3–16, Sep 1998.

[7] I. Cidon, A. Khamisy, and M. Sidi. Analysis of Packet Loss Processes in High Speed Networks. *IEEE Trans. Info. Theory*, 39(1):98–108, Jan 1993.

[8] B. Davie, Y. Rekhter, E. Rosen, A. Viswanathan, V. Srinivasan, and S. Blake. Use of Label Switching with RSVP. Internet Draft draft-ietf-mpls-rsvp-00, IETF, Mar 1998. Work in Progress.

[9] S. Floyd and V. Jacobson. The Synchronization of Periodic Routing Messages. *IEEE/ACM Trans. Network.*, 2(2):122–136, Apr 1994.

[10] O. Fourmeaux and S. Fdida. Multicast for RSVP Switching. *Telecommunication Systems Journal*, 11(1-2):85–104, Mar 1999.

[11] R. Guérin, S. Blake, and S. Herzog. Aggregating RSVP-based QoS Requests. Internet Draft draft-guerin-aggreg-rsvp-00, IETF, Nov 1997. Work in Progress.

[12] A. Leon-Garcia. *Probability and Random Processes for Electrical Engineering*. Addison-Wesley, second edition, 1994.

[13] T. Li and Y. Rekhter. A Provider Architecture for Differentiated Services and Traffic Engineering (PASTE). RFC 2430, IETF, Oct 1998.

[14] A. Odlyzko. The Internet and Other Networks: Utilization Rates and Their Implications. In *Proc.* 26th *Telecommunications Policy Research Conf.*, Oct 1998. Available from www.research.att.com/~amo/doc/networks.html.

[15] P. Pan, H. Schulzrinne, and R. Guérin. Staged Refresh Timers for RSVP. Internet Draft draft-pan-rsvp-timer-00, IETF, Nov 1997. Work in Progress.

[16] P. Sharma, D. Estrin, S. Floyd, and V. Jacobson. Scalable Timers for Soft State Protocols. USC CS-TR 96-640, University of Southern California, Sep 1996.

[17] B. Stiller. A Survey of UNI Signaling Systems and Protocols for ATM Networks. *ACM Comp. Comm. Reviews*, 25(2):21–33, Apr 1995.

[18] L. Zhang, S. Deering, D. Estrin, and D. Zappala. RSVP: A New Resource ReSerVation Protocol. *IEEE Network*, 7(5):8–18, Sep 1993.

Notes

[1] Each value of the refresh period is randomly chosen in $[R/2, 3R/2]$, with $R = 30$ sec. by default [5], to avoid message synchronisation [9]

[2] It is easy to verify that $\sum_{j=0}^{2(n-1)} p_{i,j} = 1, \quad 0 \le i \le 2(n-1)$.

[3] Indeed, for $0 \le i < 2(n-1)$, we have $\sum_{n=1}^{\infty} p_{i,i}(n) = \sum_{n=1}^{\infty} (1-p)^n = \frac{1-p}{p} < \infty$.

[4] This signalling channels includes the RSVP processes in the routers, and hence the associated queues.

[5] Such shortened refresh periods are called *establishment periods* in the rest of the paper.

[6] The period used by a node to send Resv messages is the refresh period defined in "classical" RSVP. The concept of establishment period timer does not apply to Resv messages.

CHARGING AND ACCOUNTING FOR QOS-ENHANCED IP MULTICAST

Georg Carle, Felix Hartanto, Michael Smirnov, Tanja Zseby
GMD FOKUS, Kaiserin-Augusta-Allee 31, D-10589 Berlin, Germany
{carle, hartanto, smirnov, zseby} @fokus.gmd.de

Abstract

In this paper we propose a layered framework for charging QoS-enhanced IP services with policy based configuration of its layers. As an example architecture we present our implementation - Value Added IP Charging and Accounting Service (VIPCAS). We further concentrate on VIPCAS elements for policies and data exchange. As flexible data structure for exchange of accounting information, we propose the Premium IP Network Accounting Record (PIP-NAR), which is suitable for a variety of charging schemes (e.g. charging of reserved and used resources), and which also makes provider-specific extensions possible. We specify the Tariff Formula Language (TFL) for representing tariff policies, and the Charging Information Protocol (CIP) for distributing tariff information expressed in TFL. For a fair charging of IP Multicast services, cost sharing functions should be supported at both the accounting and the charging layer. We evaluate different approaches in this area which support receiver heterogeneity with regard to the reserved QoS.

1. INTRODUCTION

In recent years there emerged an increasing number of applications such as video conferencing, distance learning, and video broadcast where data sent by a source is destined to multiple receivers. These applications also have more stringent requirements in terms of bandwidth, delay and jitter. The recent development in the Internet has been targeted to support these emerging applications. Integrated Services [33] and Differentiated Services [1] have been proposed to support service differentiation with quality of service guarantee. Multicast routing and multicast delivery have evolved from being a pure research topic and being experimentally deployed in the MBONE to being supported by major router manufacturers. Despite these developments, deployment of commercial IP multicast services is slow. One factor contributing to this is poor support for multicast charging [11].

Charging for IP multicast services introduces a number of additional problems as compared to unicast charging. One of the problems is to obtain information on the cost of a multicast tree, and to distribute the information among multiple providers. Another problem is to share the cost of the communications among receivers which may have heterogeneous QoS requirements. In addressing these problems this paper presents a layered framework for charging of multicast IP services with QoS support and support for cost sharing between receivers.

The structure of this paper is as follows. Section 2 reviews related work, focusing on support for QoS and multicast. Section 3 presents our framework for charging and accounting for QoS enhanced IP services. Section 4 describes a charging and accounting architecture based on the framework and a flexible data structure for transferring accounting information among multiple providers. Section 5 discusses some examples in configuring the framework and introduces a tariff formula language and a charging information protocol which can be used to inform users about current tariffs. Section 6 addresses the problem of cost sharing among receivers with heterogeneous QoS and presents simulation results for different cost sharing schemes. Section 7 concludes the paper and discusses future work.

2. IP SERVICE CHARGING - STATE OF THE ART

QoS Support

Service differentiation with QoS support requires charging schemes to protect the network from abusive resource reservation. Usage-based charging also supports a funding mechanism to extend network capacity at the expense of those users that actually use these resources. Charging requirements are discussed in [22], focusing on Integrated Services, and in [2], focusing on Differentiated Services. Methods for designing charging schemes for IP services with QoS have been presented in [17].

It is well accepted that flat-rate charging for QoS-enhanced IP services has severe shortcomings [30]. Usage-based charging can be based on reserved and/or consumed resources, e.g. [17] proposed charging formula based on both reserved and consumed resources. Charging can be based on link bit rate share used by the service [22], or on resource rate and buffer space [23]. In [23], models are proposed for deriving resource costs from an IntServ flow specification. Different flow measurement methods for charging and accounting purposes are considered in [13], while different measurement granularity are discussed in [12]. Further related work can be found in [16,19,24, 25,31,32].

Multicast Support

Charging for multicast services has raised several challenging tasks like the calculation of tree costs, multicast savings and cost sharing mechanisms between receivers. [8] introduces a charging and accounting architecture which supports multicast communications for IP Integrated Services over ATM. [10] suggests to use network resource cost for pricing multicast communications and derives an approximation for the cost of a multicast tree with known group size.

Group communication with payment by receivers introduces the problem of cost sharing. Additional difficulties arise for Integrated Services as each receiver can make an individual reservation. These individual reservations lead to the need of fair cost sharing techniques (see Section 6), where receivers are charged according to their reservation parameters. A scheme to share costs of a multicast tree among receivers is presented in [20,21]. The cost sharing scheme presented in [15] also allows to take distance into account.

3. QOS CHARGING: FRAMEWORK

We introduce a layered framework, the charging and accounting reference model, and an example architecture based on this framework. As part of the architecture, a data structure for exchange of accounting information has been designed. For representation of charging policies, a tariff formula language (TFL) is used. The charging information protocol (CIP) allows for distributing charging policies to charging instances at customer premises. This tariff information allows to provide online charging information to the user, and to assist users in tariff-based service selection.

The reference model classifies charging, accounting and closely related processes, and describes their interaction (see *Figure 1*). At the right, five layers are shown that encompass processing for charging and accounting. A configuration plane allows for providing configuration parameters for the processing layers.

Configuration parameters are derived from pricing policy, charging policy, accounting policy and metering policy. Since the metering layer has to provide the data needed for the charging formula, it is useful to derive the basic elements of a lower layer policy (e.g. metering) from higher layer policies (e.g. charging).These policies can be provided by interaction of dedicated policy servers with the corresponding entities of the configuration plane.

The *metering layer* provides the functions to obtain reservation information and to meter actual usage of network resources. In case of multicast, meters can be placed at the edge routers only or at multiple splitting points.

The *collecting layer* encompasses functional entities that access data provided by metering entities and forwards it for further processing to the accounting layer. For supporting multicast charging, this layer is also responsible for selecting appropriate meters (meter placement). Transfer of metering data to collectors can be initiated explicitly (the collector initiates transfer of metering data) or implicitly (after a triggering event such as detection of a new flow, the meter initiates transfer of metering data to the collector(s)). Additionally, this layer may distribute collected usage data to other domains in a multi-provider environment.

Entities of the *accounting layer* process collected usage data (from collectors within the same domain and other domains) and reservation data, consolidate them based on service parameters, and create accounting data sets (i.e., accounting records) which are passed to the charging layer for pricing assignment. To support multicast charging, this layer is also responsible for reconstructing the multicast topology including splitting points where required by the cost sharing scheme.

The *charging layer* derives costs for accounting data sets based on service specific tariff parameters. Different cost metrics may be applied to the same usage of resources, and may be evaluated in parallel. A detailed evaluation of the resource usage can be used for generating bills to the customer, or for internal analysis (auditing) by the service provider. A simple evaluation of current costs can be used for displaying an estimation of accumulated costs for the service user, or for control purposes by the customer organization or by the provider. For charging multicast services, cost allocation assigns costs to specific endpoints, such as sender(s) and receivers of a multicast group.

The *billing layer* translates costs calculated by the charging layer into monetary units and generates a bill for a customer. This process may combine technical considerations with economic considerations, such as volume of resources used by the customers, and marketing methods (e.g. offered discounts).

The left part of the figure represents the policy plane, i.e. technical and

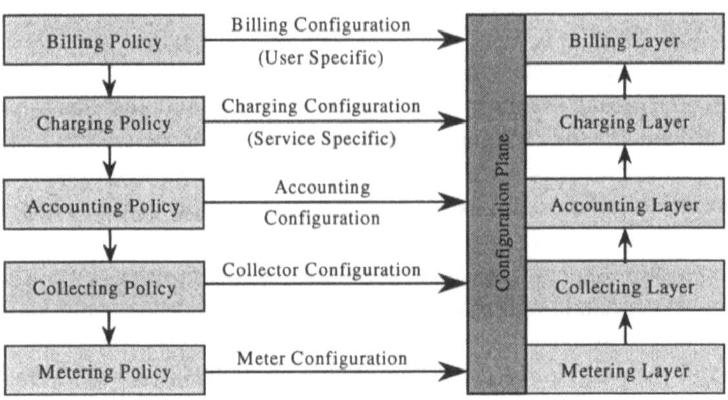

Figure 1. Charging and Accounting Framework

commercial rules for setting parameters based, e.g., on the network configuration (important for metering policies) or the market situation (important for charging and billing policies). The parameters are injected as temporary data to the layers in the right part of the figure through the configuration plane.

4. QOS CHARGING: ARCHITECTURE

Based on the framework introduced in the previous section, we designed an architecture for implementing a charging and accounting service. *Figure 2* shows a sample architecture referred to as VIPCAS (Value-Added IP Charging and Accounting Service). The architecture is being implemented in the ACTS project SUSIE. The network accounting part of the architecture is implemented using IP technology. The charging and billing part of the architecture supports TINA reference points [14] and is implemented using CORBA technology. A policy gateway and an accounting data gateway provide interfaces between these two parts.

The architecture shows that in order to support multicast charging, metering may take place in the edge routers and at the multicast routers. In order to charge, for example the sender, the collected information needs to be fed back to the sender domain (e.g. provider domain A), so that the provider can reconstruct the multicast tree structure in calculating the overall multicast costs.

The architecture uses metering conformant to the IETF Real Time Flow Measurement Architecture (RTFM) [3,5]. For configuration of a meter and for collecting of accounting data, SNMP and a special meter MIB [4,7] are used.

Data from the meters are collected by collecting entities at each domain.

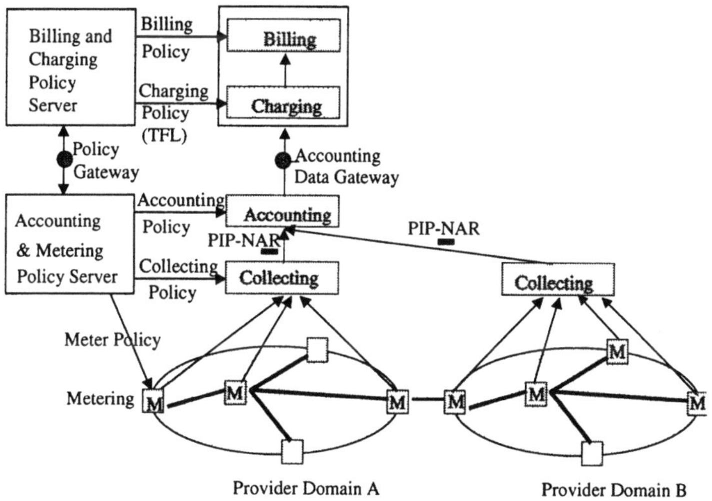

Figure 2. Architecture for Value-Added IP Multicast Charging and Accounting Service

We have specified a data structure, referred to as PIP-NAR (Premium IP Network Accounting Record), that is shown in *Figure 3*, and with more details in the appendix. This data structure is filled by the collecting layer and allows to transport usage information within one provider domain and also to exchange usage information in a multi-provider scenario.

The data structure contains reserved and used resources for an IP flow. It contains a measurement point identifier and a record description to support different styles of PIP-NARs (uni-directional/bi-directional, DiffServ/IntServ style, and others). For unique identification of the flow, a flow description is used. A detailed specification of the PIP-NAR can be found in [29].

Parameter	Type	Length [Bytes]
Record Description		
Version	Char	1
Length of Record	Char	1
Type of Record	Short	2
Measurement start time	Long	4
Measurement stop time	Long	4
Measurement point identification	**(meter IP address)**	**r_id**
Flow Description	**(src,dst IP, ports)**	**f_id**
Reserved Resources	**(e.g. flowspec)**	**rr**
Used Resources	**(#packets, #bytes)**	**umd**
Data Extension	**(e.g. distance, burstiness)**	

Flagname	Set	Not set
Uni-directional	unidirectional record	Bi-directional record
IPv6	IPv6 Flow	IPv4 Flow
Reserved Resources	PIP-NAR contains Reserved Resources	PIP-NAR contains no Reserved Resources
Used Resources	PIP-NAR contains Used Resources	PIP-NAR contains no Used Resources
DiffServ	Differentiated Services	Integrated Services
Extension	Extension Present	No Extension present

Figure 3. Selected Elements of the PIP-NAR

The content of the PIP-NAR *reserved resources* section differ for Integrated Services and for Differentiated Services. *Used resources* contain the data volume and the number of transmitted packets. The PIP-NAR record format is extensible, where future metrics can be included in the *extension* section using the TLV (type, length, value) syntax. Currently defined extensions are distance and burstiness.

Filled PIP-NARs are forwarded to a charging server where a charging scheme is applied to the data. Subsequently, calculated charges are passed to a billing server, where information about network related charges is used together with additional tariff information (user information, discounts, etc.) to generate bills and to prepare current billing information for users in real-time (hot billing).

5. QOS CHARGING: CONFIGURATION

This section discusses possible setting of the configuration plane parameters within the charging and accounting architecture.

Metering is needed at the ingress routers in order to obtain the data volume sent. The flows that should be observed are specified by attributes in a rule set that is loaded to the meter MIB by the meter reader [3-7].

For monitoring IntServ reservation information, reservation style and the flow specification parameters have to be added to the flow attributes in the rule set. RSVP Reservation messages are sent from receivers to the sender. For unicast, information about the reservation of the receiver is available at the ingress router. In this case there is no need to explicitly obtain this information from the egress router.

For multicast communication in an IntServ environment it has to be taken into account that each receiver can make an individual reservation. These individual reservations lead to the need of fair cost sharing techniques (see Section 6), where receivers are charged according to their reservation parameters. Due to the RSVP merging capability [33] by merging reservation requests on the way to the sender, the reservation message that arrives at the ingress router may contain a merged flow specification that represents only the highest QoS level reserved. This RSVP message does not allow to extract individual reservations of the receivers. Therefore, reservation information needs to be captured at egress routers. This can be done by monitoring RSVP messages with an RSVP-extended meter. Information from the egress routers can be collected by using SNMP. A further possibility arises due to the capability of RSVP to carry additional objects. Charging and Accounting (CA) objects that carry the individual reservation information can be added to RSVP messages as proposed in [8]. This allows to limit collection of metering information from the ingress router, while still supporting receivers with heterogeneous QoS. Capturing of the additional objects in the RSVP messages requires some minor changes to the meter and the flow table at the ingress router. Scalability of this solution can be improved by using the CA object aggregation technique introduced in [8].

The IntServ flow specification parameters can be captured in the ingress router by using the existing extension to the RTFM meter described in [26]. For enabling a RSVP message parser, a new variable to the control part of the meter MIB (RSVP_acc) has been introduced. Since RSVP allows the renegotiation of QoS parameters, it has to be ensured that all changes in the reservation are noticed. This can be achieved by a collection interval for accounting records that is smaller than or equal to the RSVP update interval. The accounting record collection interval can be specified with an option when the meter reader is started.

The DiffServ model uses per-packet identifiers to specify which service class a packet belongs to. These classes are specified by the provider in few parameter sets. As a result of this, the packet matching engine has to consider the DiffServ field (codepoint) in the packet header as an additional attribute [18]. Flow table and configuration files (rule sets) have to be modified so that these fields are considered in the matching process. The meaning of the codepoint in terms of QoS parameters can vary for different administrative domains (AD). A translation of codepoints to the assigned parameters can be performed above the collecting layer.

Tariff Formula Language

A tariff contains the information on how the price of a service is calculated. A tariff can consist of multiple charging formulas and some rules that define under which conditions each formula is valid. An example would be a tariff with one formula for business hours and one for the night time.

For the representation of tariffs we have developed the Tariff Formula Language (TFL). This context-free language contains essential mathematical operations (e.g. addition, multiplication) and basic mathematical and logical functions (e.g. exponential function, square root, AND, OR etc.). Furthermore, conditional expressions (if/then/else) allow to express e.g. the variation of prices for different time phases. A set of commonly used charging variables (including volume, duration, time of day) are pre-defined. The TFL provides a simple structured way to represent even complex tariffs. Tariffs are expressed in plain ASCII characters and therefore easy to parse and human-readable.

The following example presents the tariff formula from [23] for guaranteed services expressed in TFL. The approach from [23] uses virtual resource parameters: token rate and residual rate, which can be determined using the IntServ parameters token bucket rate and service rate. Two coefficients a and b represent the prices per resource unit. In our example we make the prices (parameter a and b) dependent on the time of the day (variable *td*). The globally defined variables *tr* and *sr* denote the reserved token bucket rate r and the service rate R, respectively.

```
# parameter a
a = IF(AND(td>=TIME("00:00:00"), td<TIME("05:00:00")), 0.5,
IF(AND(td>=TIME("05:00:00"), td<TIME("21:00:00"), 0.8, 0.5))
# parameter b
b = IF(AND(td>=TIME("00:00:00"), td<TIME("05:00:00")), 0.2,
IF(AND(td>=TIME("05:00:00"), td<TIME("21:00:00"), 0.4, 0.2))
# tariff formula
p = a*tr + b * (sr-tr)
```

Within our architecture, a TFL parser has been implemented using the GNU Bison tool.

Charging Information Protocol for Tariff Information Exchange

In many situations there is a desire by providers to rapidly adapt tariffs to the market situation (see current telephone market situation where newspapers hardly can follow up the tariff changes). For this purpose we developed the charging information protocol (CIP). The protocol follows the client-server approach. A charging information server maintains the information and distributes it to clients on demand.

The protocol is flexible with regard to the transport protocol. Furthermore, it can be adapted to the special needs of a small or large group of clients by using either unicast or multicast for the announcement of tariff information.

Distribution of charging information can be done by unicast or multicast transmission. Tariffs for the offered service classes are sent in a sequence of information messages (INFO). In order to allow clients to recognize a loss of a packet, the INFO messages contain sequence numbers. With these numbers it is possible to request a retransmission of lost packets.

If a unicast connection is used for the announcement of tariffs, all clients that want to receive information about current tariffs have to register with the CIP sever first. In the registration request clients can choose between two modes to get information from the server. In the push mode (default setting) information messages are sent periodically to the client. In order to prevent sending to non-existent or non-operational stations, messages are acknowledged by the client.

In the pull mode information is only sent on demand. Clients need to send a request (GET_INFO) in order to get the information messages. In the unicast case CIP uses timeout and retransmissions to provide a reliable transport. Besides the reliability and the possibility to use TCP for transport, unicast distribution allows selective individually adapted advertisements. This means that the information can be reduced to tariffs that are new to a particular client.

Furthermore, special offers for certain customers can be conveyed individually.

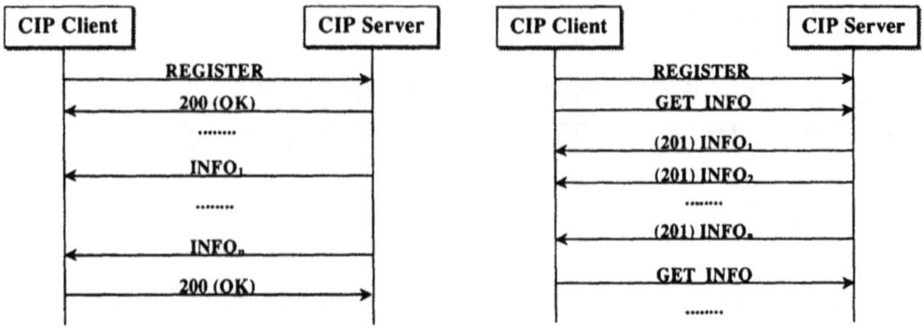

Figure 4. CIP protocol messages for push mode(a) and pull mode(b)

An alternative that provides a better scalability is the distribution of tariff information via multicast. Clients that want to obtain charging information just need to join a particular group. With multicast only the push mode is used. Since no acknowledgements and retransmissions are provided in this case, reliability is lower than for the unicast case. If an INFO message gets lost, the client can recognize this because of the sequence numbers, but he has to wait until a new INFO message is transmitted within the next regular announcement.

The information messages (INFO) contain the following fields: Identification (service name, provider), Validity, Tariff, QoS guarantees, Information about the reservation, and Transaction ID.

The identification field contains the name of the service class and the provider identification. The validity field defines the time interval for which this tariff is valid. This can be used for example to offer special tariffs for specific dates. The tariff field contains the tariff in TFL. The QoS guarantees give a service description regarding the offered QoS. Furthermore, the message gives information about the mechanism used for the reservation. Each INFO message contains a transaction ID to allow the detection of lost messages.

Selection of a service

The selection of an IntServ service can be done by sending an RSVP reservation message to the sender. In order to allow informing the service provider about the chosen tariff, a service selection mechanism is supported by CIP. To choose a service, the client sends a SELECT message to the server. The message is acknowledge by the server. SELECT messages are sent until the server responds or a timer exceeds.

This service selection mechanism is useful if multiple tariffs are offered for the same service class (for different usage profiles or different user groups, or by different providers). Furthermore, the mechanism allows the control of policy rules if the CIP server is combined with a policy server that enforces the rules within the network (accept or reject reservation requests).

6. MULTICAST CHARGING WITH COST SHARING

In general two approaches can be followed for sharing the costs for multicast communication among the participating nodes:

- Sharing the costs of individual links among all connected nodes (link cost sharing)
- Sharing the total costs of the multicast tree among all members of the multicast group (total cost sharing)

Links Cost Sharing (LCS) schemes split savings from the joint usage of a link among the nodes that are directly connected.

Total Cost Sharing (TCS) can be treated as a simplified, abstract LCS scheme, where the whole network cloud is considered as one link, with all egress routers treated as directly connected nodes. While LCS schemes usually require recursive calculation (for all nodes/links of the multicast tree) to allocate costs to the receiver, for TCS schemes it can be sufficient (depending on the total cost determination strategy) to consider only the border nodes. Therefore, it is possible to implement a TCS with less overhead than a LCS.

Simple cost sharing schemes take into account the number of receivers when evaluating the charge for a receiver, without considering differences in QoS. More sophisticated cost sharing schemes also can take into account reserved resources. As the VIPCAS architecture allows to meter individual reservations at egress routers, sophisticated cost sharing schemes can be supported. In the following, we investigate the follwing two methods for QoS-sensitive multicast cost sharing: Incremental Sharing (IS), and Proportional Sharing (PS).

The Incremental Sharing (IS) method splits the costs of a link with regard to the individual reservations made by the directly connected nodes (downstream nodes). It implies that reservations can be ordered by QoS levels. The receivers share equally the incremental cost of all QoS levels which are less than or equal to their reserved QoS [21].

The Proportional Sharing (PS) is a novel cost sharing scheme. It is based on the assumption that the shared link is of a greater value to someone who reserved a higher QoS. For PS, the share of the link costs a receiver has to pay is proportional to its reserved QoS. In comparison to IS which shares link costs only based on local information (the QoS requested by a specific receiver/node), PS takes into account the end-to-end 'value' a flow can be associated with for a specific receiver. This is achieved by sharing link costs depending on costs between the splitting point and the end point. PS can be used

as a LCS, or as TCS. If used as TCS, it allows for a QoS-sensitive multicast cost sharing which can be implemented efficiently.
We consider a generic tariffing scheme where costs of a receiver v_n may depend on the reserved resources R_{v_n}, and the distance $d_{v_n \mu_m}$ to the ingress router μ_m. This generic scheme covers more specific charging schemes such as those presented in [17] and [23]. For a unicast connection, the costs $C_{v_n, unicast}$ can be expressed as

$$C_{v_n, unicast} = f(R_{v_n}, d_{v_n \mu_n}) \tag{3}$$

The total costs of a multicast tree $C_{MC\text{-}Tree}$ depend on the number and distribution of the receivers and on their QoS parameters. To express the savings from using multicast instead of unicast, we introduce the multicast gain factor G_{MC} with

$$G_{MC} = \frac{\sum_{n=1}^{N} C_{v_n, unicast}}{C_{MC-Tree}} \tag{4}$$

By using multicast, the cost share of a receiver v_n gets reduced to

$$C_{v_n} = \frac{C_{v_n, unicast}}{G_{MC}} \tag{5}$$

This method is also useful for a simplified tariff model with a reduced implementation effort. Often, a network provider is much more interested in a comprehensive accounting scheme for the customer than in computing the actual costs of each connection. By estimating the multicast gain factor instead of ascertaining the actual costs of a multicast tree, the computation expenditure for the tariff can be significantly reduced. For N receivers with homogeneous QoS, [10] has estimated the multicast gain factor to be $N/N^{0.8}$ the 0.8 power of the multicast group size based on comparing the summation of edge costs between unicast and multicast routing.

For N receivers with homogeneous QoS, [10] has estimated the multicast tree cost to be $N^{0.8}$ the corresponding unicast costs for sparse multicast trees, resulting in a multicast gain factor of $N/N^{0.8}$.

For load-based tariffing, the reservation-based charging of Equation (1) can be extended to cover actual usage of resources by taking measurements of the effective bandwidth *BWeff* [12] into account. By including the normalized effective bandwidth BWeff into the cost function C_{vn} of Equation (1), this leads to

$$C_{v_n} = f(R_{v_n}, d_{v_n \mu_n}) \cdot (\alpha + \beta \cdot BWeff_{\mu_m}) \cdot \frac{1}{G_{MC}} \qquad (6)$$

With the weighting factors α and β, the dependence of the total costs from reserved and actually used resources can be adjusted.

Cost Sharing: Simulation Results

For investigating the impact of the two cost sharing schemes (IS, PS) we use a basic multicast scenario with a single fan-out node as topology for our simulation. We simulated the dynamic behavior of one multicast group with receivers dynamically joining and leaving. While joining, each receiver may requests an individual QoS. We set the maximum group size to 16. At each time unit receivers change their member status (join or leave the group) with a probability of 0.5. The QoS level for a joining receiver is chosen from 8 different levels and remains unchanged until a receiver leaves the group. Low QoS levels are assumed to be more likely than high QoS levels, using a *1/x* distribution. Costs were allocated in proportion to the QoS levels. We assume that the costs of the shared link depend not only on the QoS but also on other factors like distance. For a distance of 1, costs for QoS level 1 is 1 monetary unit (MU), costs for QoS level 2 is 2 MU, etc. The QoS level of the shared link is the highest requested QoS at the observed time interval. In our multicast scenario, we set the distance for the shared link to 8, resulting in a cost of 8 MU for QoS level 1, and cost of 64 MU for the maximum requested QoS level 8.

Figure 5 shows the multicast gain that can be achieved depending on the number of group members. (The unicast case is included as a reference.) The true multicast gain is compared with a theoretically derived gain using an estimation of the multicast gain according to the results of Chuang [10]. The figure shows that due to heterogeneous QoS, the results of Chuang only give a rough estimation of the true multicast gain.

Figure 6(a) shows the maximum, minimum and average costs a receiver has to pay when joining the group with a selected QoS level, if one of the two cost sharing schemes IS and PS are applied. Maximum costs occur for cases where the joined receiver is the only receiver of the group. As no cost sharing is possible in this case, the link cost share for both schemes represents the true link costs. For smaller QoS levels the mean link cost share differ only little. For high QoS levels (above level 5) the mean link cost share increases more for the IS scheme than for the DPS scheme. This shows that with the IS scheme, receivers with low QoS pay a smaller share of the common link than with the DPS scheme, while the DPS scheme is more attractive for receivers with high QoS.

For the investigation of the effects that a cost sharing schemes has to individual group members, we performed a second type of simulation. This time we looked at one particular receiver that joins the group with the maximum QoS level and remains in the group until the end of the simulation. The join/leave behavior and the QoS levels of other 15 receivers are assigned randomly like in the first experiment. The share that the receiver has to pay of the costs for the jointly used link varies depending on the number of group members and their chosen QoS level at the observed time unit. *Figure 6(b)* shows the probability of the link costs share that the observed receiver has to pay if the different cost sharing schemes are applied. In all cases the link cost share the selected receiver has to pay varies depending on the reservations of the other receivers in the observed time interval. The differences in the mean charge for the two cost sharing schemes (DPS is more attractive for receivers with high QoS) become again visible.

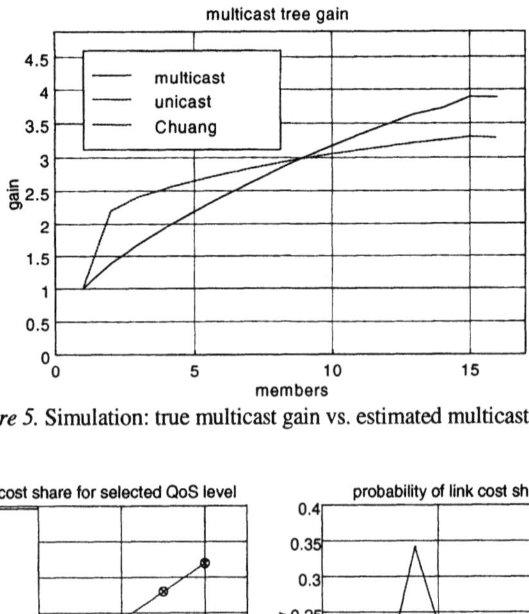

Figure 5. Simulation: true multicast gain vs. estimated multicast gain

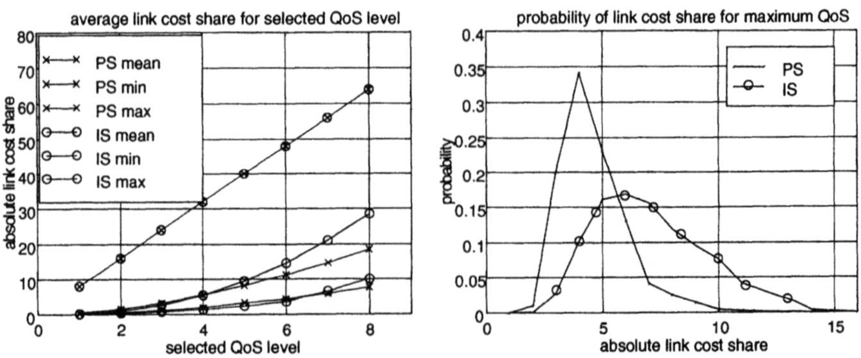

Figure 6. Simulation of end-to-end costs for cost sharing schemes PS and IS:
(a) mean/min/max costs for selected QoS, (b) costs distribution for selection of maximum QoS

7. CONCLUSION AND FUTURE WORK

We have presented a layered framework and described an initial implementation of a charging and accounting architecture based on the framework. The architecture allows its components to be configured for meeting charging and accounting requirements of IntServ or DiffServ in unicast or multicast scenarios. A data structure, the PIP-NAR, is used for transporting usage information from an accounting processing entity to a charging entity, and allows exchange of accounting information in multi-provider scenarios. We presented the Tariff Formula Language (TFL) that allows providers to express a wide variety of charging schemes. A TFL parser has been implemented based on the GNU Bison tool. We have developed a charging information protocol (CIP) that allows to inform clients about tariffs. A prototype of this protocol has been implemented using C++.

For the support of multicast charging, two cost sharing schemes which may be implemented by the architecture have been considered: a link cost sharing scheme, and a novel total cost sharing scheme. The schemes allow a fair allocation of common link costs among receivers, supporting fair charging for QoS-enhanced multicast services.

Future work is planned for deploying and testing the architecture within a multi-provider environment. For this purpose, the PIP-NAR data structure will be used by the collecting layer to exchange usage information among different providers. Future work will also cover optimal selection of IP service class by receivers based on charging information and on user preferences expressed by price limits and utility curves. For this purpose we have implemented a tool that applies numerical optimization techniques (Direction Set Method and Downhill Simplex Method) to tariffs expressed in TFL, and to user preferences expressed in a simplified version of TFL.

References

[1] S. Blake, et al. An Architecture for Differentiated Services. IETF RFC2475, December 1998.

[2] M. S. Borella, V. Upadhyay and I. Sidhu. Pricing Framework for a Differential Services Internet. European Transactions on Telecommunications, Vol. 10(2), March/April 1999.

[3] N. Brownlee, C. Mills, and G. Ruth. Traffic Flow Measurement: Architecture. IETF RFC2063, January 1997.

[4] N. Brownlee. Traffic Flow Measurement: Experiences with NeTraMet. IETF RFC2123, March 1997.

[5] N. Brownlee, C. Mills and G. Ruth. Traffic Flow Measurement: Architecture. IETF Internet draft, Work in progress, June 1999.

[6] N. Brownlee. SRL: A Language for Describing Traffic Flows and Specifying Actions for Flow Groups. IETF Internet draft, Work in progress, June 1999.

[7] N. Brownlee. Traffic Flow Measurement: Meter MIB. IETF Internet Draft, Work in progress, June 1999.

[8] G. Carle, M. Smirnow, and T. Zseby. Charging and Accounting Architecture for IP Multicast Integrated Services. Proc. of Interworking '98, Ottawa, Canada, July 1998.
[9] M. Canosa, M. De Marco, and A. Maiocchi. Traffic Accounting Mechanisms for Internet Integrated Services. Proc. of SPIE VV'98, Vol. 3529 Internet Routing and Quality of Service, Boston, MA, November 1998, pp.254-264.
[10] J. Chuang, and M. Sirbu. Pricing Multicast Communication: A Cost-Based Approach. Proc. of INET'98, Geneva, July 1998.
[11] R. Comerford. State of the Internet: Roundtable 4.0. IEEE Spectrum, Vol. 35(10), October 1998, pp. 69-79. http://www.spectrum.ieee.org/select/1098/int.html.
[12] C. Courcoubetis, F. Kelly, and R. Weber. Measurement-based Charging in Communication Networks. Statistical Laboratory Research Report 1997-19, University of Cambridge, 1997
[13] D. Decasper, M. Waldvogel, Z. Dittia, H. Adiseshu, G. Parulkar, and B. Plattner. Crossbow - A Toolkit for Integrated Services over Cell-Switched IPv6. Proc. of IEEE ATM'97 Workshop, Lisboa, Portugal, June 1997.
[14] F. Dupuy, G. Nilsson, and Y. Inoue. The TINA Consortium: Toward Networking Telecommunications Information Services. IEEE Communication Magazine, Vol. 33(11), November 1995, pp. 78-83.
[15] H. Einsiedler, and P. Hurley. Link Weighting: An Important Basis for Charging in the Internet. Proc. of Global Internet Mini-Conference, Sydney, Australia, November 1998.
[16] G. Fankhauser, B. Stiller, and B. Plattner. Arrow: A Flexible Architecture for an Accounting and Charging Infrastructure in the Next Generation Internet. NETNOMICS: Economic Research and Electronic Networking, Vol. 1(2), 1999.
[17] D. Ferrari and L. Delgrossi. Charging for QoS. Proceedings of the Sixth IEEE/IFIP International Workshop on Quality of Service - IWQoS'98, Napa, CA, May 1998.
[18] S. Handelman, N. Brownlee, G. Ruth, and S. Stibler. RTFM Working Group - New Attributes for Traffic Flow Measurement. IETF Internet draft, Work in progress, June 1999.
[19] F. Hartanto and G. Carle. Policy-based Billing Architecture for Internet Differentiated Services. Proc. of BC'99, Hong Kong, November 1999.
[20] S. Herzog. Accounting and Access Control for Multicast Distributions: Models and Mechanisms. PhD dissertation, University of Southern California, U.S.A., 1996.
[21] S. Herzog, S. Shenker, and D. Estrin. Sharing the Cost of Multicast Trees: An Axiomatic Analysis. Proc. of SIGCOMM'95, Computer Communications Review, vol. 25, Oct. 1995, pp. 315-327.
[22] M. Karsten, J. Schmitt, L. Wolf, and R. Steinmetz. An Embedded Charging Approach for RSVP. Proc. of IWQoS'98, Napa, CA, pp. 91-100, May 1998.
[23] M. Karsten, J. Schmitt, L. Wolf, and R. Steinmetz. Cost and Price Calculation for Internet Integrated Services. Proc. of KiVS'99, March 1999, Darmstadt, Germany, pp. 46-57.
[24] K. Kilkki, and J. Ruutu. Simple Integrated Media Access (SIMA) with TCP. Proc. of 4th INFORMS Telecommunications Conference, Boca Raton, FL, March 1998.
[25] J. MacKie-Mason. A Smart Market for Resource Reservation in a Multiple Quality of Service Information Network. Technical Report, University of Michigan, September 1997.
[26] A. Maiocchi. NeTraMet & NeMaC for IIS Accounting: User's Guide. CEFRIEL, Politecnico di Milan, May 1998.
[27] L.W. McKnight, and J.P. Bailey. An Introduction to Internet Economics. The Journal of Electronic Publishing 2(1), May 1996.
[28] OMG, The Common Object Request Broker: Architecture and Specification, Revision 2.1, August 1997.
[29] H. Orlamünder (Editor). Parameters and Mechanisms for Charging in IP based Networks [Network Aspects]. TR/NA-080301 V1.0.7 (1999-06), ETSI Working Group NA8 Technical Document, 1999

[30] B. Rupp, R. Edell, H. Chand, P. Varaiya. INDEX: A Platform for Determining how People Value the Quality of their Internet Access. Proceedings of the Sixth IEEE/IFIP International Workshop on Quality of Service - IWQoS'98, Napa, CA, May 1998, pp. 85-90.
[31] S. Shenker, D. Clark, D. Estrin and S. Herzog. Pricing in Computer Networks: Reshaping the Research Agenda. Communications Policy. Vol. 20(3), 1996, pp. 183-201. ftp://parcftp.xerox.com/pub/net-research/picn.ps.
[32] B. Stiller, G. Fankhauser, B. Plattner, and N. Weiler. Charging and Accounting for Integrated Internet Services – State of the Art, Problems, and Trends. Proc. of INET'98, Geneva, Switzerland, July 1998.
[33] L. Zhang, R. Braden, S. Berson, S. Herzog, and S. Jamin. Resource ReSerVation Protocol (RSVP) - Version 1 Functional Specification. IETF RFC2205, September 1997.

8. APPENDIX

Elements of the Premium IP Network Accounting Record (PIP NAR)

The types used for the PIP-NAR elements correspond to the OMG IDL syntax defined in [28].

Table 1: Measurement Point Identification and Record Type

Parameter		Type	Length [Bytes]
Record Description			
	Version	Char	1
	Length of Record	Char	1
	Type of Record	Short	2
	Measurement Start Time	Long	4
	Measurement Stop Time	Long	4
Measurement point identification			
	IP Address	String [4/16]	4/16

Table 2: Flags for the Type of Record field

Flagname	Set	Not set
IPv6	IPv6 Flow	IPv4 Flow
Reserved Resources	PIP-NAR contains reserved resources	PIP-NAR contains no reserved resources
Used Resources	PIP-NAR contains used resources	PIP-NAR contains no used resources
DiffServ	Differentiated Services	Integrated Services
Extension	Extension Present	No Extension present

Table 3: Flow Description (IPv4 Flows)

Parameter		Type	Range/unit
Flow Description			
	Destination Address	String [4]	
	Destination Netmask	String [4]	
	Source Address	String [4]	
	Source Netmask	String [4]	
	Destination Port	String [2]	
	Source Port	String [2]	
	Flow Start Time	Long	
	Protocol	Short	(UDP=17,TCP=6)
	Flow Owner	Short	QoS Setup Protocol, Flow, management or others

Table 4: Reserved Resources for Integrated Services

Parameter		Type	Range/unit
Reserved Resources			
	Service	Short	Guaranteed Delay=1, Controlled Load=2
	Rate	Long	[bits/s]
	Depth	Long	[bytes]
	Peak Rate	Long	[bytes]
	Service Rate	Long	[bytes]
	Min. Transmission Unit	Long	[bytes]
	Max. Transmission Unit	Long	[bytes]
	Backlog	Integer	[Bytes]
	Delay	Integer	[μs]
	Slack Term	Integer	[ms]

Table 5: Used Resources

Parameter		Type	Range/unit
Used Resources			
	Volume sent	Long	[bytes]
	# of IP packets sent	Long	

Table 6: Extension Element

Parameter		Type	Range/unit
Number of TLVs		Short	
Data Extension			
	Type	Short	
	Length	Short	
	Value	Dependent on type	

PART 5

VIRTUAL NETWORKS

A TRAFFIC MANAGEMENT MODEL FOR VIRTUAL PRIVATE NETWORK LINKS

Leila Lamti
Ecole Nationale Supérieure des Télécommunications
2 Rue de la châtaigneraie, BP 78 35512 Cesson Sévigné - France
Tel: (+33) 2.99.12.70.51
Fax: (+33) 2.99.12.70.30
Leila.Lamti@enst-bretagne.fr

Abstract

A Virtual Private Network (VPN) is a solution that provides corporate networking between geographically dispersed sites. VPN sites consist of local area networks (LANs). Their interconnection is based on a public network infrastructure. Links connecting VPN sites are allocated with a peak rate and the VPN customer pays for the reserved bandwidth. The goal of this work is to develop a control model able to manage traffic on these links. By maximizing bandwidth utilization, an optimum balance for the allocation of bandwidth on each link can be found. To respond to such needs, we propose to introduce in each LAN of the VPN a control architecture that we call The Hierarchical Bandwidth Manager. This manager is able to cope with best-effort and guaranteed flows so that bandwidth left unused by guaranteed flows is dynamically distributed among best-effort ones. It uses a tree representation of the LAN nodes and regulation of link bandwidth is done in a hierarchical and distributed manner. Each node in the tree respects either an inter-node bandwidth share protocol or an intra-host regulation protocol. The bandwidth manager relies on the implementation of both protocols in the tree node. Results of the implementation of the bandwidth manager in the ns network simulator are described in this paper.

1. INTRODUCTION

Efficient bandwidth sharing among multiple sessions has been analyzed in several research studies. Heterogeneity is one of the main problems in Quality of Service (QoS) provision and multiple traffic classes with different QoS requirements may be multiplexed on the same path. Integration of applications with different QoS needs and traffic characterizations in a local network in general and at the network outlet in particular is an important problem to solve. It is even more critical in the presence of known or predicted resource contentions.

With the advent of constrained traffic (real-time applications, jitter or delay constrained sources, ...), the interest for the specification and development of new mechanisms able to cope with such traffic characterizations has increased.

Major networking communities have contributed in this field. The Traffic Management specifications for ATM networks [1] allow flexible bandwidth allocations at high speeds. They also allow a scalable architecture especially in the context of local area networks (LANs). The IETF community has also contributed in this field by designing and developing a new signaling mechanism called ReSerVation Protocol (RSVP) [4]. This protocol is used for resource reservation on the Internet. Both communities has defined several service classes. Each of these service classes is designed to provide certain QoS guarantees to traffic flows. Applications are expected to use one of these classes according to their needs.

In addition to QoS provisioning, a new concept for virtual sub-networking has emerged. This concept known as *Virtual Private Network (VPN)* [2] enables the interconnection of geographically dispersed sites. It provides corporate networking between geographically dispersed sites using the public switched network infrastructure. It can be accessed from any inter-working unit (a router, a LAN multiplexer) and it allows LANs interconnection. VPNs were more marketable products than well-defined telecommunication services because of a lack of standardization. The VPN concept is receiving more attention now. Several research projects as well as international standardization activities are involved in this field. Major networking communities have contributed in this field, especially within the IETF community where a significant amount of work is being done for the specification of the VPN service deployment over the IP backbone [8]. ATM backbones may also support a VPN service deployment and in the literature, several papers propose the use of ATM Virtual Paths for the provision of VPN services [7], [15].

A VPN may be built over an ATM network or over the Internet backbone. In both IP-based and ATM-based implementations, VPN nodes are connected to each other through virtual links. These virtual links are allocated with a peak rate and the VPN customer pays for the reserved bandwidth even when he does not use it.

In this paper, we focus on virtual links bandwidth allocation. Since traffic characterization is a difficult process, customers tend to over-allocate bandwidth on virtual links in order to prevent their traffic from any congestion, leading to an inefficient network resources utilization. To avoid such inefficiency, a reasonable solution would be to try to enhance statistical multiplexing on each virtual link. In order to obtain differentiated and customized Quality of Service (QoS) for flows multiplexed on the same virtual link, an adequate and sufficient bandwidth amount should be allocated. Also, the statistical multiplexing should be coupled to an efficient control of the bandwidth distribution between flows sharing the same virtual link. Traffic has to be managed so that each flow receives the amount of bandwidth it has been agreed to use.

Our proposal will rely on two important features: flow isolation and traffic shaping. Flow isolation is necessary since sensitive applications with stringent QoS requirements could malfunction due to bandwidth lack or network congestion (caused by an unfairness in bandwidth share or by greedy applications). On the other hand, traffic shaping, when performed, ensures that the overall multiplex of flows sharing the same virtual link does not exceed the maximum allocated capacity. Without traffic shaping, non conforming packets may be sent and discarded by the policing functions of the public network.

To meet these requirements, we propose to introduce in each LAN of the VPN a control model that we call *The Hierarchical Bandwidth Manager.* It uses a tree representation of the LAN nodes and regulation of link bandwidth is done in a hierarchical and distributed manner. Each node in the tree respects either an inter-node bandwidth share protocol or an intra-host regulation. Control algorithms are performed by each node in the hierarchy in order to reach the 2 above-cited goals. By reaching these goals, bandwidth utilization could be maximized.

The paper is organized as follows: In section 2, we explain how the proposed manager may be combined to a VPN implementation and present its principle. In section 3, we introduce two new protocols called *the inter-node bandwidth share protocol* and *the intra-host regulation protocol* that constitute the control components of the hierarchical bandwidth manager. We explain how these protocols dynamically enforce bandwidth regulation on LAN virtual links. We also present a novel algorithm called the *fair shaper* used to schedule packets in hosts and aimed at implementing the intra-host regulation protocol. In Section 4, we explain how the inter-node bandwidth share protocol can be implemented in existing equipments. The achieved results of both protocols in the *ns* network simulator [14] show that bandwidth regulation goals are reached.

2. TRAFFIC CONTROL REQUIREMENTS

Each company site represents a LAN. The purpose of a VPN service is to interconnect these LANs through a public network infrastructure. As mentioned above, a VPN service may either be offered over the IP backbone or through a public ATM network. We can represent VPN sites and their interconnection by means of a unique model. Some definitions are given in the following:

Customer Edge Device: It is the edge device at the customer side that connects the LAN to the provider network. This consists of the IP router that connects the LAN to the Internet backbone. It may also consist of the ATM switch that connects the LAN to the public ATM network.

Provider Edge Device: It is the edge device at the provider side to which the customer edge device is connected. As for the customer edge device, it may be an IP router or an ATM switch.

Virtual link: Depending on the VPN implementation, it may consist in the virtual link that connects 2 customer edge devices in the VPN or the one that connects a customer edge device to the provider edge device.

Figure 1 presents the generic VPN connectivity model that we will use for the rest of the paper and resumes all the above-mentioned definitions.

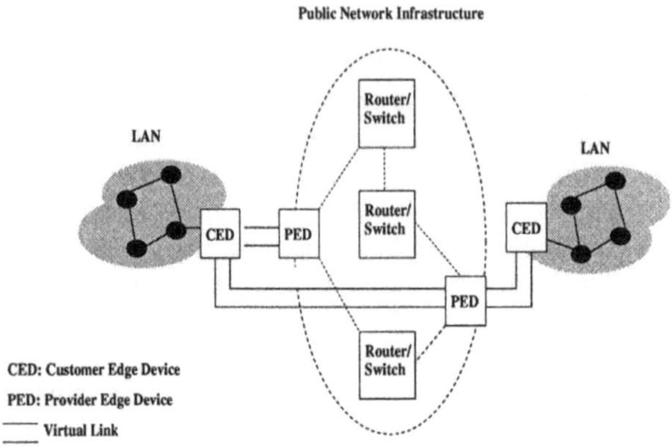

Figure 1 The generic VPN connectivity model

Requirements

In the generic VPN connectivity model, the LAN is connected to the VPN through a virtual link. For a VPN customer, an important task is to allocate the virtual links with sufficient capacities to deal with the external traffic needs. The high peak-to-mean ratios in LAN outgoing traffic volume allow high multiplexing gains. The statistical multiplexing should be coupled to an efficient control of the bandwidth distribution between flows sharing the same virtual link. Traffic should be managed efficiently so that each flow receives the amount of bandwidth it has been agreed to use.

In this paper, we suppose that each virtual link is allocated an amount of bandwidth that we propose to share fairly. The sharing model we propose consists of a *hierarchical bandwidth manager* able to control the access to a VPN link from within a VPN site. The hierarchical bandwidth manager has two components: an *inter-node bandwidth share protocol*, and an *intra-host regulation protocol.*

The inter-node bandwidth share protocol is a dynamic hierarchical bandwidth allocation scheme. The top level of the hierarchy is the VPN link access device, what we called the customer edge device; the next level consists of gateway routers of subnets. And the last level consists of individual hosts. Starting from an initial set of bandwidth allocations, each parent machine monitors the bandwidth usage of each child machine, and periodically reallocates the excess bandwidth among the children machines that are not under-using their bandwidth allocations. The intra-host regulation protocol uses a rate regulator for guaranteed traffic, best-effort traffic is kept in a separate queue. Whenever no guaranteed traffic is eligible to send, best-effort traffic, if any, is served.

The Traffic Management Model

In our model, the *root node* consists of the customer edge device (defined above in section 2). A *gateway* is the equipment that connects a sub-network to the other subnetworks of the LAN and to the root node. Throughout this study, we consider a LAN as composed of subnetworks $S_1, S_2, \ldots\ S_n$ (see Figure 2). Gateways $G_1, G_2, \ldots\ G_n$ are connected by transmission links with

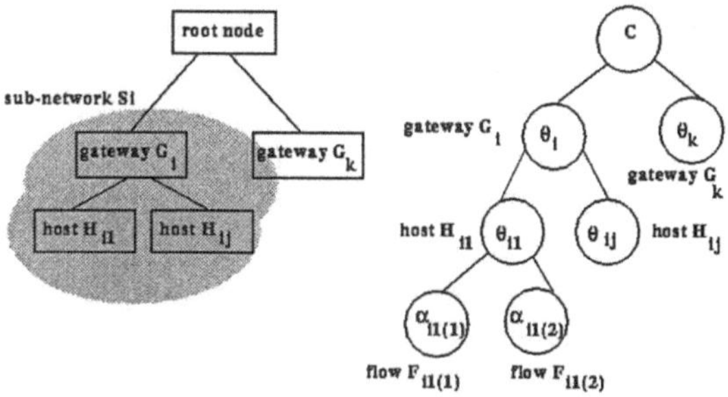

Figure 2 A tree representation of LAN outgoing links

fixed capacity to the root node.

During the VPN configuration, the root node negotiates with the provider edge device the establishment of a virtual link and the allocation of its peak bandwidth. Several gateways may share a virtual link (an ATM VP is a multiplex of ATM VCs). The root node manages bandwidth on a virtual link (e.g. a VP) by sharing it between gateways (e.g. a VC per gateway). We attribute to each gateway G_i a static weight Φ_i that represents the minimum amount of bandwidth it can use. Gateways should then cooperate with the root node to dynamically re-adjust bandwidth allocations depending on the effective bandwidth utilization. The root node periodically computes new weights and informs the gateways about them. Depending on real bandwidth needs and traffic evolution, the root node decides whether to negotiate with the provider edge device the increase or the decrease of bandwidth allocation on a specific virtual link.

A gateway G_i in each subnetwork S_i is responsible for all outgoing traffic generated by hosts enclosed in S_i. It shares this amount of bandwidth among all hosts using the same virtual link (a weight is given to each host). After receiving its weight from the root node, a gateway is then responsible for sharing this amount of bandwidth among hosts enclosed in S_i.

Finally, each host should ensure that bandwidth is fairly shared between applications (flows) set up on the same virtual link. Generally, we can distinguish at least two traffic service classes: *the guaranteed service class* and *the best-effort service class.* Each flow belongs to one of these 2 classes and packets should be scheduled by the host according to the traffic class they belong to.

Our model is inspired from the *Hierarchical Link Sharing* concept proposed in the literature [6]. According to this concept, each node in a hierarchy is assigned a weight and the main idea is that each node, by means of a set of control functions, should receive its allocated bandwidth (which is proportional to its weight). According to the link sharing concept, a node can be a traffic class (e.g the real-time class), a traffic type (e.g. telnet traffic), etc ...

An example of link sharing algorithms is *The Hierarchical Fair Service Curve Algorithm* by Stoica and Zhang [13]. Another proposal is *The Class Based Queueing CBQ* by Floyd and Jacobson [6]. In [3], Bennet and Zhang presented an overview of *The Hierarchical Packet Fair Queueing Algorithms H-PFQ*. These algorithms define a class hierarchy (a tree) for each link. A class represents a collection of flows grouped into organizations, protocol families, types of traffic, etc ... Each class receives a minimum bandwidth (expressed as a weight) totally consumed if sufficient traffic is generated. Otherwise, the unused bandwidth (or excess bandwidth) is fairly shared between active classes.

The above-mentioned models differ from each other in the definition of the class scheduling technique and in the applied policy in case of excess bandwidth distribution. In case of congestion, some packets may be lost since neither shaping nor policing is performed. They also assume that the root node of the tree performs packet scheduling on the aggregate traffic in a centralized manner. All intermediate nodes in the tree (other than the root node) are virtual. They are used by the root node to decide which class to serve with a given priority. These models are proposed for public network routers.

The same need for link sharing exists in a LAN since we can divide a LAN into administrative groups, give priority to some traffic types and share bandwidth of outgoing links by statically assigning weights to each node. The model we propose is also based on the hierarchical link sharing concept. Nevertheless, our model differs from previously presented models (CBQ and H-PFQ) regarding 4 points:

- In our model, intermediate nodes in the tree (other than leaf nodes and root node) do not only represent aggregate flows but also control entities.
- These control entities are aimed at performing traffic shaping as well as flow isolation between guaranteed applications sharing the same virtual link.
- In our model, excess bandwidth is distributed among only best-effort flows since we consider that excess bandwidth is not a guaranteed resource and can not be used by guaranteed flows.
- The implementation of our model is distributed. Not only the root node is serving packets (like for CBQ since the tree representation is logical) but also intermediate nodes perform control functions and schedule packets before sending them to the root node.

The Hierarchical Bandwidth Manager

The hierarchical bandwidth manager relies on two protocols performed by the nodes of the hierarchy [10]. Each node in the tree respects either an *Inter-Node Bandwidth Share* protocol or an *Intra-Host Regulation* protocol. In the following, we will focus on the management of a single virtual link. By applying the same mechanism on each virtual link, all VPN virtual links are controlled.

The link capacity C is to be shared between gateways G_1, G_2, ... G_n. If Γ is the set of gateways, then we have:

$$C = \sum_{i \in \Gamma} r_i, \text{ where } r_i = \Phi_i \times C \tag{1}$$

r_i represents the bandwidth share of gateway G_i and Φ_i its weight. Each host H_i^j connected to gateway G_i has a weight Φ_i^j that could be attributed on an administrative hierarchy basis. If Γ_i is the set of hosts connected to gateway G_i, the traffic generated by a host H_i^j should be limited to:

$$r_i^j = \Phi_i \times \Phi_i^j \times C, \text{ where } \Phi_i = \sum_{j \in \Gamma_i} \Phi_i^j \tag{2}$$

Host H_i^j is intended to share r_i^j between its active applications depending on their networking parameter needs. A flow can either belong to the guaranteed service class or to the best-effort service class. In order to deliver QoS to all guaranteed flows, the host has to perform an admission control function. This function evaluates available bandwidth in order to decide whether to accept a new guaranteed flow or not. This is to ensure that already established guaranteed flows continue to receive the committed QoS parameters for the whole lifetime of the connection. Beyond connection admission control, it is necessary to apply a traffic shaping on guaranteed flows and to share unused bandwidth between best-effort ones.

To explain the principle of this bandwidth sharing, we present a hierarchy example in Figure 3. In this hierarchy, the maximum capacity C of the link is 5Mb/s. Gateway G_1 is allowed to send $4Mb/s$ and host H_{11} $3Mb/s$. If the total guaranteed traffic at host H_{11} is less than $3Mb/s$, it is useful to make the unused bandwidth available for best-effort flows that may be set up on host H_{11} (best-effort flows are not represented in this figure since they don't have any minimum bandwidth allocation). If host H_{11} has no sufficient traffic (guaranteed and best-effort flows included) to consume these $3Mb/s$, excess bandwidth may be used by host H_{12}. Moreover, if the aggregate traffic at gateway G_1 is less than $4Mb/s$, it is reasonable to make gateway G_2 consume the excess bandwidth. Only best-effort flows are authorized to share the excess bandwidth. This is because we assume that guaranteed flows are constantly shaped. Also, excess bandwidth can not be considered as a guaranteed resource.

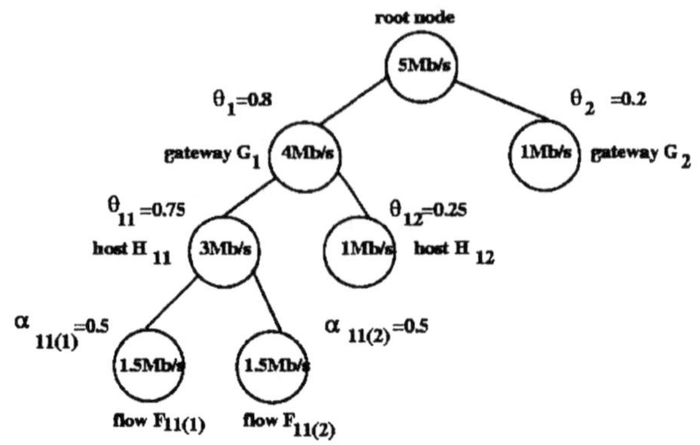

Figure 3 A hierarchy example

3. CONTROL COMPONENTS OF THE HIERARCHICAL BANDWIDTH MANAGER

Each host applies traffic shaping on guaranteed flows. When guaranteed flows are idle (or should be idle due to traffic shaping conditions), the host sends best-effort packets taking into account the maximum allowed rate (it will be explained later how this rate can be dynamically evaluated). Each host is entitled to send at its maximum capacity. This concept is referred to as intra-host regulation protocol and is implemented through a mechanism called the *fair shaper* (it will be explained in section 3).

A dynamic weight computation scheme ensures that when some nodes are idle or sending less than their allocated bandwidth, the excess bandwidth will be distributed between active sibling nodes. Each parent node periodically estimates current load, re-evaluates its children weights and informs them about their new weights (always greater or equal to initial ones). Similarly, children nodes re-compute weights of their descendant nodes. This process is done recursively to share the excess bandwidth along the tree nodes. In our model, only the root node and gateways are concerned with such dynamic weight computations. This concept is referred to as the inter-node bandwidth share protocol.

The Inter-node Bandwidth Share Protocol

Consider a parent node N_i (the root node or a gateway) with weight Φ_i and capacity C_i [1]. Let Γ_i be the set of its children. Let N_i^j be a child node, Φ_i^j its weight, Δ_i^j the excess bandwidth it can borrow from sibling nodes in addition to its share. λ_i^j represents its actual transmission rate.

If U_i denotes the set of under-loaded nodes (i.e. $\{ N_i^j \mid \lambda_i^j < \Phi_i^j \times C_i \}$), then:

[1] $\Phi_i = 1$ for the root node and $C_i = C \times \Phi_i$

Definition 1 *A bandwidth allocation is said to provide inter-node bandwidth share if for each node N_i^j, there exists an excess bandwidth Δ_i^j defined as follows:*

$$\Delta_i^j = \begin{cases} \frac{(C_i - \sum_{j \in \Gamma_i} \lambda_i^j) \times \Phi_i^j}{\sum_{k \notin U_i} \Phi_k} & \text{if } N_i^j \notin U_i \\ 0 & \text{otherwise} \end{cases} \tag{3}$$

whenever $Cardinality(U_i) \neq 0$ and the new weight becomes:

$$\Phi_i^j := \Phi_i^j + \frac{\Delta_i^j}{C_i} \tag{4}$$

According to this definition, an inter-node bandwidth share is optimal whenever:

$$\sum_{j \in \Gamma_i} (\Delta_i^j + \lambda_i^j) = C_i$$

A parent node N_i needs to keep information on the actual transmission rate of its children and their initial and current weights. New weights are computed according to equation (4) and periodically sent. A theoretical evaluation of the update interval optimal value depends on the LAN architecture and available buffers in gateways.

Intra-host Regulation Protocol: The Fair Shaper

Our purpose is to share, on a host machine, bandwidth between flows using the same outgoing link. We assume that a multi-task operating system (Solaris 2.5) is running on the host machine. We suppose that each application belongs to a certain service class. Depending on its networking parameter needs, an application requests a set of traffic parameters. It is then expected to respect this set of parameters. The operating system must manage end-system resources so that processing needs implied by the bandwidth and delay requirements of each connection could be satisfied.

In current operating system implementations, flow isolation is not respected and traffic shaping is not performed. Guaranteed flows may send more traffic than what has been negotiated. The overall multiplex may consequently exceed the link capacity. Moreover, a guaranteed flow may also be "disturbed" by a best-effort one when they both compete for accessing common resources (CPU, memory access, network driver access, ...).

In this context, we propose to perform traffic shaping at the source so that any bursty source is prevented from sending non conforming packets. Each flow is confined to respect its negotiated traffic parameters. Also, by using an adequate packet scheduling algorithm, flow isolation can be ensured.

The Algorithm Design

In order to perform traffic shaping coupled with packet scheduling, we have designed a new algorithm that we call *the Fair Shaper* to be implemented in the network driver of the Solaris 2.5 operating system. Such an algorithm applies traffic shaping per connection with a very small probability to block any application process when a non conforming packet arrives to the network driver (process blocking is very costly). It also uses the *Self Clocked Fair Queuing* algorithm proposed by Golestani [9] as a packet scheduler. We first explain the main idea behind the fair shaper algorithm before justifying the choice of combining traffic shaping with packet scheduling.

In a classical network driver (the IP driver in our case), all flows are multiplexed in the driver queue. This driver is managed by a single process, i.e. all flows share the same environment. All packets (from different flows) are stored in this common queue and are served in a FIFO (First In First Out) manner. This FIFO queueing discipline does not ensure flow isolation and does not take into account the networking parameters of guaranteed flows. In order to ensure flow isolation, we propose to modify this queueing discipline by integrating a simple and efficient mechanism.

The proposed mechanism computes for each guaranteed packet a departure time and an insertion tag before it inserts it in the driver queue. Insertion tags can be computed according to a Generalized Processor Sharing GPS-like policy [12]. Since we are concerned with a packet system (the network driver), we propose to use a packet approximation of the GPS policy. One of the Packet Fair Queueing algorithms PFQ [5] could be used. As explained above, the SCFQ algorithm will be used since it is the simplest one and presents good fairness properties, especially in the context of our work (more explanations on this choice can be found in [11]). The SCFQ algorithm computes insertion tags so that flows are served proportionally to their traffic parameters. Packets are then inserted in the driver queue in the increasing order of these tags.

For traffic shaping, we compute a theoretical departure time for each arriving guaranteed packet. This theoretical departure time is computed according to the flow traffic parameters. If the packet comes in advance (e.g. if the source is bursty), it is blocked in the driver queue waiting for a timer to expire.

Since we will use the same queue for traffic shaping and for packet scheduling, we propose to combine the two mechanisms into a single algorithm that we call *the fair shaper*. More details on this algorithm and its motivations are described in [11].

The Fair Shaper Algorithm

The fair shaper consists of a packet scheduling server implemented in the network driver. It is composed of an arrival module and a service module (see Figure 4). When a guaranteed packet arrives, the arrival module computes its position in the queue based on the SCFQ algorithm. This position is called *virtual finishing service tag*. The arrival module also computes its *theoretical departure time* based on a minimal packet inter-arrival time. The packet is then inserted in the driver queue. When a best-effort packet arrives, the arrival module has to insert it in the first empty entry in the server queue. This ensures that the server will maximize bandwidth utilization when sufficient traffic is available. The arrival module links empty entries (in the driver queue) to form a second queue. This queue is used to store best-effort packets. The service

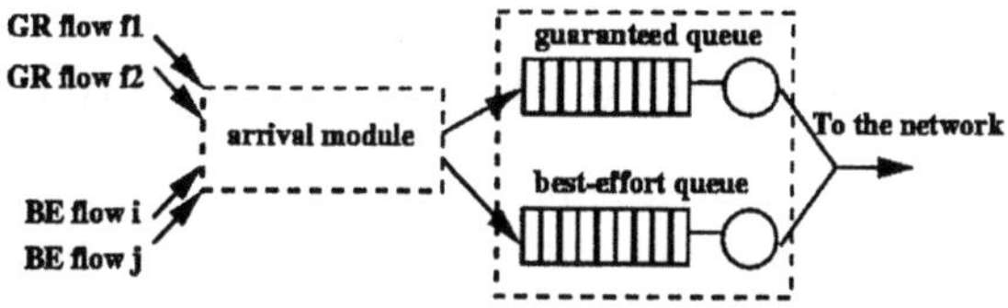

Figure 4 The fair shaper architecture

module is back-logged whenever packets are still in the driver queue. It extracts the first packet from the guaranteed queue and sends it only if its theoretical departure time is reached. Otherwise, it sends the head of the best-effort queue.

For each guaranteed flow i, a weight α_i is computed proportionally to its traffic parameters (for example one could consider CBR flows with α_i proportional to PCR). When the kth packet P_i^k of length l_i^k arrives at time a_i^k from guaranteed flow i, the arrival module computes its virtual finishing service tag F_i^k according to the SCFQ algorithm and its theoretical departure time D_i^k as follows:

$$F_i^k = \max(F_i^{k-1}, v(a_i^k)) + \frac{l_i^k}{\alpha_i} \quad (5)$$

$$D_i^k = \max(D_i^{k-1} + T_i, a_i^k) \quad (6)$$

The virtual time function $v(t)$ is equal to the service tag of the packet in service at time t. T_i corresponds to the minimum inter-arrival time between packets considered as bursts. In the case of an ATM-based VPN, this parameter is computed so that the burstiness caused by the fragmentation of an IP packet into ATM cells is absorbed (more details on this computation can be found in [11]). The following theorem proves the correctness of this algorithm by demonstrating that theoretical departure times and service tags are coherent:

Theorem 1 *For any pair of packets P_i^k, P_j^l which have virtual finishing service tags F_i^k, F_j^l respectively, and theoretical departure times D_i^k, D_j^l respectively,*

$$F_i^k \leq F_j^l \Leftrightarrow D_i^k \leq D_j^l \quad (7)$$

The proof of this theorem can be found in [11] and is based on the GPS and SCFQ algorithms properties.

4. IMPLEMENTATION

The hierarchical bandwidth manager controls bandwidth utilization on all virtual links of a VPN. It consists of a proposal for site-level traffic management. In this section, we present the guidelines for the implementation of the inter-node bandwidth share protocol within the root node and the gateways. A detailed description of the fair shaper implementation can be found in [11].

The Inter-node Bandwidth Share Protocol

The protocol we propose is completely distributed, i.e., gateways do not need to keep state information on each other. A gateway just communicates with the root node and its children nodes. For the sake of simplicity, we explain how the protocol works in a gateway. At the root node, we use the same protocol with some name translation (e.g. we just replace host by gateway and gateway by root node to determine the algorithm at the root node).

The gateway needs to keep some information on its own weight, the bandwidth capacity of a link, the weights of all its children and their actual transmission rates. Two tables are defined by the gateway: the first one, called *links table*, stores information about the available links, their capacities, the gateway initial and current weights. An entry in this table has the following structure:

Link identifier	Link capacity	Initial weight	Current weight

The second table, called *hosts table*, stores information about hosts. An entry in this table is composed as follows:

Host identifier	Initial weight	Current weight	Effective rate

The initial weight is a float number that is attributed statically by a network manager to a specific host. The current weight is used to keep track of the current share. The effective transmission rate is a counter of received bytes from a host during an update interval. At the end of an update interval, the gateway follows these steps to compute new weights:

1. It reads the hosts table to determine the set of under-loaded hosts (as defined in section 3).

2. The gateway tests if this set is empty.

    (a) If it is empty, no excess bandwidth is to be distributed.

    (b) Else, new weights are computed according to equations 3 and 4.

3. The gateway verifies if its parent node has sent a control message with a new weight.

(a) If the weight has changed (an excess bandwidth is to be shared at the parent node or a sibling node becomes active and wants to recuperate its bandwidth share), the gateway updates the links table with its new current weight.

(b) Else, nothing is to be done.

4. The gateway sends to all its children (hosts), within control messages, its new bandwidth share (new current weight read from links table) and their new weights computed in step 2.a (read from hosts table).

Notes

- When a node temporarily sends at a lower rate, the unused bandwidth will be viewed as an excess at the parent node and is reallocated to the other nodes. When this same node speeds up to its regular rate in the next period, the total traffic at the parent node will exceed its maximum capacity. We use for this purpose at the parent node a specific queue that stores packets in excess and schedules them in the next period since no space is left for the current period.

  Clearly, such a solution may violate a guaranteed flow. Nevertheless, this violation may be reduced if the period duration is chosen according to the LAN dimensions, to the traffic variability etc, ... We should hence choose a period small enough so that queue overflow and guarantees violations are avoided. If this situation occurs, at the end of the period, the parent node re-attributes to its children their initial weights.

- It is to be noted that in the hosts table, we always keep the initial weight in order to be able to decrease the transmission rate of some hosts when under-loaded ones become able to use their full share. We keep information on the current weight to determine if the host is under-loaded or not.

- In the links table, we keep information on the gateway initial weight in order to be able to decrease its share when other gateways become able to use their initial share.

- IP packets are exchanged between the tree nodes to update state information.

Simulation Results

We use the ns [14] network simulator from Lawrence Berkeley National Laboratory (LNBL) for our simulations. We implemented the fair shaper algorithm as a new scheduling discipline. This consists of a new class implemented as a module added to the available package. In each node created by the simulator, a classifier object receives packets, examines their fields and then maps the values to an outgoing interface. We modified the classifier object to support the algorithm described in 4. We use the simple topology presented in 2.

Experiment 1

We first test the implementation of the fair shaper. We suppose that all nodes of the hierarchy are idle except for host H_{11}. In host H_{11}, we establish a best-effort flow BE_{11} and 2 guaranteed flows, GR_{11} and GR_{12}. Both guaranteed flows have the same weight (0.5) and are intended to share the amount of bandwidth of their parent node ($3Mb/s$). Since all the other nodes of the hierarchy are idle, H_{11} can use up to $5Mb/s$. Guaranteed flows should be shaped so that each one can uses up to $1.5Mb/s$ and the best-effort flow will consume the remaining bandwidth $2Mb/s$. We measured the instantaneous rate of each flow. As it can be seen in Figure 5, guaranteed flows GR_{11} and

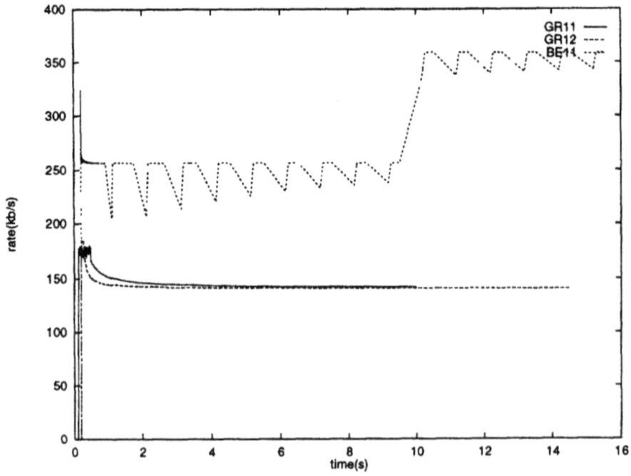

Figure 5 The fair shaper results

GR_{12} are well shaped and the best-effort BE_{11} has a variable rate with a mean rate of approximately $2.2Mb/s$. When flow GR_{11} is stopped (at time 10), flow BE_{11} sees its rate grow up to $3.5Mb/s$.

Experiment 2

In this experiment, we suppose that gateway $G1$ is active during [0..30]. Gateway $G2$ is active during [0..20], idle during]20..25] and again active at]25..30]. At time 20, when $G2$ becomes idle, gateway $G1$ should be enabled to consume the total capacity of the link ($5Mb/s$). Also, at time 25, when gateway $G2$ is enabled again, this latter should be able to speed up to its allocated rate

($1Mb/s$) and at the same time, $G1$ is attributed again its initial weight (sending rate less or equal to $4Mb/s$).

In the following experiment, we only represent the behavior of flows belonging to gateway $G1$. The behavior of the other flows (from gateway $G2$) can be easily guessed. During the whole duration of the experiment, we establish a guaranteed flow GR_{11} (shaped to $2.5Mb/s$) and a best-effort flow BE_{11} in host H_{11}. During [0..15], a guaranteed flow GR_{12} (shaped to $0.8Mb/s$) and a best-effort flow BE_{12} are active in host H_{12}. As it can be seen in Figure 6,

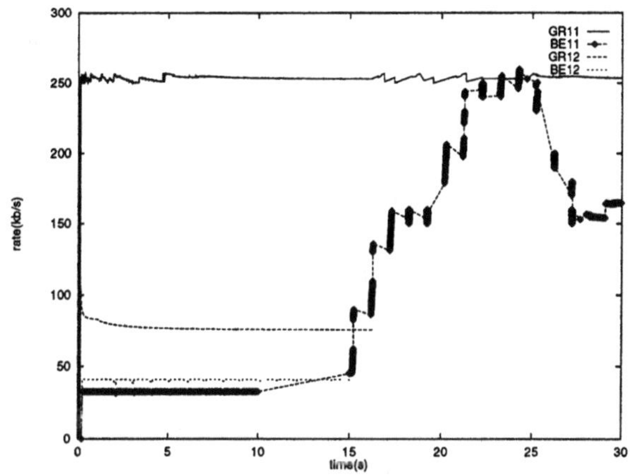

Figure 6 The inter-node bandwidth share protocol results

at time 15, when host H_{12} becomes idle, flow BE_{11} is enabled to consume the excess bandwidth (its rate approximates $1.5Mb/s$). At time 20, when gateway $G2$ becomes idle, flow BE_{11} sees its rate grow up to $2.5Mb/s$. At time 25, when gateway $G2$ becomes active again, best-effort flow BE_{11} sees its rate reduced to $1.5Mb/s$ since flows from gateway $G2$ are now able to consume their allocated bandwidth ($1Mb/s$).

5. CONCLUSION

In this paper, we have presented a bandwidth regulation mechanism able to control link bandwidth in a LAN connected to a VPN. The mechanism copes with best-effort and guaranteed flows so that bandwidth left unused by guaranteed flows is divided among best-effort ones throughout the LAN. We used a tree representation of the LAN nodes. We introduced two new concepts called inter-node bandwidth share and intra-host regulation. We explained how both of them dynamically enforce bandwidth regulation over the whole network. We also presented a new algorithm called the fair shaper used at the leaf nodes and introduced some implementation details in a Solaris 2.5 operating system. The bandwidth manager is shown to achieve near to optimal bandwidth use and traffic regulation.

REFERENCES

[1] ATM-Forum. Traffic Management Specification, version 4.0. ATM Forum/af-tm-0056.000, April 1996.

[2] R. Bell. Virtual private Networks: The Major Issues, problems and Opportunities. Presented at the IEE half-day Colloquium on Virtual Networking, October 1993.

[3] J. Bennet and H. Zhang. Hierarchical Packet Fair Queueing Algorithms. Presented at ACM SIGCOMM'96, August 1996.

[4] B. Braden, L. Zhang, S. Berson, S. Herzog, and S. Jamin. Resource ReSerVation Protocol (RSVP) – Version 1 Functional Specification. IETF RFC 2205, September 1997.

[5] A. Demers, S. Keshav, and S. Shenker. Analysis and Simulation of a Fair Queueing Algorithm. *Journal of Internetworking Research and experience*, pages 3–26, October 1990.

[6] S. Floyd and V. Jacobson. Link-Sharing and Resource Management Models for Packet Networks. *ACM/IEEE Transactions on networking, Vol. 3, No. 4*, pages 365–386, 1995.

[7] S. Fotedar, M. Gerla, P. Crocetti, and L. Fratta. ATM Virtual Private Networks. *Communications of the ACM*, pages 101–109, February 1995.

[8] B. Gleeson and J. Heinanen. A Framewrok for IP based Virtual Private Networks. Work in progress draft-gleeson-vpn-framework-00.txt, October 1998.

[9] S.J. Golestani. A Self-Clocked Fair Queueing Scheme for Broadband Applications. In *Proceedings of IEEE INFOCOM'94*, pages 636–646, April 1994.

[10] L. Lamti and H. Afifi. A Hierarchical Bandwidth Manager for Local Area Network Outlets. Presented at IEEE Globecom'98, November 1998.

[11] L. Lamti and H. Afifi. The Fair Shaper: An Efficient Mechanism for Internet Bandwidth Share over ATM in a Multi-Tasks OS. In *IEEE ATM workshop ATM'98*, pages 56–64, May 1998.

[12] A. Parekh and R. Gallager. A Generalized Processor Sharing Approach to Flow Control - The Single Node Case. *ACM/IEEE Transactions on networking Vol. 1, No. 3*, pages 344–357, 1993.

[13] I. Stoica and H. Zhang. A Hierarchical Fair Service Curve Algorithm for Link-Sharing Real-Time and Priority Services. Presented at ACM SIGCOMM'97, September 1997.

[14] Berkley University. *ns [online]*. available http://www-nrg.ee.lbl.gov/ns, 1998.

[15] S. Walters and M. Ahmed. Broadband Virtual Private Networks and their Evolution. Presented at XIV ISS, October 1992.

CIRCUIT EMULATION OVER IP NETWORKS

Raffaele Noro, Maher Hamdi and Jean-Pierre Hubaux
Institute for computer Communications and Applications,
EPFL-DI-ICA, 1015 Lausanne, Switzerland
{noro, hamdi, hubaux}@epfl.ch

Abstract

Recent developments in transmission and switching technology has made available low-cost gigabit network capacity for packet-based WANs (e.g., IP over WDM), that will not require the intermediate SONET/SDH multiplexing layer. For competitive operators that want to minimize their investment by deploying *native* IP over WDM networks, Circuit Emulation over IP gives support to the important class of legacy circuit-based equipment (e.g., T1/E1 multiplexers), which otherwise will require the deployment of an expensive telecommunication infrastructure, including SONET/SDH equipment. At the user interface, Circuit Emulation is required to maintain the same service of a circuit-based network, including synchronization and structured data delivery. In this paper we design the algorithm and the protocol that provide these two features. First, we identify the protocols and mechanisms used in the Internet and their ability to be used for Circuit Emulation. Second, we address the problem of synchronization and we propose an algorithm for efficient source clock recovery and handling of delay variations. Finally, we show through simulations that Circuit Emulation over IP provides the needed service performance at the user interface.

1. INTRODUCTION

In recent years, important progress has been done in transmission and swithing technology and is becoming possible to deploy low-cost, high-speed *packet-based backbones* for Wide Area Networks (WAN), for example by running the Internet Protocol (IP) directly over Wavelength Division Multiplexing (WDM) layers. Native IP over WDM will be the preferred solution for the large majority of new network operators: indeed, it allows to more efficiently transport the increasing amount of Internet traffic across their high capacity transmission infrastructure (e.g., CATV and/or fiber), and without investing in expensive telecommunication equipment used for Synchronous Optical Network/Synchronous Digital Hierachy (SONET/SDH) networks.

However, given the increasing demand for circuit-based leased lines (i.e., T1/E1 and T3/E3), these new operators would maximize their benefits by providing support to legacy *circuit-based equipment.* Circuit Emulation over IP permits to map T1/E1 traffic (as well as other digital signals of the Plesiochronous Digital Hierarchy- PDH), in IP packets to be transported over an Internet-optimized infrastructure.

The mapping of isochronous traffic, like T1/E1, into IP packets presents several challenges which are only partially addressed in the literature. In particular, as already highlighted in the case of Circuit Emulation over ATM [8], the service offered by Circuit Emulation at the user interface (i.e., the edge between the network and the user equipment) must include *synchronization* and *structured data delivery.*

On the contrary of PDH signals transported in SONET/SDH networks, synchronization cannot be transferred end-to-end in a transparent way, since IP does not provide any mechanism for synchronous transport, such as in the Time Division Multiplexing (TDM) of PDH and SONET/SDH. As a consequence, *clock recovery* and *dejittering* must be performed in the receiver of the IP packets. While the problem of dejittering is somehow similar to the case of packet audio and packet video applications (e.g., [1, 14]), the problem of clock recovery cannot be solved with conventional algorithms based on Phase Locked Loops (PLLs). Under normal conditions of jitter in the Internet, the duration of the convergence period become prohibitively long with PLLs (in the order of minutes or more [9]) for good performance in the steady state, thus causing loss due to overflow/underflow of the dejittering buffer.

The contribution of this paper is twofold. The first contribution consists of a *method for clock recovery* that relies on a Least-square Linear Regression (LLR) algorithm that, unlike PLLs, achieves accurate synchronization within few processing cycles, thus overcoming the limitation of PLLs. The second contribution consists in the *design of the protocol* for supporting the encapsulation and synchronization of PDH traffic in an IP packet stream. The protocol is based on existing features of the Real-Time Protocol/Real-Time Control Protocol (RTP/RTCP [13]), such as the Time Stamp (TS) field -used for dejittering-, and also some extended functionality of the RTP/RTCP, such as the Source Clock Indication (SCI) and the Spacing fields -used for clock recovery and data structure delivery, respectively.

The paper is organized as follows. In Section 2 we define the role of the Circuit Emulation adapter, which is the device implementing the interface between the IP network and the user equipment. In Section 3 we describe the problem of synchronizing a circuit-emulation receiver, we survey past work in this area and we propose a solution based on the LLR algorithm. In Section 4 we describe the protocol designed for Circuit Emulation. In Section 5 we evaluate the performance of the protocol through simulations and in Section 6 we give some concluding remarks.

2. DESIGN OF CIRCUIT EMULATION

Circuit Emulation is implemented as a network adapter which permits to the PDH user equipment to plug in the IP network as it was a conventional circuit-switched network (Fig. 1).

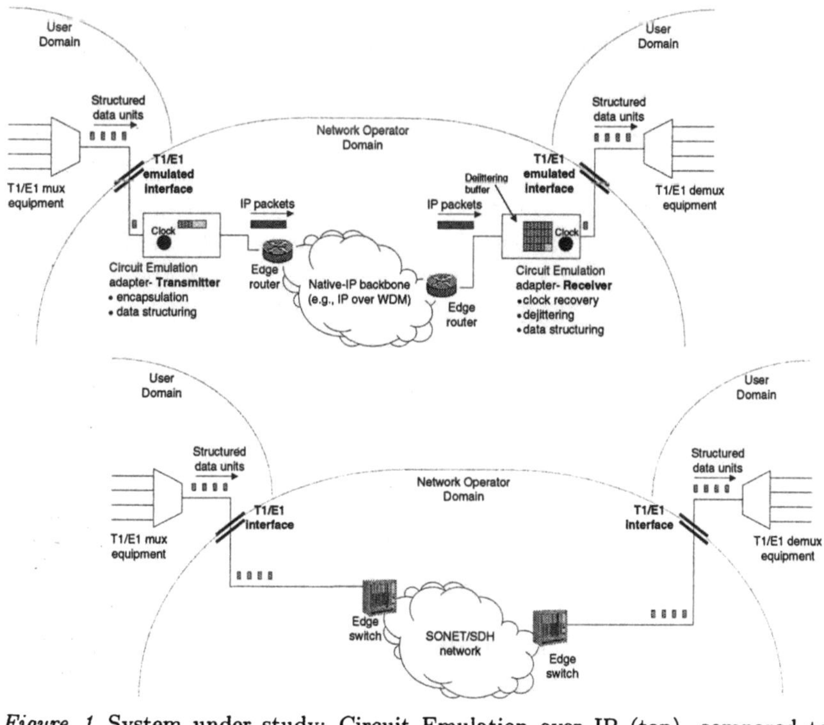

Figure 1 System under study; Circuit Emulation over IP (top), compared to the conventional circuit-switched case (bottom)

In the case of Fig. 1, the T1/E1 multiplexer is able to send/receive data units in *structures*, which correspond to groups of bits to write/read simultaneously. The *Transmitter* collects data units from the T1/E1 equipment and write them in packets. The *Receiver* receives packets out of the IP network interface, writes them in a receiver buffer and delivers each data unit at a precise delivery instant, under the control of the receiver clock that needs to be properly synchronize.

Designing Circuit Emulation consists of designing the functionality allocated to both Transmitter and Receiver. To accommodate the requirements of different synchronous applications [8], the circuit emulation service should provide:

- structuring of the data units to be output (any group of bits and bytes - including a whole packet)
- delivery of data units at the specified, varying rate (the traffic generated by the multiplexer may vary, according to the number of input lines that are simultaneously active)[1]
- constant end-to-end delay (of individual data units)
- handling of data losses (this point is not treated in this paper and is left for further study)

It can be observed that the need for constant *end-to-end delay* puts stringent requirements on the *synchronization* between Transmitter and Receiver. Indeed, to provide constant end-to-end delay, the Receiver must be equipped with a buffer that absorbs early arrivals of packets. The stability of this buffer (i.e., no overflow/underflow) is guaranteed only when the clock rates of the Transmitter and of the Receiver are strictly the same, that is, when clocks are synchronized.

Source clock recovery is therefore the first functionality to consider for Circuit Emulation.

3. SOURCE CLOCK RECOVERY

Clock recovery (or synchronization) is a critical issue in any synchronous system. Fig. 2 shows the effect on the receiver buffer occupancy when the receiver clock is 1% slower than the transmitter clock. The x-axis is the time seen by the source, and the y-axis is the level of

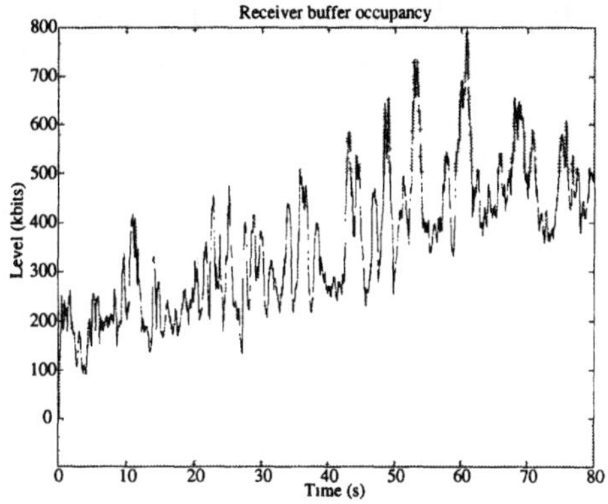

Figure 2 Overflow due to a slower receiver clock

a receiver buffer. Buffer overflow will occur since the rate seen by the receiver is different of the rate seen by the sender

The skew between source and receiver clock is responsible for the long term variation of buffer level observed in Fig. 2. The short term fluctuations of the buffer level are due to the varying network delay and play-out rate.

Although synchronization schemes without any synchronized clock have been proposed, optimal performance is clearly achieved when the receiver clock is somehow synchronized to the source clock. Clock synchronization schemes consists of a protocol and a mechanism. The protocol is based either on information contained in the data stream itself (e.g., SRTS of AAL type 1 [8]) or on a synchronization flow independent of the main data stream (e.g., NTP [9]). In the last case the synchronization is either global (e.g., such as provided by the GPS) or point-to-point.

There are numerous synchronization mechanisms that are described in the literature. PLLs are extensively used to synchronize telecommunications equipment [4] as well as multimedia systems [12]. In [5] a probabilistic method for reading remote clocks in distributed systems subject to unbound communication delay is proposed. The method becomes more accurate as the round-trip time becomes shorter. Moon et al. [10] have recently proposed a scheme for removing clock skew in traces of network delay measurements. This scheme, based on a linear programming algorithm, seems most appropriate for post-processing of network delay measurements.

In the Internet, the Network Time Protocol (NTP, [9]) consists of a set of time servers dispersed worldwide. NTP messages are processed by servers and clients in order to synchronize clocks with an absolute time base, the Coordinated Universal Time (UTC). NTP is built on top of IP and uses UDP. A digital PLL is employed as synchronization mechanism. PLL design is such that in the presence of an high amount of jitter, such as in the Internet, synchronization is maintained only at the expense of an intolerable long transient period [11]. It may be therefore difficult to maintain synchronization of dispersed host with the required accuracy, even if it looks substantially appropriate for LAN applications.

We propose an alternative synchronization method based on a Least-square Linear Regression (LLR) algorithm, which slaves the receiver clock to the transmitter clock with greater accuracy. We define the following terminology used for the LLR:

- clock indication: sample of the source clock,
- source clock: master time measured at the source,
- receiver clock: free-running time measured at the receiver,
- recovered clock: slaved time obtained with synchronization,
- t_s: measurement of the source clock,
- t_r: measurement of the receiver clock when source clock is t_s,
- $\hat{t}_s$: estimate of the recovered clock at t_s,
- t_{si}: value of the i-th clock indication issued by the source,
- t_{ri}: receiver clock when the i-th clock indication is received,
- a: actual clock skew between source clock and receiver clock (i.e., frequency ratio),
- b: initial clock offset between source clock and receiver clock,
- $\hat{a}$: estimate of the clock skew,
- $\hat{b}$: estimate of the clock offset.

The time model [5] that relates source and receiver clock is of the form

$$t_s = a \cdot t_r + b \tag{1}$$

a and b are typically unknown and the goal of any clock recovery method consists in estimating $\hat{a}$ and $\hat{b}$ such that the error between t_s and the estimate $\hat{t}_s = \hat{a} \cdot t_r + \hat{b}$ is minimized. Our approach is based on the observation that the points (t_{si}, t_{ri}) are distributed close to a straight line (i.e., on the straight line if network delay is constant) whose slope and offset are, respectively, the estimate of clock skew and the estimate of clock offset (minus the average of the network delay). The values of $\hat{a}$ and $\hat{b}$ are computed by minimizing the Mean Square Error (MSE) with least-square linear regression

$$\hat{a} = \frac{m\sum t_{si}^2 - (\sum t_{si})^2}{m\sum(t_{si}t_{ri}) - (\sum t_{ri}\sum t_{si})}, \tag{2}$$

$$\hat{b} - \frac{\sum t_{si}\sum(t_{ri}t_{si}) - (\sum t_{ri}\sum t_{si}^2)}{m\sum(t_{si}t_{ri}) - (\sum t_{ri}\sum t_{si})} \tag{3}$$

Only the m last received clock indications are processed by the algorithm. This is known as the Durbin algorithm and is based on the assumption of stationary distribution of jitter. Similar methods for non-stationary distribution also exist. The method discussed here has a shorter duration of the transient period, since m (the upper bound) does not need to be very large (in the order of 100). It is also much faster than a PLL with equivalent steady-state accuracy of the recovered clock [11]. This avoids severe losses due to overflows and underflows of the receiver buffer during the transient period. Furthermore, the method can be as simple as a second-order PLL when recursion is used [11].

Performance

The source clock recovery method is simulated in the following conditions:

- Simulated duration of 160 s;
- Source clock indication generated at 100 ms rate;
- $m = 1000$;

For the network jitter, we refer to the model of [2] which is further discussed in the Section 5 for the simulation of the network delay. Fig. 3 shows the distribution of the network delay around its average value.

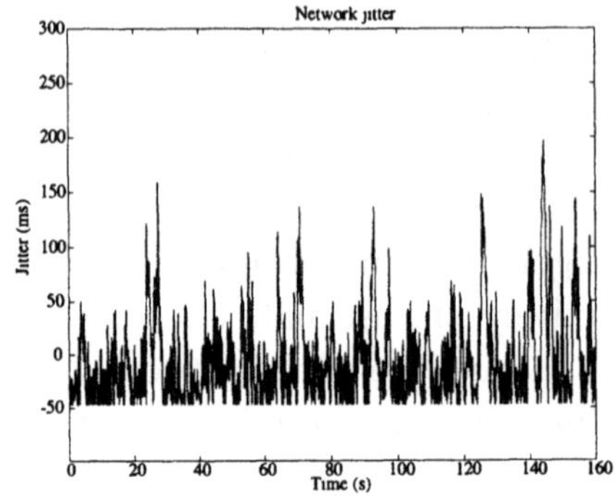

Figure 3 Jitter during the experiment

Fig. 4 (left) and Fig. 4 (right) illustrate the performance of the clock recovery method in the presence of the network jitter. The x-axis represents the master time measured at the source. In Fig. 4 (left) we plot the accuracy of the recovered clock, defined as the difference $t_s - \hat{t}_s$ and measured in ms. In Fig. 4 (right) we plot the stability of the estimate clock skew, defined as the difference between the output of the Eq. 3 and its actual value (expressed in parts per million, ppm).

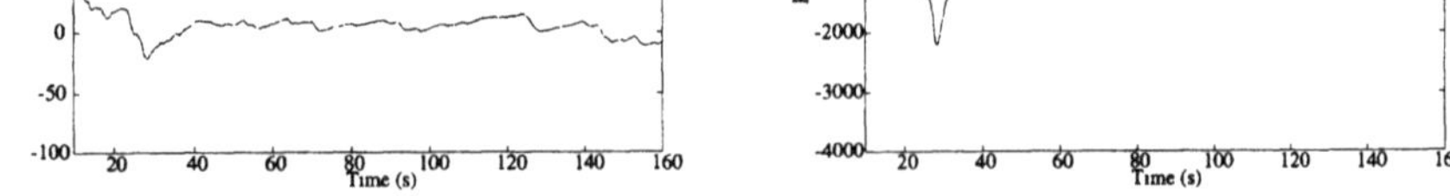

Figure 4 The accuracy of the recovered clock (left), and the stability (right)

The comparison of Fig. 3 and Fig. 4 (left) shows that the residual jitter of the recovered clock is 10 times smaller than the network jitter in the steady state. We can also observe a transient period of around 40 s. The steady-state is reached when a sufficient number (i.e., 400 in this case) of source clock indications have been processed by the LLR algorithm. As shown in [11] the transient period is around 100 times shorter than the transient period of a PLL with an equivalent steady-state accuracy.

4. CIRCUIT EMULATION FUNCTIONALITY

In this section we analyze in greater detail the functionality needed for Circuit Emulation and we define the use of RTP/RTCP for this application. In the context of packet audio and packet video over the Internet, the RTP/RTCP [13] is well established as the standard for transporting time-sensitive data. Its native functionalities include timestamping of packets and sequencing. A number of implementations of real-time applications is based on RTP as the transport layer of audiovisual data (e.g., [6]).

In our case, we extend the features of the RTP in order to implement the functionalities of Circuit Emulation: handling of data structures, the handling of delay variation, and the clock recovery at the receiver.

Functional Blocks

The Fig. 5 illustrates both Transmitter and Receiver. We define the *spacing* as the time (corresponding to the emission rate) between two consecutive structured data units which enter the system, the *timestamp* as the time at which a packet leaves the source, *structure* as the number of bits that compose a data unit and *d_max* as the maximum packing delay of a data unit.

The maximum network delay influences the design of the receiver buffer. This bound can be a guaranteed value, a stochastic value (i.e., via a reservation mechanism [3]) or an estimated value (e.g., in best effort Internet). Separate reservation mechanisms are clearly necessary to optimize the end-to-end performance of circuit emulation.

The payload of a packet is filled-up by consecutive data units and is transmitted either when its fullness has reached a predefined level (i.e., a bound of the packing delay) or when a change in the spacing of arrival units has been detected[2]. Therefore, packets can be of variable size.

While packets suffer from *network jitter*, individual data units suffer also from *packing jitter*. The purpose of the receiver buffer is thus to absorb both transmission and packing delay [8], while the role the clock recovery method is to guarantee that the spacing between two data units at the output is the same of the input (which does not mean

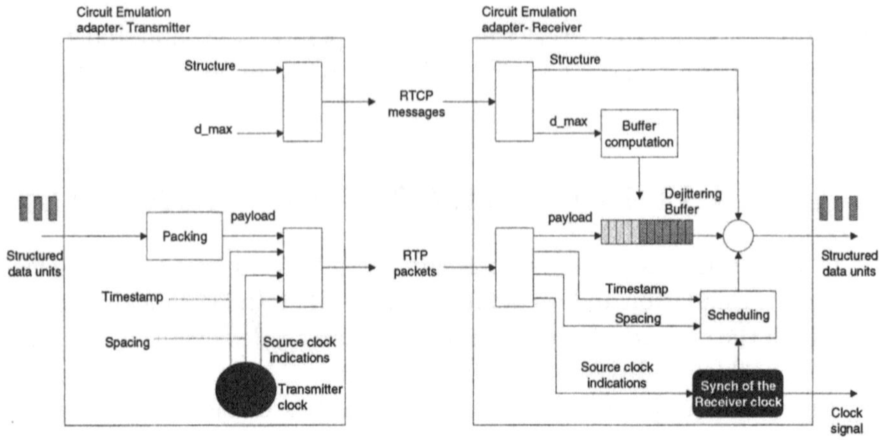

Figure 5 Functional blocks of Circuit Emulation adapters

that all data units have the same spacing - the rate can be variable). The receiver clock can optionally generate a synchronization signal, if specifically required by some of the equipment attached to the output lines (e.g., video decoders) of the demultiplexer.

The data structure is identified at the beginning of the session and must be communicated during the session setup phase via an RTCP message. Even if under normal conditions is not supposed to change, it can optionally be dynamically modified during the session with a successive RTCP message. Data structures can be any group of bits or bytes and even whole packets[3] that are exchanged between the circuit emulation adapter and the application. The spacing between consecutive data units is expressed in units of the Transmitter clock and is encoded in each RTP packet header. The spacing is combined with the timestamp to obtain the delivery instant of every individual data unit.

The receiver buffer handles the variability of delay. The design of the buffer depends on several factors: the network delay, the packing delay, the input rate and the maximum packet size. The design of the receiver buffer is a well studied problem [1, 14] which is not tackled here. The maximum packing delay is provided through RTCP messages, while the characteristics of the network delay (e.g., average and maximum value) has to be provided by the reservation protocol (or estimated in the case of best effort).

The source clock recovery method has been described in Section 3. The source clock indications are carried in an extension to the RTP packet header. For interoperability with existing implementations, we consider that the common timebase has a frequency resolution f_n equivalent to the 4.3 GHz resolution of the NTP (at most). The source frequency is expressed as f_n/x, where x is a rational. Information about the source clock is periodically inserted by the source to allow the receiver to adjust its clock drift. It is important to note that the receiver can ignore this information and operate with the local clock or NTP (i.e., reducing the accuracy of the clock synchronization).

RTP/RTCP Extensions

Circuit Emulation with RTP/RTCP is supported by two types of *RTCP messages*, to indicate *d_max* and *structure*, and by two types of *RTP packet extensions*, for carrying source clock indications and/or spacing.

A 32-bit field of a Sender Report (SR) or Application-defined (APP) RTCP message supports this function. It is partitioned in two 16-bit fields: the first field carries the value of d_max in units of the source clock, the second field indicates the length of data units in bits. Fig 6 illustrates both cases.

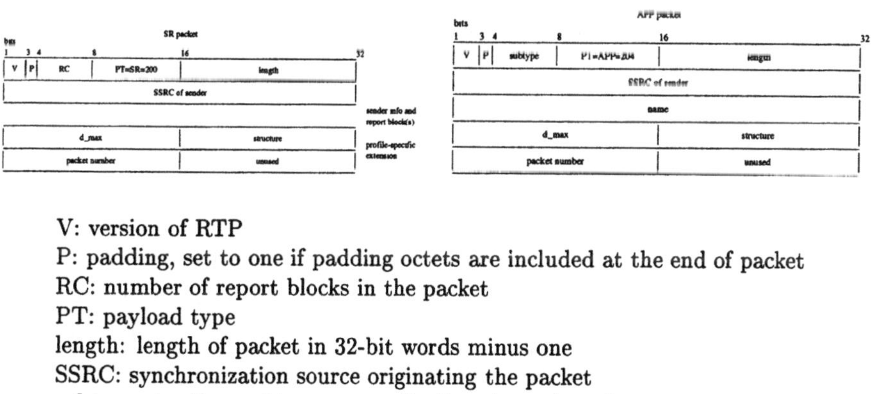

V: version of RTP
P: padding, set to one if padding octets are included at the end of packet
RC: number of report blocks in the packet
PT: payload type
length: length of packet in 32-bit words minus one
SSRC: synchronization source originating the packet
subtype: to allow subtypes or application-dependent data
name: 4 octets to identify the name of the APP

d_max: maximum packet delay in source clock units (zero if undefined)
structure: length of data units (in bits, zero means one bit)
packet number: first RTP data packet subject to d_max and structure

Figure 6 Usage of RTCP packets

RTP packet header extensions contain the spacing, the source clock indication and the timestamp. The RTP packet payload contains the user data. In the header extension, a first 16-bit field is used to encode the spacing in units of the Transmitter clock, a second 64-bit field (if present) carries the source clock indication. The overhead introduced by the latter must be kept within a reasonable limit (e.g., not exceed the 1 % of the session traffic, for example one source clock indication field each 64 ms for a 1 Mbit/s session). This is illustrated by Fig. 7

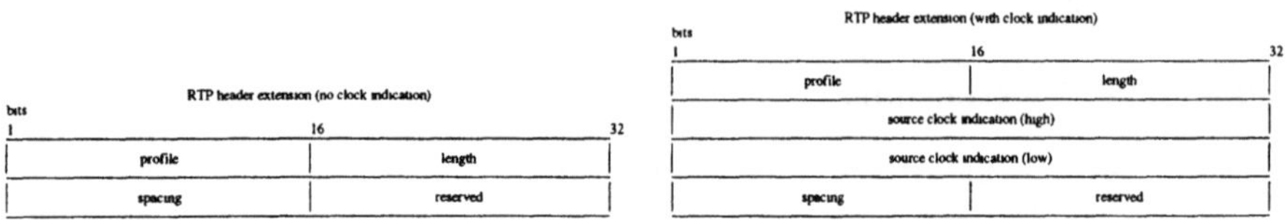

profile: defines the CES
length: length of header extension in 32-bit words minus one (either 1 or 3)

spacing: temporal distance between data units in Transmitter clock units
source clock indication: absolute value of source clock in units of 4.3 GHz
reserved: for future use

Figure 7 Usage of RTP packets

5. RESULTS

We have carried out simulations of Circuit Emulation for the transport of coded audiovisual information in MPEG-2 Transport Stream [7] format. The goal is to show that the delay jitter of data units, i.e., the end-to-end performance, is below the threshold of ±4 ms defined for this particular type of applications. The parameters of the simulation are the following:

- Source emission rate varying between 1 Mbit/s and 250 kbit/s;
- Size of data units of one byte;
- Size of RTP packet payload of 188 bytes;
- Geometric distribution of the network jitter with 100 ms of minimum delay, 780 ms of maximum delay and 154 ms of average delay (Fig. 3);
- Window length of the source recovery method $m = 1000$;

- Source clock indication generated every 100 ms;
- Simulated duration of 160 s

The network jitter model is consistent with the results presented in [2]. The inter-arrival process of packets emitted at regular intervals δ fits with a geometric distribution

$$\text{Prob}\{(t_r^{i+1} - t_r^i) = k \cdot \delta, k \geq 0\} = p \cdot (1-p)^k \tag{4}$$

where p is a decreasing function of δ. In our experiment we have taken $\delta = 3.4$ ms and $p = 0.52$ [4]. We also assumed lossless transmission.

directly affected by the residual jitter of the recovered clock (see Section 3). Fig 8 (left) shows the delay experienced by each delivered data unit during 16 s of the experiment.

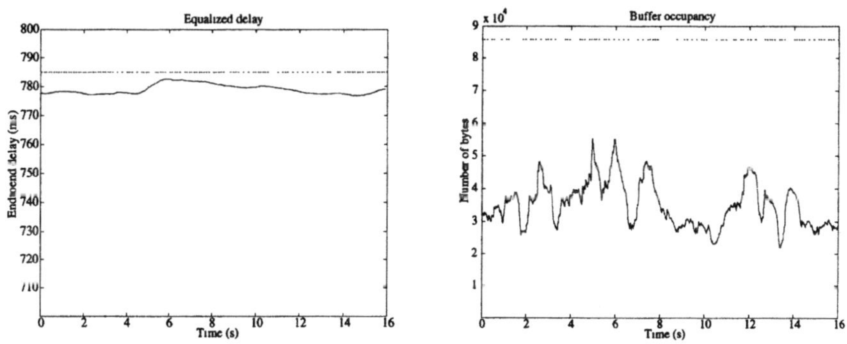

Figure 8 Effect of residual jitter in (left), and buffer occupancy (right)

Fig. 8 (left) shows that circuit emulation provides the required end-to-end performance by maintaining the jitter below ± 4 ms.

The receiver buffer occupancy reflects the fact that data units are generated and consumed at different rate. As shown by Fig. 8 (right), occupancy increases during bursts and tends to be lower during low-activity periods.

It is important to note that the overhead induced by the source clock indication has been maintained below the 1 % of the average rate.

6. CONCLUSION

In this paper we described the design of Circuit Emulation over IP. The Circuit Emulation allows legacy circuit-based equipment to be supported by IP-based networks. Two purposes are served: network operators has to deploy and maintain only one network infrastructure while users with traditional network access does not need to upgrade their equipment. We identified three key features of Circuit Emulation: handling of data structure, handling of delay variations and clock recovery. We discussed the ability of protocols and mechanisms of the Internet to support the circuit emulation service.

The clock recovery method is the second contribution of this paper. As an improved alternative to NTP, we proposed a method for clock recovery which slaves the Receiver clock to the Transmitter clock in the presence of clock skew and network jitter. The method is based on a Least-square Linear Regression algorithm. Our simulation results show its ability to compensate for severe amounts of network jitter in a short convergence period.

Finally, at the protocol level, we fit the functionality of Circuit Emulation with the features of RTP/RTCP. Clock indications, data rate, and data structure information are some additional feature added to RTP/RTCP. The proposed protocol has a number of characteristics in common with the circuit emulation in ATM. In fact, RTP over UDP/IP plays the same role of AAL type 1 on top of ATM (while the Least-square Linear Regression mechanism plays the same role of the SRTS mechanism). One additional feature is the ability to support variable rate streams.

We emphasize that these conclusions are based on the assumptions used in this paper. Factors not taken into account can alter the conclusions. Examples of these factors are the effects of packet loss on the clock recovery process, the handling of data loss at the delivery process and the appropriate interface of the protocol to external reservation protocols (i.e., the user-to-control plane interface). The impact of these factors on Circuit Emulation are interesting subjects for future research.

Notes

[1] This represents an optional feature. However, the adapter itself can be arranged in order to not transmit the idle time slots of the PDH signal, since they can be easily regenerated by the Receivers. The usage of network bandwidth results optimized

[2] assumption is made on the fact that emission rate is changed only at packet boundaries

[3] in RFC2250 [6] a single Transport Stream packet can be encapsulated in an RTP packet (although it is not an efficient scheme). In this case it is the whole payload of the RTP packet that is delivered to the Transport Stream decoder

[4] This means that 52 % of packets are assumed to reach the receiver in bursts, as a consequence of network overload. δ is the average of the packet emission interval

REFERENCES

[1] H. M. Ahmed, "Adaptive Terminal Synchronization in Packet Data Networks", *in Proc. of Globecom'89*, pp. 728–732, Dallas, Texas, Nov. 1989.

[2] J.-C. Bolot, "Characterizing End-to-End Packet Delay and Loss in the Internet", *Journal of High-Speed Networks*, vol. 2, pp. 305–323, Dec. 1993.

[3] R. Braden, L. Zhang, S. Berson, S. Herzog, and S. Jamin, "Resource ReServation Protocol (RSVP) - Version 1 Functional Specification", IETF RFC 2205, Sept. 1997.

[4] S. Bregni, "A Historical Perspective on Telecommunications Network Synchronization", *IEEE Communications Magazine*, vol. 36, pp. 158–166, June 1998.

[5] F. Cristian, "Probabilistic clock synchronization", *Distributed Computing*, vol. 3, pp. 146–158, Dec. 1989.

[6] D. Hoffman, G. Fernando, V. Goyal, and M. Civanlar, "RTP Payload Format for MPEG1/MPEG2 Video", IETF RFC 2250, Jan. 1998.

[7] ISO/IEC, *Information technology - Generic coding of moving pictures and associated audio information - Part 1: Systems*, Oct. 1994, DIS 13818-1.

[8] ITU-T Study Group 13, "B-ISDN ATM Adaptation Layer Specification, Type 1 AAL", ITU-T Recommendation I.363.1, Aug. 1996.

[9] D.L. Mills, "Internet Time Synchronization: The Network Time Protocol", *IEEE Transactions on Communications*, vol. 39, pp. 1482–1493, Oct. 1991.

[10] S. B. Moon, P. Skelly, and D. Towsley, "Estimation and Removal of Clock Skew from Network Delay Measurements", *in Proc. of Infocom'99*, pp. 227–234, New York, Mar. 1999.

[11] R. Noro and J.-P. Hubaux, "Clock Synchronization of MPEG-2 Services over Packet Networks", *Telecommunication Systems*, vol. 11, pp. 3–16, Mar. 1999.

[12] M. Perkins and P. Skelly, "A Hardware MPEG Clock Recovery Experiment in the Presence of ATM Jitter", ATM Forum contrib. #94-0434, Apr. 1994.

[13] H. Schulzrinne, S. L. Casner, R. Frederick, and V. Jacobson, "RTP: A Transport Protocol for Real-Time Applications", IETF RFC 1889, Jan. 1996.

[14] H. Schulzrinne, "Voice Communication Across the Internet: A Network Voice Terminal", Technical Report 92-50, Univ. of Massachusetts, July 1992.

PART 6

WIRELESS

ON THE ANALYSIS OF CELLULAR IP ACCESS NETWORKS

András G. Valkó
Ericsson Research
andras.valko@lt.eth.ericsson.se

Javier Gomez, Sanghyo Kim, Andrew T. Campbell
Center for Telecommunications Research, Columbia University, New YorK
[javierg,shkim2,campbell] @comet.columbia.edu

Abstract

Mobile IP represents a simple and scalable global mobility solution but lacks support for fast handoff control and real-time location tracking found in cellular networks today. In contrast, third generation cellular systems offer seamless mobility support but are built on complex and costly connection-oriented networking infrastructure that lacks the inherent flexibility, robustness and scalability found in IP networks. Future wireless networks should be capable of combining the strengths of both approaches without inheriting their weaknesses. In this paper we present analysis of Cellular IP, a new host mobility protocol which represents one such approach. Cellular IP incorporates a number of important cellular system features but remains firmly based on IP design principles. The protocol presented in this paper is implemented as extensions to the ns simulator.

1. INTRODUCTION

Recent initiatives to add mobility to the Internet mostly focus on the issue of address translation [2] through the introduction of location directories and address translation agents. In these protocols (e.g., Mobile IP [8]), packets addressed to a mobile host are delivered using regular IP routing to a temporary address assigned to the mobile host at its actual point of attachment. This approach results in simple and scalable schemes that offer global mobility support. It is not appropriate, however, for fast mobility and smooth handoff because after each migration a local address must be obtained and communicated to a possibly distant location directory or home agent (HA). Cellular mobile telephony systems are founded on radically different concepts. Instead of aiming at global mobility support, cellular systems are optimized to provide fast and smooth handoff in a restricted geographical area. In the area of coverage mobile users have wireless access to the mobility unaware global telephony network. A scalable forwarding protocol interconnects distinct cellular networks to support roaming between them.

Restricting the cellular coverage to a limited geographical area limits the potential number of connected users. This makes it feasible to maintain per mobile states which we believe is key to delivering fast handoff support to mobile hosts. Having per-mobile location information allows the cellular system to support location independent addressing avoiding the need to change addresses during each intra-network migration. Even in limited geographical areas, however, the number of users can grow to a point where using fast lookup techniques for per user data bases is no longer viable. In addition, mobility management requires mobile hosts to send registration information after migration. The resulting signaling overhead has significant impact on the performance of the wireless access network. To overcome this problem, cellular telephony systems require mobiles to register every migration only when they are engaged in "active" calls. In contrast, "idle" mobile hosts send registration messages less frequently and as a result can roam in large areas without loading the network and the mobility management system. The location of idle mobile hosts is only approximately known to the network at any one time. To establish a call to an idle mobile, the mobile host must be searched for in a limited set of cells. This feature called *passive connectivity* allows the cellular network to accommodate a very large number of users at any instance without overloading the network with large volumes of mobility management signaling information and messaging.

Cellular networks offer a number of desirable features which if applied correctly could enhance the performance of future wireless IP networks without loosing any of important flexibility, scalability and robustness properties that characterize IP networks. However, there are fundamental architectural differences between cellular and IP networks that make the application of cellular techniques to IP challenging. Cellular telephony systems rely on a restrictive "circuit" model that requires connection establishment prior to communication. In contrast, IP networks perform routing on a per packet basis. In addition, today's cellular systems are strictly based on hierarchical networks and use costly mobile-aware nodes (e.g., MSC). We believe that a future Cellular Internet should be founded on IP, inheriting its simplicity, flexibility and robustness. A Cellular Internet should leverage mobility management and handoff techniques found in cellular networks. A single scalable host mobility protocol should be capable of flexibly supporting pico, campus and metropolitan area networks based on a set of simple and cheap network nodes that can be easily interconnected to form arbitrary topologies that operate without prior configuration.

In this paper, we present analysis of *Cellular IP* [10] [11], a new mobile host protocol that is optimized to provide access to a Mobile IP enabled Internet in support of fast moving wireless hosts. Cellular IP incorporates a number of important cellular principles but remains firmly based on IP design principles. Because of its IP based design and the feature of passive connectivity, Cellular IP can scale from pico to metropolitan area installations. The Cellular IP distributed location management and routing algorithms lend themselves to a simple, efficient and low cost implementation for host mobility requiring no new packet formats, encapsulation or address space allocation beyond what is already present in IP. The paper is structured as follows. In Section 2, we present an overview of the Cellular IP protocol. Following this in Section 3 we analyze the protocol which is implemented as extensions to the ns simulator. In particular we discuss the handoff performance and cost of mobility management. We present some concluding remarks in Section 4.

2. PROTOCOL OVERVIEW

Features

The universal component of a Cellular IP network is a *base station* which serves as a wireless access point but at the same time routes IP packets and integrates the mobility specific control functionality traditionally found in Mobile Switching Centers (MSC) and Base Station Controllers (BSC). Base stations are built using the regular IP forwarding engine, however, IP routing is replaced by Cellular IP routing and location management. Cellular IP access networks are connected to the Internet via *gateway* routers. Mobile hosts attached to an access network use the IP address of their gateway as their Mobile IP care-of address. Figure 1 illustrates the path taken by packets addressed to a mobile host.

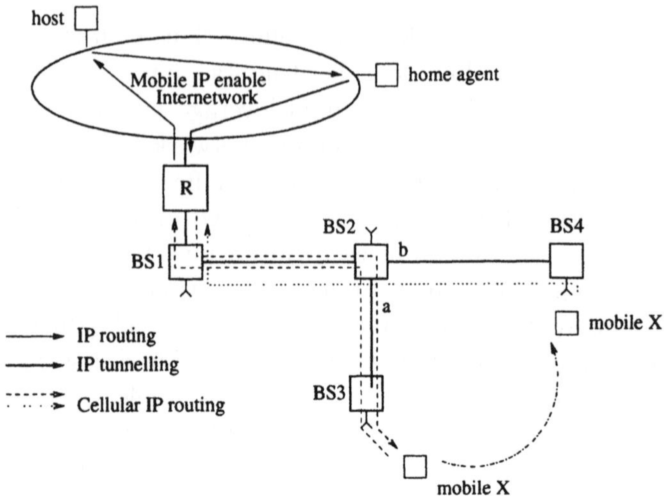

Figure 1 A Cellular IP Access Network Interconnected to a Mobile IP enabled Internet

Assuming Mobile IPv4 [8] and no route optimization [5], packets will be first routed to the host's home agent and then tunneled to a gateway. The gateway "detunnels" packets and forwards them toward the base stations. Inside the Cellular IP network, mobile hosts are identified by their home addresses and data packets are routed without encapsulation, tunneling or address conversion. The Cellular IP routing protocol ensures that packets are delivered to the host's actual location; that is, the base station that serves as the mobile host's point of attachment to the Cellular IP access network. Packets transmitted by mobile hosts are first routed to a gateway and from there on to the global Mobile IP enabled Internet.

In Cellular IP, location management and handoff support are integrated with routing. To minimize control messaging, regular data packets transmitted by mobile hosts are used to establish host location information. *Uplink* packets are routed from mobile hosts to the gateway on a hop-by-hop basis. The path taken by these packets is cached by intermediate base stations. To route *downlink* packets addressed to a mobile host the path used by recently transmitted packets from the mobile host is reversed path routed. When the mobile host has no data to transmit it sends empty IP packets to the gateway to maintain its downlink "soft" routing state. Following the principle of passive connectivity mobile hosts that have not received packets for some period allow their downlink soft-state routes be cleared from the caches. In order to route packets to idle hosts a Cellular IP mechanism called *paging* is used. In what follows we provide a brief overview of the Cellular IP functions. For a full discussion of Cellular IP see [10] and for a full specification of the protocol see [11].

Routing

The Cellular IP gateway periodically broadcasts a beacon packet that is flooded in the access network. Base stations record the interface they last received this beacon through and use it to route packets toward the gateway. All packets transmitted by mobile hosts regardless of the destination address are routed to the gateway using these routes.

Packets transmitted by a mobile host traverse the access network nodes destined for the gateway. As these packets pass each node on route to the gateway their route information is recorded as follows. Each base station maintains a "soft-state" *routing cache.* When a data packet originated by a mobile host enters a base station the local routing cache stores the IP address of the source mobile host and the interface over which the packet entered the node. In the scenario illustrated in Figure 1 data packets are transmitted by a mobile host with IP address **X** and enter base station **BS2** through its interface **a**. In the routing cache of base station **BS2** this is indicated by a mapping **(X,a)**. This mapping remains valid for a system specific time called the *route-timeout* and its validity is renewed by each data packet that traverses the same interface coming from the same mobile host. As long as the mobile host is regularly sending data packets then base stations along the path (between the mobile's actual location and the gateway) maintain valid entries in their routing cache forming a soft-state route between the mobile host and gateway nodes. Packets addressed to the same mobile host are routed on a hop-by-hop basis using the established routing cache.

A mobile host may sometimes wish to maintain its routing cache mappings even though it is not regularly transmitting data packets. A typical example for this is when a mobile host is the receiver of a stream of UDP packets and has no data to transmit. To keep its routing cache mappings valid the mobile host transmits the *route-update packets* at regular intervals called *route-update time.* These packets are empty data packets addressed to the gateway. Route-update packets have the same effect on routing cache as normal data packets, however, they do not leave the Cellular IP network.

Handoff

The Cellular IP *hard handoff* is based on a simply approach that tolerates some potential packet loss in exchange for minimizing handoff messaging rather than guaranteeing zero packet loss. Handoff is initiated by mobile hosts in a Cellular IP access network. Hosts listen to beacons transmitted by base stations and initiate handoff based on signal strength measurements. To perform a handoff a mobile host has to tune its radio to the new base station and send a route-update packet. This creates routing cache mappings on route to a gateway hence configuring the downlink route to the new base station. Handoff latency is the time that elapses between the handoff and the arrival of the first packet through the new route. For hard handoff, this time will be equal to the round-trip time between the mobile host and the cross-over point which is the gateway in the worst case. During this time downlink packets may be lost. Mappings associated with the old base station are not cleared explicitly during handoff. Rather, they are cleared by a soft-state routing mechanism resident at each node in the Cellular IP access network on expiration of the route-timeout.

Before these mappings timeout a period exists when both the old and new downlink routes are valid and packets are delivered through both base stations. This feature is used in the *semisoft handoff* procedure that improves handoff performance but suits the lightweight nature of the base protocol by providing probabilistic guarantees instead of fully eliminating packet loss by, for example, retransmissions. Semisoft handoff adds a single temporary state to the soft state protocol in mobile hosts and base stations and scales well for a large number of mobile hosts and frequent handoffs.

The semisoft handoff procedure has two components. First, in order to reduce handoff latency, the routing cache mappings associated with the new base station must be created before the actual handoff takes place. When the mobile host initiates a handoff it first sends a *semisoft packet* to the new base station and immediately returns to listening to the old base station. While the host is still in connection with the old base station, the semisoft packet configures routing cache mappings associated with the new base station. After a *semisoft delay*, the host performs a regular handoff. The semisoft delay can be anything between the mobile-gateway round-trip time and the route-timeout. (In our ns simulation environment we use a conservative value of 100 ms). This delay ensures that by the time the host tunes its radio to the new base station its downlink packets are being delivered through both the old and new base stations.

Paging

Cellular IP defines an *idle mobile host* as one that has not received data packets for a system specific time called the *active-state-timeout.* Idle mobile hosts let their respective soft-state routing cache mappings timeout. These mobile hosts transmit *paging-update packets* at regular intervals defined by the *paging-update-time.* The paging-update packet is an empty IP packet addressed to the gateway that is distinguished from a route-update packet by its IP type parameter. The mobile host sends its paging-update packets to the base station that has the best signal quality. Similar to data and route-update packets, paging-update packets are routed on a hop-by-hop basis toward the gateway. Base stations may optionally maintain *paging cache.* A paging cache has the same format and operation as a routing cache with two differences. First, paging cache mappings have a longer timeout period called the *paging-timeout.* Second, paging cache mappings are updated by any packet sent by mobile hosts including paging-update packets. In contrast, routing cache mappings are updated by data and route-update packets sent by mobile hosts. This results in idle mobile hosts having mappings in paging caches but not in routing caches. In addition, active mobile hosts will have mappings in both types of cache. Packets addressed to a mobile host are normally routed by routing cache mappings. Paging occurs when a packet is addressed to an idle mobile host and the gateway or base stations find no valid routing cache mapping for the destination. If the base station has no paging cache, it will forward the packet on all its interfaces except the one the packet came through. Paging cache is used to avoid broadcast search procedures found in cellular systems. Base stations that have paging cache will only forward the paging packet if the destination has a valid paging cache mapping for the mobile host and only to the mapped interface(s). Without any paging cache the first packet addressed to an idle mobile is broadcast in the access network. While the packet does not experience extra delay it does, however, load the access network. Using paging caches, the network operator can restrict the paging load in exchange for memory, processing and bandwidth cost.

Idle mobile hosts that receive a packet move from idle to active state and start their active-state-timer and immediately transmit a route-update packet. This ensures that routing cache mappings are established quickly potentially limiting any further flooding of messages to mobile hosts in Cellular IP access networks.

3. ANALYSIS

In this section we analyze the handoff performance of Cellular IP access networks. We quantify the performance penalty associated with the Cellular IP handoff scheme which trades performance (e.g., packet loss and delay) for simplicity. Furthermore, we investigate the "cost" of mobility management for routing and paging in Cellular IP access networks. Determining the mobility management cost is important because different cellular system installations (e.g., pico-cellular and macro-cellular access networks) will operate under different mobility conditions.

Simulation Environment

The Cellular IP protocol is implemented as extensions to the ns simulator [7] which is widely used by the networking community to analyze IP networks. The Cellular IP simulation environment used for the reported results is shown in Figure 1; note that the simulator supports Cellular IP access networks of arbitrary topology. The assumptions and limitations of the Cellular IP ns simulation environment are as follows. First, an "ideal wireless interface" is used; that is, packets transmitted over the wireless interface encounter no delay, bit error or loss and congestion over the air interface is not modeled. Next, the beacon messages transmitted by a Cellular IP gateway are not modeled. The network is configured when the simulation session is initiated and the topology remains constant for the duration of the simulation. Finally, wireless cells are assumed to overlap and mobile hosts move from one cell to another in zero time. This does not limit the ns simulator's ability to study packet loss during handoff because such packet loss is mainly a product of misrouted packets.

Handoff Performance

The design of a fast and efficient handoff algorithm is central to the performance of a cellular access network especially in the case of networks that are comprised of small wireless cells with fast moving mobile hosts. One of the design goals of Cellular IP is to operate efficiently at very high handoff frequencies. In accordance with this design goal, the Cellular IP handoff algorithm avoids explicit signaling messages (used for example in cellular telephony and Mobile IP systems) and buffering or forwarding of packets [1] [4]. As a result Cellular IP packets may be lost during handoffs. In such cases we assume that packet loss is dealt with by higher layer protocols (e.g., TCP). In this section we analyze the performance of Cellular IP handoff to determine the performance penalty we pay for our simple approach to host mobility.

Delay

The impact of handoff on ongoing sessions is commonly characterized by the *handoff delay.* Handoff delay is usually defined as the time taken to resume normal traffic flow after a mobile host performs handoff. Though this does not fully determine the performance seen by applications, it is a good indication of the handoff performance. In [3] handoff delay is decomposed as *rendezvous* and *protocol time.* Rendezvous time refers to the time taken for a mobile host to attach to a new base station after it leaves the old base station. This time is related to wireless link characteristics, particularly to the inter-arrival time of beacons transmitted by base stations. Protocol time refers to the time taken to restore traffic flows/sessions once a mobile host has received a beacon from the new base station. In the following analysis we assume that the rendezvous time is small and handoff performance is determined by the protocol time. Rather than adopting the notations proposed in [3], we define the handoff delay as the time it takes a mobile host to receive the first packet through the new base station after it moved from the old to the new base station, which, as discussed earlier, we assume to take zero time.

In Cellular IP, handoff delay and packet loss are consequences of the time it takes for the distributed routing state to follow host mobility. As described in Section 2, immediately after handoff, mobile hosts transmit a route-update packet to reduce this time to a minimum. The route-update packet travels from the new base station to the gateway configuring the new soft-state downlink route toward the mobile host's new point of attachment. The old and new downlink routes both originate at the gateway but while the former routes packets to the old base station, the latter leads to the base station the host has just moved to.

A handoff scenario is illustrated in Figure 1. The node where the old and new routes join base station (**BS2**) in Figure 1 is referred to as the *cross-over node*. The new downlink route becomes operational when the first route-update packet transmitted through the new base station reaches the cross-over node. The time period during which time the mobile host is not receiving packets after initiating handoff represents the the time taken for the route-update packet to reach the cross-over node plus the time taken for the first downlink packet to travel from the cross-over node to the new base station. Handoff delay is equal to the round-trip time between the new base station and the cross-over node.

Packet Loss

In addition to handoff delay, application level service quality is also related to packet loss during handoff. To determine handoff packet loss, let us assume that a periodic stream of packets is being transmitted from the Internet to a mobile host. Before a handoff is initiated packets are routed along the old route. In the following calculation, we will assume that the cross-over node knows in advance which of the stream's packets will be the last one to reach the mobile host at the old location. Let us assume that the cross-over node marks this packet. Upon receiving the marked packet, the mobile host performs a handoff and immediately transmits a route-update packet through the new base station. Downlink packets routed by the cross-over node after the marked packet but before the arrival of the route-update packet are routed to the old base station and are lost. This time interval is equal to the sum of the time taken for the marked packet to propagate from the cross-over node to the mobile host and the time taken for the route-update packet to reach the cross-over node. The loss of packets at handoff is related to the "handoff loop time" which is defined as the transmission time from the cross-over node to the mobile host's old location plus the transmission time from the mobile host's new location to the cross-over node. Specifically, the number of lost packets at handoff n_{loss} is equal to the number of packets arriving at the cross-over node during the handoff loop time T_L, that is

$$n_{loss} = wT_L \tag{1}$$

where w is the rate of downlink packets. Since the average handoff

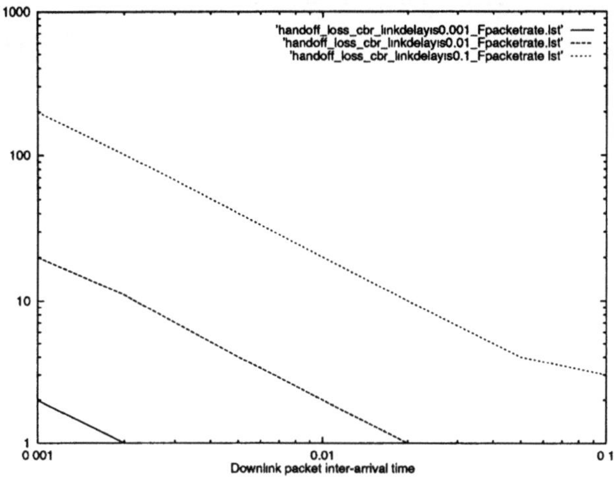

Figure 2 Packet Loss vs. CBR Packet Inter Arrival Time

loop time is equal to the average handoff delay, the expected number of packets lost at handoff can equally be calculated using the handoff delay. In what follows we do not differentiate between these two values.

Handoff packet loss for a Constant Bit Rate (CBR) source using our simulation environment is plotted in Figure 2. The curve represents the average number of packets lost during handoff against down link packet inter-arrival time in seconds. The three curves correspond to T_L values of 0.002, 0.02 and 0.2 seconds, respectively (twice the link delay shown in Figure 2). The simulation results closely match the calculations presented above. These results are achieved with neither mobile hosts nor base stations having special states associated with handoff. In exchange for this simplicity, however, handoff performance is dependent upon the traffic conditions. In a highly loaded network the handoff delay and packet loss will be higher.

Real time Internet applications (e.g., voice over IP) are sensitive to packet delay and cannot typically tolerate the delay associated with the retransmission of lost packets. For these applications, the number of lost packets characterizes handoff performance. Other applications, however, use end-to-end flow control to respond to network and traffic conditions and retransmit packets and/or reduce transmission rate if errors occur. In what follows, we focus on TCP performance in the presence of handoff. TCP represents the most typical traffic type over today's Internet

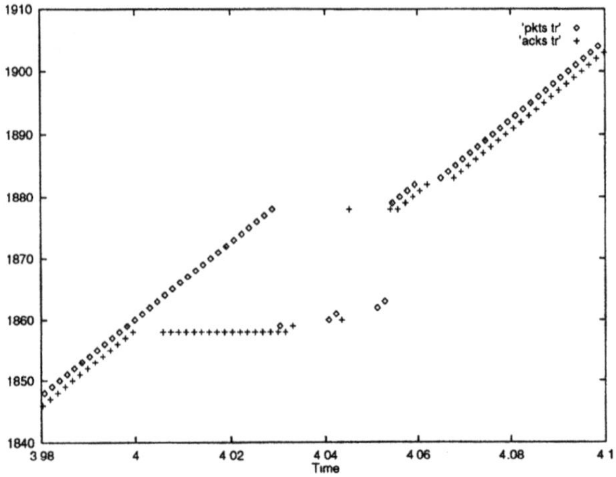

Figure 3 TCP Sequence Numbers at Handoff (Downlink Case)

which carries World Wide Web, file transfer, remote login and other applications. Investigating TCP performance is important because its flow control has been shown to operate sub-optimally in wireless environments.

TCP Behavior

We will first use simulation to look at the behavior of a TCP session during handoff. The simulated configuration is identical to the Cellular IP simulation environment shown in Figure 1. In the first example TCP is used to download data to a mobile host. The TCP packet size is 1000 bytes and a mobile user has up to 5 Mbps downlink bandwidth, that is, the downlink packet rate w is 625 packets/sec. Packet transmission time between nodes in the simulated configuration is 2 ms, resulting in a handoff delay of 4 ms.

Figure 3 shows the sequence numbers of downlink data packets and uplink acknowledgments observed at the gateway during handoff; note that TCP Tahoe flow control is operational throughout. Handoff is initiated by the mobile host at 4 seconds into the simulation. In accordance with Equation 1 three consecutive packets get lost as indicated by the three consecutive missing acknowledgments. After the handoff delay packets continue to arrive at the mobile host. These packets are, however, out of sequence and cause the receiver to generate duplicate acknowledgments as indicated by the horizontal line of acknowledgment sequence numbers. The duplicate acknowledgments inform the TCP transmitter about the losses and cause it to retransmit the lost packets. The first retransmitted packet arrives approximately 20 ms after the handoff (see Figure 3). Using Tahoe flow control, the transmitter remains silent until this packet is acknowledged and increases its transmission window size as further acknowledgments arrive. The full TCP rate is regained at 4.07 sec into the simulation as shown in Figure 3. The figure represents TCP sequence numbers at the client side transmitter for both packets and acknowledgments against time in seconds.

Cellular IP handoff is interpreted by a transmitter in the wired IP network as congestion which causes it to reduce its transmission rate. Using Tahoe flow control the handoff triggers slow-start which increases the performance impact of handoff packet loss. From the simulation results we observe that normal operation is resumed approximately 70 ms after handoff is initiated as shown in Figure 3.

In the next experiment TCP is used to carry data from the mobile host. In this case handoff packet loss affects acknowledgments instead of data packets. Figure 4 shows simulation results for a configuration that is identical to the previous one. Before handoff is initiated the TCP sender at the mobile host uses its maximum window size of 20 packets which is reflected in the difference between data packet and acknowledgment sequence numbers. At 4 sec (simulated time) the mobile host performs a handoff and stops receiving acknowledgments for a period of approximately 4 ms, which represents the handoff delay. During the handoff delay the sender does not transmit any packets since its window size is used up and it needs incoming acknowledgments to advance its transmission window.

In the next experiment (as shown in Figure 4) handoff is initiated when the TCP session is in a stabilized phase and acknowledgments keep arriving at the mobile host in a paced and continuous manner. After the handoff delay, acknowledgments are routed to the mobile host's new location. Due to the cumulative nature of TCP acknowledgments, the first acknowledgment that arrives at the mobile host after handoff informs the sender that all its transmitted packets have arrived at the receiver (up to the sequence number shown in the acknowledgment). This causes the transmitter to advance its transmission window and continue transmitting at the maximum available data rate. In the simulation example this rate is slightly higher than the rate dictated by TCP flow control which represents the long term average capacity. This results

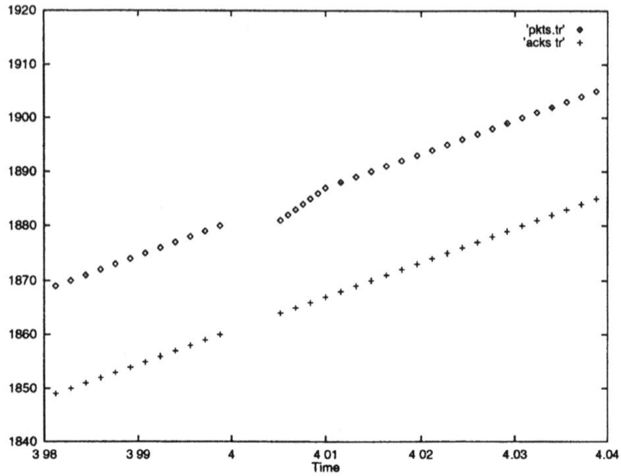

Figure 4 TCP Sequence Numbers during Handoff for the Uplink Case

in a curve of data packet sequence numbers that is somewhat steeper during handoff. As observed in Figure 4, normal operation is resumed quickly with the result that handoff has little impact on the active data session.

We observe that the behavior is different if handoff occurs when a TCP session is in its initial slow start phase and acknowledgments are not regularly arriving at the mobile host. In this case the new downlink route is established after the handoff delay but no acknowledgments arrive to the sender. If at this point the sender has used up all its transmission window and is waiting for acknowledgments then TCP can suffer a delay equal to the sender's retransmission timer. Mechanisms to avoid this problem are for further study.

Mobility Management Cost

Route Maintenance Overhead

The network operator will typically set the route-timeout to be a small multiple of the route-update time. This ensures that the mobile host's routing cache mappings remain valid even if a few route-update packets are lost. Let T_{ru} denote the route-update time and αT_{ru} the route-timeout where α is a small integer. To choose an optimal value for T_{ru}, the following trade-off should be observed. After an active host performs a handoff, its old routing cache mappings remain valid for a duration determined by route-timeout. During this time, packets addressed to this host continue to be delivered to the old base station increasing the network load and reducing network performance. A small value of T_{ru} should be used to minimize this condition. On the other hand, an active host that has no data to send must transmit route-update packets at a rate of $1/T_{ru}$. This load increases with decreasing T_{ru}. Let the cost of carrying a packet to or from the mobile host be defined as the size of the packet in bits. This model neglects differences in uplink and downlink cost due to different traffic conditions but is sufficient to characterize the T_{ru} trade-off. Consider a mobile host that is receiving data at a constant rate r bps (including headers) and let p denote the fraction of the time when it is not sending packets and is forced to transmit route-update packets instead. (We note that in some typical IP applications downlink traffic is considerably higher than uplink traffic. This, however, does not necessarily cause p to be high if acknowledgments are transmitted over the uplink.) The cost of transmitting route-update packets during time T is $R_{ru}pT/T_{ru}$ where R_{ru} is the size of a route-update packet in bits. During this time the mobile performs T/T_H handoffs where T_H (dwell time) is the mean time spent in a cell. After each handoff, the old route remains active for at most αT_{ru}, the exact value depending on when it was last updated before handoff. Hence the mean cost of sending packets along the old route after handoff is $rT_{ru}(\alpha - 1/2)$ and the total cost of misrouted packets during time T is $rTT_{ru}(\alpha - 1/2)/T_H$. The optimal route-update time $\hat{T}_{ru}$ is the one that minimizes the sum of these costs and is calculated as

$$\hat{T}_{ru} = \sqrt{\frac{pR_{ru}T_H}{r(\alpha - 1/2)}}$$

This theoretical result is plotted in Figure 5. The mobile host performs handoffs every 30 seconds while it is receiving data at a rate of 128 kbps. The size of route-update packets is 102 bytes, α is 3 and p is 0.1. The plot shows that the optimal route-update time in the described scenario is 87 ms. We also plotted the sum of these costs which can be interpreted as the total cost associated with the mobility of an active host and is calculated as

$$C_a = \frac{pR_{ru}}{\hat{T}_{ru}} + \frac{r\hat{T}_{ru}(\alpha - 1/2)}{T_H} = \sqrt{\frac{4pR_{ru}r(\alpha - 1/2)}{T_H}}$$

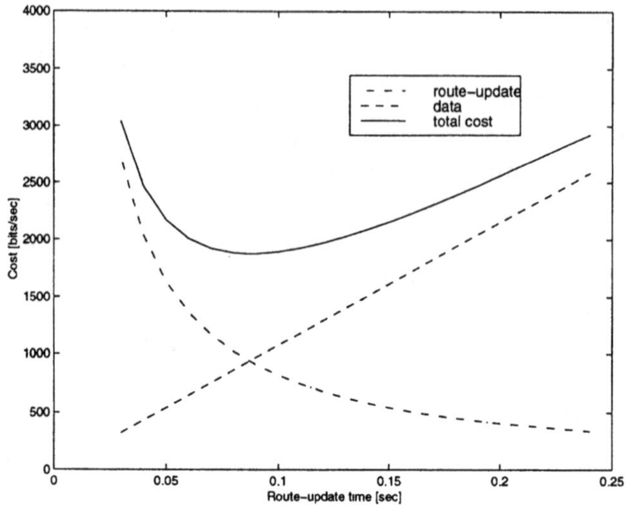

Figure 5 Location Management Cost vs. T_{ru} (Dotted Lines Represent Simulation Measurements)

This cost is not proportional to the migration frequency but to its square root. In keeping with the original design goals, this shows Cellular IP's efficiency in supporting highly mobile hosts. Note that the mobility cost increases with increasing user data rate. This property applies to most mobility schemes (e.g., when data must be forwarded from one base station to another after handoff) but is more apparent in Cellular IP. This is related to the soft-state nature of Cellular IP. Since there is no explicit signaling during handoff, which makes handoff transparent to the base stations, the base station is unaware that mobile hosts move into or out of its cell. Transmitting data to mobile hosts that have left the cell adds to the cost of mobility.

Paging Overhead

The paging-update time T_{pu} is subject to a similar trade-off as T_{ru}. A selected value that is too small will result in very frequent paging-update packets being sent by idle mobile hosts. On the other hand, considering that the paging-timeout is a small multiple of the paging-update time, increasing T_{pu} will result in an increase in the number of cells that an idle mobile host is paged in.

Paging is initiated when a new data session starts by a downlink packet, for instance a TCP connection is initiated *to* the mobile host. Let λ_P denote the arrival rate of such sessions and R_P the mean amount of traffic (bits) sent in paging packets. The paging packets are delivered to all the cells to which the mobile host has valid paging cache mappings. Let us first assume that all base stations have paging caches and that the probability of immediately revisiting a cell is negligible. Paging occurs in the 'primary' cell that the target mobile host resides in plus any other 'secondary' cells where the mobile host has valid paging cache mappings. Secondary cells represent cells that the mobile host has recently visited and that have valid paging cache for the target mobile host. Paging secondary cells is a waste of transmission resources and reflects the cost of our paging scheme. The mean number of secondary cells paged is $(\beta - 1/2)T_{pu}/T_H$, where β is the ratio between the paging-timeout and the paging-update time. The optimal paging-update value $\hat{T}_{pu}$ is the one that minimizes the sum of paging-update traffic and wasted paging traffic and is obtained as

$$\hat{T}_{pu} = \sqrt{\frac{R_{pu}T_H}{\lambda_P R_P(\beta - 1/2)}}$$

where R_{pu} is the size of paging-update packets in bits. Using this optimal paging-update time, the total cost C_i associated with the mobility of an idle host is

$$C_i = \sqrt{\frac{4R_{pu}\lambda_P R_P(\beta - 1/2)}{T_H}}$$

These results take a similar form to those obtained for the route-update time. However, the downlink data rate r (an important parameter in the route-update time trade-off) is now replaced by $\lambda_P R_P$ which is the rate at which data arrives at the mobile host in paging packets. This rate depends largely on the application but will be in most cases orders of magnitude lower than r which justifies selecting a higher paging-update time than route-update time. This also accounts for the fact that the cost C_i associated with the mobility of idle hosts is significantly lower than the mobility cost of active users which is the basis of passive connectivity.

4. CONCLUSION

In this paper we have presented analysis of the Cellular IP protocol. Cellular IP represents a new approach to IP host mobility that incorporates a number of important cellular system features but remains firmly based on IP design principles. A fundamental design objective of Cellular IP is implementational and functional simplicity. To reduce complexity, we omitted explicit location registrations and replaced them by implicit inband signaling. As a result, nodes in a Cellular IP access network need not be aware of the network topology or of the mobility of hosts in the service area. This design choice deliberately trades off performance for simplicity. As a result packets may be lost at handoff rather than explicitly buffered and redirected to mobile hosts as they move. Our analysis has focused on the performance of the Cellular IP hard handoff algorithm and on the network traffic overhead imposed by mobility management. We have found that a simple approach can offer fairly good service quality. We have presented an analytical and empirical study of protocol parameters that can be set to configure a Cellular IP access network to match local mobility and traffic characteristics. Future work is addressing new mechanisms to provide quality of service support while maintaining the same simple lightweight protocol approach to host mobility and wireless access to the Internet.

5. ACKNOWLEDGMENTS

The authors wish to thank members of the IETF Mobile IP Working Group for their comments on the first version of this protocol. In addition, the COMET Group would like to thank Ericsson, IBM and Intel for their on-going support of the Cellular IP Project (comet.columbia.edu/cellularip) at Columbia University.

REFERENCES

[1] H. Balakrishnan, S. Seshan, R. Katz, "Improving Reliable Transport and Handoff Performance in Cellular Wireless Networks," ACM Wireless Networks 1(4), December 1995.

[2] Pravin Bhagwat, Charles Perkins, Satish Tripathi, "Network Layer Mobility: an Architecture and Survey," IEEE Personal Communications Magazine, Vol. 3, No. 3, pp. 54-64, June 1996.

[3] Ramon Cáceres, Venkata N. Padmanabhan, "Fast and Scalable Handoffs for Wireless Internetworks," Presented at ACM Mobicom, 1996.

[4] John Ioannidis, Dan Duchamp, Gerald Q. Maguire Jr., "IP-Based Protocols for Mobile Internetworking," Proc. ACM Sigcomm'91, pp. 234-245, September 1991.

[5] David B. Johnson, Charles Perkins, "Route Optimization in Mobile IP," Internet Draft, draft-ietf-mobileip-optim-07.txt, November 1998, Work in Progress.

[6] M. Mouly, M-B. Pautet, "The GSM System for Mobile Communications," published by the authors, ISBN 2-9507190-0-7, 1992.

[7] "Network Simulator - ns (version 2)", ns home page, http://www-mash.cs.berkeley.edu/ns/ns.html.

[8] Charles Perkins, editor, "IP Mobility Support," Internet RFC 2002, October 1996.

[9] Charles Perkins, "Mobile-IP Local Registration with Hierarchical Foreign Agents," Internet Draft, draft-perkins-mobileip-hierfa-00.txt, Work in Progress, February 1996.

[10] András G. Valkó, "Cellular IP: A New Approach to Internet Host Mobility," ACM Computer Communication Review, pages 50-65, January 1999.

[11] A. Valkó, A. Campbell, J. Gomez, "Cellular IP," Internet Draft, draft-valko-cellularip-00.txt, Work in Progress, November 1998.

ROUTING AND HANDOVER ISSUES OF RSVP MESSAGES IN MOBILE IP ENVIRONMENT

I. Mathes and T. Dagiuklas
Advanced Communications Technologies
Development Programmes Department
INTRACOM SA
Peania Attica
Athens, GREECE
Tel: ++ 30 1 669 0368
Fax: ++30 1 686 0312
Email: {imath, ntan}@intracom.gr

ABSTRACT

This paper addresses the problems of interworking of RSVP and IP in order to support QoS in hosts within a mobile environment. Two important issues are discussed. The first regards routing of RSVP messages combined with Mobile IP (both IPv4 and IPv6) and the second concerns the impact of handover in the operation of RSVP. The problems associated with each issue are discussed for both Mobile IPv4 and IPv6 and possible solutions have been proposed.

1. INTRODUCTION

Recent advances in the mobile computing, personal wireless communications and the Internet have led to the explosion of applications (e.g. WWW, multimedia, audio and video) to the mobile user [1]. There are three reasons, which has led to this explosion. The first regards the latest advances in the increasing computing power in the PCs capable to support multimedia applications. The second concerns the evolution towards Universal Mobile Telecommunication System (UMTS). Finally, the Internet has experienced in the last decade a great explosion due to the innovation of new multimedia services (e.g. WWW, Internet Telephony) containing video and audio elements.

Originally, the Internet had been designed to provide "best effort" service to IP datagrams with no guarantees in loss and delay. However, the provision of multimedia applications must use methods to provide Quality of Service (QoS) guarantees to services such as video and audio. One of the methods proposed to provide QoS in the Internet, is the use of Resource

Reservation (RSVP) protocol in the routers along the path from the sender to the receiver [4], [19].

The provision of QoS in mobile environment is more complicated due to handover. Handover occurs when either the host moves from one location to another or when the radio resources gets exhausted to the current cell (access point) and therefore the host is handed over a neighboring cell. Mobile IP has taken into account the fact that a host may move around. On the other hand, RSVP considers that the users are always attached to the same access point in the network. There are two important aspects of RSVP interworking with the Mobile IP. The first considers the routing of RSVP packets that may follow different paths from those of the IP datagrams. As an effect, reservation may take place at different path, which may lead to the reduction of the service to the "best effort" category. The second regards the reservation of resources to a new location area when handover occurs.

This paper is organised as follows. Section 2 presents an outline of RSVP. Section 3 and 4 describe the routing problems of RSVP combined with Mobile IPv4 and Mobile IPv6 respectively and proposed solutions are presented. Section 5 discusses the impact of handover in the RSVP and solutions are proposed for both Mobile IPv4 and IPv6. Finally, conclusions are given in section 6.

2. RSVP OUTLINE

RSVP is a setup protocol designed for integrated services. It is used by a host to request specific QoS from the network for a particular flow [4], [6], [19]. RSVP is also employed by routers to deliver QoS requests to all nodes along the path(s) of the flows, establish and maintain states to provide the requested service. RSVP is not a transport or routing protocol. Routing is handled by current routing protocols and transport of data is carried out by protocols like TCP, UDP, RTP and ST2. It operates over the IP layer and employs soft state and refresh policy, so that the generated states in intermediate routers are timed out, unless they are refreshed [4], [6], [19].

The two basic message types of RSVP are PATH and RESV. PATH messages are sent by the transmitters towards the receivers, as illustrated in Figure 1 [7]. They are routed on end-to-end basis as normal data and establish "PATH states" in the intermediate routers. PATH states include information such as the sender of the message, the IP address of previous hop and the requested QoS. Intermediate routers modify PATH messages to describe the service they can provide and forward it to the next hop. On the reception of the PATH message, the receiver generates the appropriate RESV message, which is sent to the previous node using the previous hop field of the PATH state. The RESV messages follow exactly the same route as the PATH ones. On the reception of the RESV messages, the routers reserve the appropriate resources and transmit a RESV message towards the node sending the PATH message.

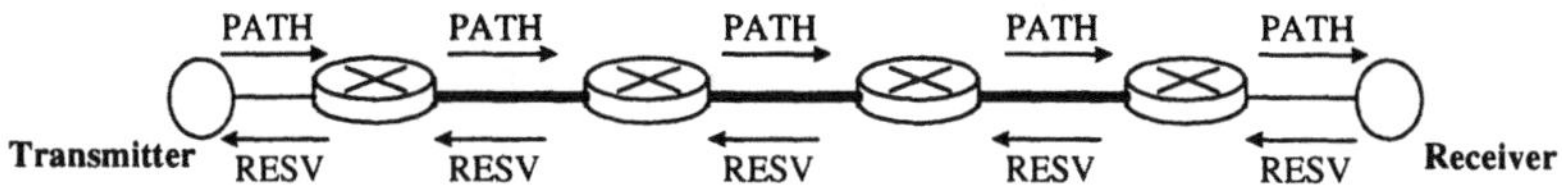

Figure 1: RSVP set-up operation

3. ROUTING of RSVP MESSAGES

Routing of RSVP with Mobile IPv4

In standard Mobile IPv4, all data destined to a Mobile Node (MN) from a Correspondent Node (CN) are routed through the MN's Home Agent (HA) [15], [16]. The CN sends the packets using the MN's home address (ha) as destination. IP packets arriving at the HA, are encapsulated in another IP datagram where the MN's care of address (coa) is used as destination. IP datagrams are delivered to the MN's Foreign Agent (FA) or directly to the MN if it owns a collocated coa (this is an temporary address assigned to the MN itself) [15], [16]. A de-capsulation procedure follows prior to sending packets to MN's IP processing module. Transportation of data within the IP tunnel is carried out transparently, so that intermediate routers do not notice the payload of the inner IP datagrams. Routing of IP packets through the HA occurs only in the case when the CN is a transmitter, since in the reverse direction packets are sent directly to the CN without the need for tunneling.

The same procedure is applied to the RSVP PATH and RESV messages, which are sent from the CN towards the MN, as illustrated in Figure 2. In the reverse direction, PATH messages are routed directly to the CN (if routing decisions are based on the destination address and not the source one), without passing through the tunnel. RESV messages also avoid tunneling since they are routed using the previous hop value kept in the "PATH state" of each router traversed by the PATH messages.

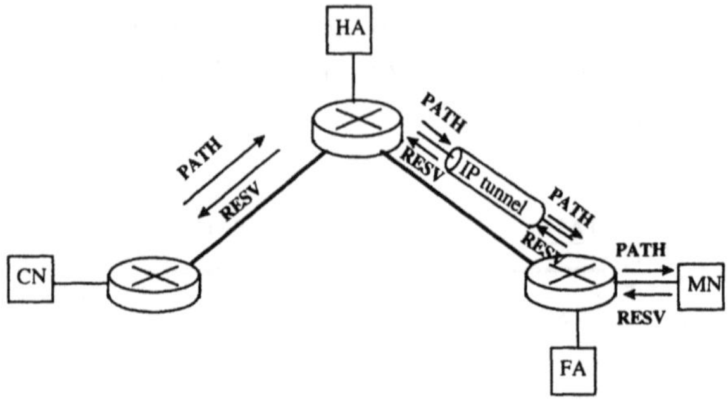

Figure 2: RSVP messages routing in combination with Mobile IPv4.

When the CN transmits a RSVP PATH message towards the MN, it uses MN's ha as the destination address. As an effect, PATH messages reach the HA where they will be IP encapsulated and are sent to MN using its coa. However, the outer header of the IP tunneled packet will not carry a notification indicating a RSVP message, which must be processed by the intermediate routers. Normally, a Router-Alert option must be carried and the protocol id must be set to 46 indicating a RSVP message. All intermediate routers in the tunnel, until the one at the exit will discard the PATH message. In the same way, the routers within the tunnel will neglect the RESV messages traveling in the opposite direction and no reservation will be made inside the tunnel. Additionally, even if it is possible to reserve resources inside the tunnel, it would be difficult to determine whether the tunneled packets must be handled in a different way or not. This is due to the fact that current IP-in-IP encapsulation scheme moves all distinguishing information to the inner IP header adding only a standard IP header as the external wrapper.

A solution to the tunnelling problem has been proposed by IETF [18]. The entry router (Rentry) of a tunnel recognizes the end to end RSVP PATH [16], [18]. Subsequently, a tunnel PATH message is sent from Rentry towards the exit router of the tunnel (Rexit). This message is not IP encapsulated and the intermediate routers inside the tunnel process it. When this message is received at Rexit, it is processed and deleted. The original end to end PATH message is encapsulated at Rentry and is sent to Rexit. This PATH message carries a new RSVP object. The purpose of this object is to associate the end to end session with the relevant tunnel session. Encapsulated end-to-end PATH messages are decapsulated at Rexit. Prior to forwarding the message to the next hop along the path to the destination, Rexit records the association of the tunnel session with that of the end-to-end session, and sets the previous hop field of the end-to-end session to Rentry. At the reverse direction when an end to end RSVP RESV message reaches Rexit, it triggers a tunnel RESV message from Rexit to Reentry, which makes reservations at all intermediate routers inside the tunnel. The end to end RESV message is encapsulated at Rexit and forwarded upstream to Rentry, where it is de-capsulated and forwarded to the next hop. When data packets arrive at Rentry, if there is no resource reservation for them, then they are normally IP encapsulated and forwarded into the tunnel. Otherwise, the encapsulation procedure adds a UDP header within the IP outer header.

We propose an alternative solution to bypass the tunneling problem. In this approach, the intermediate routers in the tunnel process the encapsulated IP datagrams in order to identify RSVP messages, as well as the IP data flows. Such a scheme is illustrated in Figure 3. The RSVP PATH messages travelling in the tunnel are encapsulated into two IP datagrams. When a packet reaches an intermediate router, the router must strip out both the outer and inner IP headers before submitting the PATH message to the RSVP module. In order to strip out the outer header, this message must carry a Router-Alert indication and the Protocol ID field must indicate the transportation of RSVP message within the IP datagrams (a new protocol ID number has to be defined). In order to strip out the inner IP header, a Router-Alert option must be carried in the header and the protocol ID is set to 46. RESV messages travelling in the reverse direction will not be encapsulated so there is no need for special treatment. Additionally, the correct classification of encapsulated IP datagrams inside the tunnel requires processing based on the inner and not on the outer IP header. By employing a protocol ID to identify IP encapsulation in the outer IP header, intermediate routers can be notified to classify incoming IP packets, using the inner IP header. Then the classification would be correct and match the reserved resources.

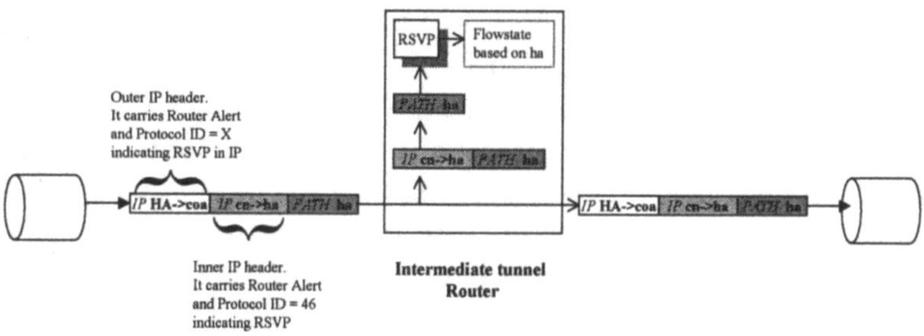

Figure 3: Proposed RSVP Tunneling using Mobile IPv4

Routing of RSVP Using Mobile IPv6

In Mobile IPv6, a MN can send binding updates to inform CNs of its current coa [12], [14], [16]. Binding updates may be sent after a binding request has arrived from a CN. CNs may respond binding acknowledgments to notify MNs for the receipt of a binding update message. When a CN wants to send an IP packet to a MN, a look up of the binding cache is generated prior to the formulation of the IP header. If there is a relevant entry, then MN's coa is obtained from the binding cache and is used as the destination address. MN's ha is placed in an IPv6 Routing Extension Header. It must be emphasised that, by default, in IPv6 all coa are collocated and the employment of FAs is unnecessary [12], [14]. Once IP packets reach the MN, the IPv6 Routing Header will be processed, the ha will be identified as the ultimate destination and the IP datagram will be delivered to the upper layers.

The employment of binding caches alters considerably the routing of IP datagrams, which are sent from the CN towards the MN [12], [14], [16]. IP datagrams are no longer routed through the ha. Instead they follow the optimal route directly to MN's coa. When the CN does not know MN's coa, the MN's ha will be used. As an effect, IP datagrams are sent through the HA to the MN. In this case, when the MN receives the first tunneled IP packets, it can understand that the CN does not know its coa and may send a binding update to the CN. After receiving the binding update, the CN can send IP packets to the MN through the optimal route. The same modifications must be considered for the routing of the RSVP messages, when Mobile IPv6 is employed. Routing RSVP messages using Mobile IPv6, two different cases have been studied. In the first, CN does know MN's coa whereas in the second case CN knows MN's coa. The problems and possible solutions associated with each case are examined in the following sections.

Routing of RSVP Messages when the CN does not know MN's coa.

When the CN sets up a RSVP session in the route to a MN, it will transmit an initial PATH message to the MN. The RSVP module in the CN operates over the IPv6 module and the associated binding cache. So the CN will employ MN's ha when constructing the outgoing PATH message. Additionally, MN's ha will be used as the destination address in the IP datagrams carrying the PATH message, since there is no relevant entry in the binding cache. Therefore, the PATH message will be routed through MN's HA making no reservation inside the IP tunnel.

When the PATH message reaches the MN, it will understand that the CN does not have an entry in its binding cache associating its ha with the corresponding coa. In this case, a binding update may be sent to the CN. After receiving the binding update, the CN is able to send IP datagrams to the MN through the optimal route, bypassing the HA. However, some IP datagrams may already have been transmitted from the CN. Additionally, the CN must send a new PATH message to reserve resources through the optimal route. We propose two solutions to alleviate this problem:

- In the first approach, the MN does not send a RESV message as a reply to the initial received PATH message. Instead, it sends a binding update message towards the CN. When the binding update message arrives at the CN, its corresponding RSVP module is notified of the MN address association. However, this solution requires modifications on the operation of RSVP and binding updates, both at the MN and the CN.
- Another solution is to allow the HA to recognise the incoming (from the CN) RSVP message and instead of tunneling it, a binding update is sent towards CN. Then, the CN can initiate a new RSVP session directly to MN. This approach requires modifications in the Mobile IP operating at the HA (a binding update is sent instead of tunneling the received PATH message) and also alterations at the binding update and RSVP operation at the CN (the binding update notifies the RSVP module of the coa-ha association).

Routing of RSVP Messages when the CN knows MN's coa.

The RSVP PATH message that is sent by the RSVP module of the MN towards the CN, contains the MN's ha. This message is delivered to the IPv6 module for transmission assuming that an entry exists in the binding cache associating MN's ha and coa. The IP datagrams include MN's coa as the destination address. As an effect, the PATH message is routed to MN through the optimal route without traversing MN's HA. However, since the RSVP PATH message within the IP datagrams contain MN's ha, flowstates at routers will be based on the ha (as illustrated in Figure 4). The IP datagrams requiring a certain QoS, are identified by the session spec (the triple destination address, protocol id and optional destination port) and filter spec (sender id). IP datagrams, though, transmitted by the CN use MN's coa as destination address. CN assumes that an entry exists in the binding cache associating MN's ha and coa. Although, QoS reservations may exist at the routers, IP datagrams will not be identified as the flow to obtain the reserved QoS since they include MN's coa.

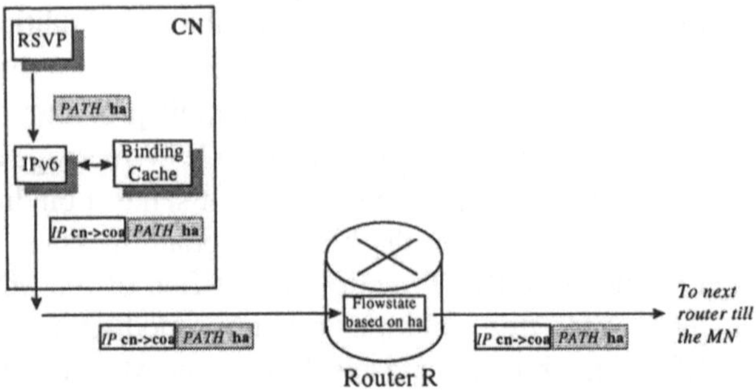

Figure 4: Transmission of PATH message from CN towards the MN using Mobile IPv6

We propose three solutions in order to resolve the aforementioned problem:

- The first one regards the employment of MN's coa instead of its ha in the RSVP PATH message which is sent from the CN towards the MN. Then in the intermediate routers, "path states" and reservations must be assigned according to the MN's coa and are compliant with the destination address employed in IP datagrams. This solution can be implemented by modifying the RSVP module so that when the PATH messages are created, the binding cache is accessed to retrieve MN's coa. As an effect, both Mobile IPv6 and RSVP must be modified. Mobile IP must provide a method for enabling RSVP to retrieve binding cache information and RSVP module must access the binding cache prior to the formulation of the PATH message. Another alternative option of including MN's coa in the PATH message, regards the modification of Mobile IPv6 module to recognize the RSVP PATH message. In this case, MN's ha is swapped with MN's coa in the PATH message. This method does not impose modifications in the RSVP module but it requires extensions in Mobile IPv6 to parse all RSVP messages and swap the addresses. This extension may slow down considerably the operation of the Mobile IPv6 module. It must be emphasized that both approaches require modifications at the MN when creating the RSVP RESV message.
- A second solution necessitates the employment of binding caches at the routers. When IP datagrams arrive from the CN using MN's coa as destination address, it is swapped with MN's ha prior to transferring it to the router's decision whether the data belong to a flow or not. As an effect, flow classification is based on MN's ha which is compliant with the employment of ha when the initial QoS reservation at the router is carried out. One method to keep binding caches at the intermediate

routers, is to process the binding update messages at every visited router along the path from the CN towards the MN. This method requires modifications at the Mobile IPv6 software at the routers. However, the main disadvantage of this approach regards its scalability when the dimension of the caches gets large. Another approach to update binding caches, is to process the outer IP header containing the PATH messages, which includes both MN's coa and ha. This method exhibits the same scalability drawback as the previous one.

- A third solution is to make QoS reservations at the routers based on both MN's coa and its ha. In order to achieve this, the outer header of the IP datagrams carrying the RSVP PATH message must be provided to the RSVP module residing at the routers. Then the RSVP module will be informed of both MN's coa and ha and a path state is created according to MN's coa. However, the header of the IP datagram including the RSVP RESV message, which is transmitted in the reverse direction, will not contain both addresses (since it is routed hop by hop). Only MN's ha will be included in the inner RESV message. Thus, the RSVP module must maintain a mapping between MN's coa and ha (something like the binding cache), to create correctly the QoS reservation when the RESV message arrives.

4. RSVP and Handover

In a wireless/mobile IP environment, Mobile IP can be used in order to handle mobility and RSVP can be employed (assuming an integrated service model) to handle the reservation resources part. As a mobile host moves from one Access Point (AP) to another, mobility and resource reservation procedures must be employed in order to register the MN with the new AP [10], [13]. If the applications running at the MN are adaptive, a re-negotiation of the QoS that was originally allocated can be made, which could even degrade the service offered to "best effort" [2]. However some connections may not accept QoS re-negotiation. These connections will either be dropped or an alternative method should be employed to assure the existence of enough resources in the new AP [2], [8], [9]. In a Mobile IP based network, RSVP module must manage the reservations in the new path when the MH experiences handover. This necessitates possible extensions of the RSVP and interactions of RSVP module with Mobile IP to operate while MH experiences handover. These issues will be addressed in the following sections both for Mobile IP v4 and v6.

Handover and RSVP in Mobile IPv4

In standard Mobile IP (Mobile IPv4, or Mobile IPv6 without using binding cache option), all IP datagrams from a CN to a MN are routed through the MN's HA. The HA tunnels the arriving datagrams either to the MN's FA or directly to the MN (if a co-located address scheme is employed). In this scenario, resource reservation is carried out in the routers from the CN to the FA through the HA. No reservation exists inside the tunnel, unless specific extensions for RSVP are employed. When the MN hands over from a FA1 to a FA2, the path from CN to HA remains the same and new resource reservation is necessary only at FA2. The following steps occur while handover is performed:

1. The MN moves from FA1 to FA2.
2. The MN listens to the FA2 advertisements and registers with it
3. The HA is notified for the MN's new position.
4. Once "refresh timeout" period is expired, the HA sends a PATH message towards the MN. These messages will be transmitted through a new IP tunnel between the CN and the FA2.
5. Once the PATH message arrives at FA2, a new PATH state is created which is forwarded towards the MN.
6. In the next step, the MN sends the appropriate RESV message to FA2, which completes the resource reservation at FA2.
7. Resource reservation at FA1 will be deactivated at the expiration of the "cleanup timeout" interval at FA1.

Figure 5 illustrates the handover procedure regarding the RSVP operation with standard Mobile IP (v4).

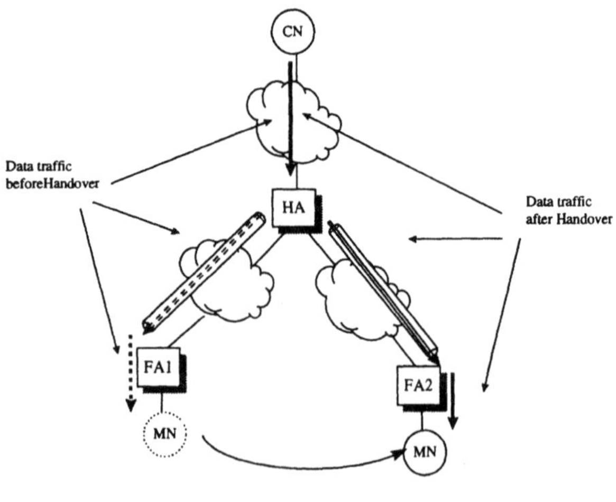

Figure 5: The handover procedure in combination with Mobile IP v4 and RSVP

The drawback of the above procedure is that the new resource reservation at FA2 is performed only after the expiration of the "refresh timeout" period at the HA. As an effect, a limited number of datagrams from the CN to the MN will traverse the path towards MN receiving "best effort" QoS at FA2. Additionally, it must be noted that steps 2-6 are based on "best effort" transport, which extends also the duration of handover/resource reservation procedure.

Mobile RSVP (MRSVP) has been proposed in order to solve the aforementioned problem of the RSVP operation during handover [17]. The main idea of MRSVP is that the MN makes in advance resource reservations in all possible cells it may visit. In order to achieve this, the MN must be capable of a mobility specification (Mspec), which is a set of locations, the MN may visit. However, the main disadvantage of MRSVP is the over-reservation of resources, which are wasted.

We propose an alternative scheme, which alleviates the over-reservation drawback of MRSVP. In this approach, the initiation of the new resource reservation at FA2 is employed by forcing the HA to send the PATH message towards FA2 immediately after being notified about MN's new position (coa2). Additionally, a PATH Tear message can be also sent towards the FA1 in order to tear down the old reservation at FA1 and release the resources dedicated to this flow. In order to implement this solution, the RSVP module at the HA must interact with Mobile IP. Once Mobile IP informs the HA about the movement of the MN towards a new AP, it triggers the RSVP module to modify the coa address of the MN. By employing this procedure, the HA is enabled to send the PATH message before the expiration of the relevant "refresh timer". However, this method requires modifications both in the RSVP module and Mobile IP at the HA.

Handover and RSVP in Mobile IPv6

The employment of binding caches in Mobile IPv6 allows the CN to communicate directly with the MN without routing its traffic through the HA. This option in Mobile IPv6 necessitates the employment of the optimum route from the CN to MN and permits the reservation of resources throughout the entire path (there is no tunnel present). When a MN moves from a FA1 to a FA2, a new resource reservation is carried out from the CN to the new location of the MN. The following procedures are carried while handover is performed:

1. The MN listens to the FA2 advertisements and registers with it
2. The HA is notified for the MN's new position (coa2).

3. The MN sends binding updates to the CN to notify about its current location (coa2).
4. The CN sends a new PATH message to trigger a new resource reservation procedure along the new path.
5. The MN will transmit back a RESV message as a response to the received PATH message, completing the resource reservation procedure.
6. The connection can now proceed in the new cell.

Figure 6 illustrates the handover procedure regarding the RSVP operation with Mobile IPv6.

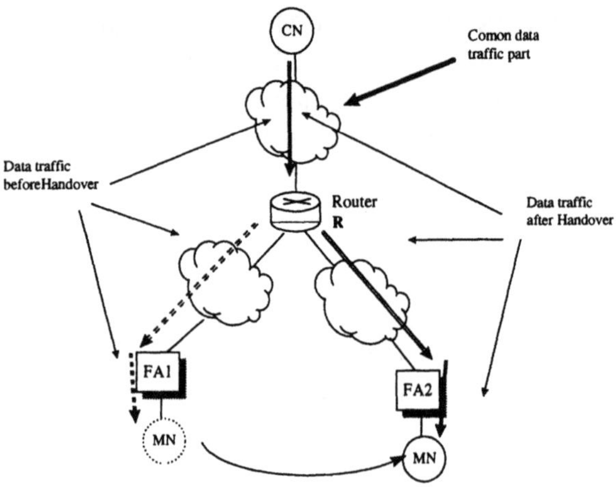

Figure 6: The handover procedure in combination with Mobile IPv6 and RSVP

The above procedures experience the following problems:

- Steps 2-5 are performed based on the "best effort" QoS, which may slow down and deteriorate the overall handover procedure. Additionally, the initiation of the new resource reservation at step 4 is not triggered by the reception of the binding update message at step 3 but only after the expiration of the "refresh timeout" period at the CN. This implies that in the meantime, some datagrams belonging to a flow from CN to MN may be treated by the routers as "best effort". This problem occurs due to the fact that the delivery of both the binding updates messages (they are sent by MN to both HA and the CN) and the RSVP messages (interchanged between the CN and the MN during the new resource reservation procedure) use the standard "best effort" IP service. Although in general, the delay of this procedure may not be considerable, its overhead is rather significant for the effective operation of the handover. Solutions such as the one used in connection oriented protocols (e.g. ATM) where a predefined channel is reserved for signaling [1], [18], can not be employed due the connectionless nature of the IP. We propose a more suitable approach, which must mark/tag the appropriate IP packets (note that both Mobile IP binding updates and RSVP messages are transported within IP datagrams) as time sensitive in order to obtain special care in the routers. This can be achieved by using the Traffic Class field in the header of the IPv6 datagram (or the TOS field in an IPv4 datagram) as described also in the differentiated services approach [5]. This requires interaction between the RSVP and IPv6 modules so as the IPv6 module will mark the RSVP messages correctly.

- The initiation of the new resource reservation procedure. After the initial resource reservation along the path to the MN has been set up, the CN will continue to transmit PATH refresh messages at regular intervals, since this is required by the RSVP's "soft state" operation. Then a binding update arrives from the MN, informing CN of its current coa (coa2 after the handover). When the "refresh timeout" period expires at CN, a PATH message is transmitted towards MN's new location (coa2) which establishes resource reservation along the new path. The default average period between transmissions of RSVP messages is 30 seconds [6], [7]. This period is quite long for the fast handover process. In the meantime, IP datagrams will be delivered to the MN using "best effort" service. We propose the following solutions to solve this problem:
  - ✓ Reduction of the RSVP retransmission period. The shorter this period is, the faster the response of the RSVP module at the CN about the change of the coa of the MN. However, the disadvantage of this approach is the increase of signaling overhead in the network, due to the fact that PATH messages are sent more frequently.
  - ✓ Another solution considers the triggering of the RSVP module when the binding update message arrives at the CN. This arrival subsequently triggers the transmission of the PATH message immediately. However, this method requires modification of RSVP operation at the CN, so that CN is informed of the arrival of the binding update message.
- Resource Reservation along the common path. Resource reservation will be made along the entire path from the CN to the MN. However, this may not be necessary for the common part between the old and new route (i.e. from CN to router R). This occurs because data flow classification at the routers is based on MN's coa. This address changes after the handover has been performed (coa1 and coa2 the are the addresses before and after handover respectively). Although QoS reservation exists in the routers

comprising the common path (from CN to R), the data flow will not be identified as the one obtaining the reserved QoS. Data flow classification is based on the session spec (the triple destination address, protocol id and optional destination port) and sender id (source address, source port). MN's coa is employed to identify in the routers the IP datagrams requesting a certain QoS. When handover is triggered, the MN's coa changes and as an effect a new resource reservation must be made along the path although the appropriate resources have already been reserved in the common part from the CN to router R. This is illustrated in Figure 6. QoS reservation at routers is based on MN's ha not its coa. However, data traffic carries MN's coa as the destination address. Although QoS reservations may exist at the routers (based on MN's ha), IP datagrams (including MN's coa) will not be identified as the flow to obtain the reserved QoS. Therefore, we propose the following solutions:

- ✓ Binding caches are employed at the routers. Routers record the bindings of the MNs and use this binding in order to route the RSVP messages towards the MNs. When a MN moves to a new AP, a binding message is sent from the MN to the CN. This message is also used by the routers to perform binding update and renew their cache with the new MN's coa (coa2). Thus the arriving packets coa2 will be identified as the ones which must receive the reserved resources in the routers along the common path (from CN to R) where the reservation has been employed by using coa1. However, the main disadvantage of this approach regards scalability due the extra memory requirements at the expense of resolving the handover issue.
- ✓ Reservations are made at routers by using both MN's addresses (ha and coa). This approach alleviates the handover problem. This is due to the fact that when RSVP PATH messages have been processed along the entire path, the RSVP module has been updated using MN's coa2. However, in this case QoS reservation still has to be reestablished along the entire path. Additionally, the longer the path is, the longer the delay to update the RSVP module with the new MN coa. This approach may also lead to low throughput when the MN's movement is high.

- The soft state of RSVP does not require canceling the reservations in the old path (before handover) since this occurs when the relevant timers expire. The RSVP "soft state" approach defines that the RSVP states created at routers, are deleted if no matching refresh message arrives before the expiration of a "cleanup timeout" interval at the router. However the actual soft state timers are too long (around 30 secs) for fast handover purposes, which may lead to unnecessary resource reservation thus wasting the network's resources. This problem can be resolved by reducing the soft state timers at the expense of extra overhead in the RSVP messages. Another approach regards the employment of RSVP Teardown messages which remove path or reservation state immediately. There are two types of RSVP teardown message called PathTear and ResvTear [4], [6], [7], [19]. A PathTear message travels towards all receivers downstream from the point of initiation and deletes path state, as well as all dependent reservation state. A ResvTear message deletes reservation state and travels towards all senders upstream from the point of initiation. A PathTear (ResvTear) message may be visualised as a reversed-sense Path message (Resv message, respectively). Once it is initiated, a teardown request must be forwarded hop-by-hop without delay. A teardown message deletes the specified state in the received node. Based on this option, the CN can initiate a PathTear message towards FA1 immediately after receiving the binding update message from the MN. Then a new resource reservation along the path may be initiated. It must be emphasized that in this way the reservation along the common part of the path (from CN to R) is torn down and a new one is re-created. The most efficient approach is to allow router R initiating the PathTear message towards the FA1 and subsequently the Path message is sent towards the MN. However but this approach lacks implementation simplicity.

5. CONCLUSIONS

This paper has addressed the problem of routing and handover of RSVP messages within mobile hosts. It has been demonstrated that RSVP suffers from serious problems of operation when combined with Mobile IP, due to fact that it has been designed for users attached to fixed network points. The problems of interworking of RSVP and Mobile IP is of great importance in order to provide QoS guarantees in mobile hosts. The issues of routing and handover associated with RSVP have been addressed when both Mobile IPv4 and IPv6 are employed and possible solutions have been proposed.

6. REFERENCES

[1] A. Acharya et al, "Mobility Management in Wireless ATM Networks", *IEEE Communications Magazine*, pp. 20-30 , Nov. 1997.

[2] B. Balachandran et al, "Active Filters: Delivering Scalable Media to Mobile Devices", *Proc. 7th Int. Workshop on Network and Operating System Support for Digital Audio and Video*, May, 1997.

[3] B. Bardinath et al, "Ipv6+Mobile-IP+MRSVP = Internet Cellular Phone", *Fifth IFIP Workshop on QoS*, May 1997.
[4] B. Barzilai et al, "Design and Implementation of an RSVP-Based Quality of Service Architecture for an Integrated Services Internet", *IEEE J. Selected Areas on Comm.*, pp. 397-413, April 1998.
[5] Y. Bernet et al, "A Framework for Differentiated Services", *IETF*, Work in progress, May 1998.
[6] R. Braden et al, "RSVP- Version 1: Functional Specifications", *RFC-2205*, Sept. 1997.
[7] R. Braden et al, "RSVP- Version 1:Message Processing Rules", *RFC-2209*, Sept. 1997.
[8] A. Campbell, "QOS-Aware Middleware for Mobile Multimedia Communications", *J. on Multimedia Tools and Applications*, Kluwer Academic Publishers, pp. 67-82, July 1998.
[9] J. Gomez and A. Campbell, "Delivering Adaptive Flows to Mobile Hosts over the Internet", *Advance Project Report*, Columbia University, January 1997.
[10] S. Hadjiefthymiades et al, "Mobility Management in an IP-based Wireless ATM Network", *ACTS Mobile Summit*, Rhodos, Greece, June 1998.
[11] *IEEE Internet Computing Magazine*, January 1998.
[12] D. Johnson and C. Perkins, "Mobility support in IPv.6", *IETF*, Internet Draft, Work in progress, November 1996.
[13] A. Kaloxylos et al, "Mobility Management and Control Protocols for Wireless ATM Networks", *IEEE Network Magazine*, pp. 19-27, July/August 1998.
[14] C. Perkins and D. Johnson, "Mobility support in IPv6", *ACM Mobicom* ,November 1996.
[15] C. Perkins, "IP Mobility Support", *RFC-2002*, October 1996.
[16] C. Perkins, Mobile IP: Design Principles and Practices, *Addison-Wesley*, 1998.
[17] A. Talukdar, "MRSVP: A Reservation Protocol for an Integrated Services Packet Network with Mobile Hosts", *DCS-TR-337*, Rutgers University, 1997.
[18] A. Terzis et al, "RSVP Operation over IP tunnels", *IETF*, Internet Draft, Work in progress, August 1998.
[19] L. Zhang et al, "RSVP: A new resource reservation protocol", *IEEE Network Magazine*, pp. 8-18, Sept. 1993.

AUTHOR INDEX

PFHSN VI - 1999

AUTHOR INDEX '99

1989-1999 PfHSN INDEX

1989–1999
TABLE OF CONTENTS INDEX

IFIP WG6.1/WG6.4
International Workshop on Protocols for High Speed Networks

PfHSN IV–VI are co-sponsored by the IEEE Communications Society Technical Committee on Gigabit Networking

IFIP PfHSN I – Zürich, May 1989

HARRY RUDIN and ROBIN WILLIAMSON

North-Holland / Elsevier, Amsterdam 1989 0-444-88536-6

WORKSHOP CO-CHAIRS:

Harry Rudin	
Robin Williamson	*IBM Zürich Research, Switzerland*

PROGRAM COMMITTEE:

Greg Chesson	*Protocol Engines, Inc., USA*
André Danthine	*Université de Liège, Belgium*
Marjory Johnson	*RIACS, NASA Ames, USA*
Radu Popescu-Zeletin	*GMD-FOKUS, West Germany*
Otto Spaniol	*Technical University Aachen, West Germany*

PART 1: ARCHITECTURE, EXPERIENCE I-1

PART 2: PERFORMANCE ISSUES I-55

PART 6: FIBER OPTICS, ACCESS I-217

PART 7: HIGHER LAYERS, APPLICATIONS, REQUIREMENTS I-255

IFIP PfHSN II – Palo Alto, November 1990

MARJORY J. JOHNSON

North-Holland / Elsevier, Amsterdam 1991 0-444-88932-9

WORKSHOP CHAIR:

Marjory Johnson	*RIACS / NASA Ames Research Center, USA*

PROGRAM COMMITTEE:

Eduardo Bergamini	*Instituto de Pesquisas Espaciais, Brazil*
Greg Chesson	*Silicon Graphics, USA*
André Danthine	*Université de Liège, Belgium*
Jeff Derby	*IBM Research Triangle Park, USA*
Per Gunningberg	*Swedish Institute of Computer Science, Sweden*
Simon Lam	*University of Texas at Austin, USA*
Gerard LeLann	*INRIA, France*
Bryan Lyles	*Xerox PARC, USA*
Radu Popescu-Zeletin	*GMD-FOKUS, Germany*
Harry Rudin	*IBM Research Zürich, Switzerland*
Nachum Shacham	*SRI, USA*
Otto Spaniol	*Technical University Aachen, West Germany*
Richard Watson	*Lawrence Livermore Labs, USA*
Robin Williamson	*IBM Austin, USA*
Yechiam Yemini	*Columbia University, USA*

PART 1: CONGESTION/FLOW CONTROL II-1

PART 2: ROUTING II-73

PART 3: IMPLEMENTATION TECHNIQUES II-105

PART 4: TRANSPORT LAYER II-269

PART 5: MAC LAYER II-351

IFIP PfHSN III – Stockholm, May 1992

BJÖRN PEHRSON, PER GUNNINGBERG,

and STEPHEN PINK

North-Holland / Elsevier, Amsterdam 1993 0-444-89925-1

WORKSHOP CO-CHAIRS:

Per Gunningberg Björn Pehrson Stephen Pink	*Swedish Institute of Computer Science, Sweden*

PROGRAM COMMITTEE:

Sudhir Aggarwal	*SUNY Binghamton, USA*
Geoffrey Baehr	*Sun Microsystems, USA*
André Danthine	*Université de Liège, Belgium*
Jeff Derby	*IBM Research Triangle Park, USA*
David Greaves	*Olivetti Research, UK*
Marjory Johnson	*RIACS, NASA Ames, USA*
Toshiki Kato	*KDD, Japan*
Bryan Lyles	*Xerox PARC, USA*
Hideo Miyahara	*Osaka University, Japan*
Sape Mullender	*Twente University, Netherlands*
Craig Partridge	*Bolt, Baranek & Newmann, USA*
Harry Rudin	*IBM Research Zürich, Switzerland*
R.P. Singh	*Bellcore, USA*
Morten Skov	*NKT Elektronik, Denmark*
Otto Spaniol	*Technical University Aachen, West Germany*
James P.G. Sterbenz	*IBM HPCC, USA*
Richard Watson	*Lawrence Livermore Labs, USA*
Tommy Westin	*Ellemtel, Sweden*
Robin Williamson	*IBM Research Zurich, Switzerland*
Yechiam Yemini	*Columbia University, USA*

PART 4: APPLICATIONS AND RESOURCE MANAGEMENT III-119

PART 5: ATM I III-153

PART 6: ATM II III-183

PART 7: HOST INTERFACE I III-201

PART 7: HOST INTERFACE II III-233

IFIP PfHSN IV – Vancouver, August 1994

GERALD NEUFELD and MABO ITO

Chapman & Hall, London 1995 0-412-71180-X

WORKSHOP CO-CHAIRS:

Mabo Ito	
Gerald Neufeld	*University of British Columbia, Canada*

PROGRAM COMMITTEE:

Gregor Bochmann	*University of Montrael, Canada*
Steve Deering	*Xerox PARC, USA*
David Feldmeier	*Bellcore, USA*
David Greaves	*Olivetti Research, UK*
Per Gunningberg	*University of Upsalla, Sweden*
Marjory Johnson	*RIACS, NASA Ames, USA*
Bryan Lyles	*Xerox PARC, USA*
Hideo Miyahara	*Osaka University, Japan*
Bernhard Plattner	*ETH Zurich, Switzerland*
Allyn Romanow	*Sun Microsystems, USA*
Harry Rudin	*IBM Research Zurich, Switzerland*
James P.G. Sterbenz	*GTE Laboratories, USA*
David Tennenhouse	*MIT, USA*
Joe Touch	*USC/ISI, USA*
Carey Williamson	*Canada*
Martina Zitterbart	*TU Braunschweig, Germany*

PART 4: PARALLEL IMPLEMENTATIONS AND ERROR HANDLING IV-121

PART 5: PROTOCOLS IV-169

PART 6: IMPLEMENTATION AND PERFORMANCE IV-241

PART 7: POSTERS IV-293

IFIP PfHSN V – SophiaAntipolis, Oct 1996

WALID DABBOUS and CHRISTOPHE DIOT

Chapman & Hall, London 1997 0-412-75850-4

WORKSHOP CO-CHAIRS:

Wallid Dabbous	
Christophe Diot	*INRIA Sophia Antipolis, France*

PROGRAM COMMITTEE:

Ernst Biersak	*EURECOM, France*
Gregor Bochmann	*University of Montreal, Canada*
Torsten Braun	*IBM ENC, Germany*
Andrew Campbell	*Columbia University, USA*
Jon Crowcroft	*UCL, UK*
Michel Diaz	*LAAS, France*
Julio Escobar	*SENACYT, France*
David Feldmeier	*Bellcore, USA*
Serge Fdida	*MASI, France*
Per Gunningberg	*University of Upsalla, Sweden*
Mabo Ito	*University of British Columbia, Canada*
Marjory Johnson	*RIACS / NASA Ames, USA*
Gerald Neufeld	*University of British Columbia, Canada*
Ramon Puigjaner	*UIB, Spain*
Bernhard Plattner	*ETH Zürich, Switzerland*
Harry Rudin	*IBM Research Zürich, Switzerland*
Nachum Shacham	*SRI International, USA*
Aruna Seneviratne	*UTS, Australia*
James P.G. Sterbenz	*GTE Laboratories, USA*
Ahmed Tantawy	*IBM Research, USA*
Joe Touch	*USC/ISI, USA*
Giorgio Ventre	*Universita di Napoli, Italy*
Martina Zitterbart	*TU Braunschweig, Germany*

KEYNOTE ADDRESS

PART 1: TRANSMISSION CONTROL V-1

PART 2: VIDEO OVER ATM V-47

PART 3: COMMUNICATION SYSTEM ARCHITECTURE V-75

WORKING SESSION 1

PART 4: GROUP COMMUNICATION V-107

PART 5: ILP V-165

WORKING SESSION 2

PART 6: QOS V-199

WORKING SESSION 3

IFIP PfHSN VI – Salem, August 1999

JOSEPH D. TOUCH and JAMES P.G. STERBENZ

Kluwer Academic Publishers, Boston 1999

WORKSHOP CO-CHAIRS:

James P. G. Sterbenz	*BBN Technologies, GTE, U.S.A.*
Joseph D. Touch	*USC / ISI, U.S.A.*

PROGRAM COMMITTEE:

Sujata Banerjee	*Univ. of Pittsburgh, U.S.A.*
Ernst Biersack	*Eurecom, France*
Gregor von Bochmann	*University of Ottawa, Canada*
Jon Crowcroft	*UCL, United Kingdom*
Christophe Diot	*Sprint Advanced Technology Lab, U.S.A.*
Julio Escobar	*SENACYT, Panama*
Per Gunningberg	*Uppsala University, Sweden*
Marjory Johnson	*RIACS/NASA Ames Research Center, U.S.A.*
Guy Leduc	*University of Liege, Belgium*
Bryan Lyles	*Sprint Advanced Technology Lab, U.S.A.*
Gerald Neufeld	*Siara Systems, U.S.A.*
Craig Partridge	*BBN Technologies, GTE, U.S.A.*
Harry Rudin	*IBM Zürich Research Lab, Switzerland*
Douglas C. Schmidt	*Washington University, U.S.A.*
Ahmed Tantawy	*IBM, U.S.A.*
Martina Zitterbart	*Tech. University Braunschweig, Germany*

1989-1999 AUTHOR INDEX

A

B

C

D

E

F

G

H

I

J

K

L

M

N

O

P

Q

R

S

T

V

W

Y

Z